THE PRINCE OF THE POWER OF THE AIR

AND THE LAST DAYS

THE PRINCE OF THE POWER OF THE AIR

AND THE LAST DAYS

Satanology - History - Prophecy - Technology

JEFFREY W. MARDIS

DEFENDER
Crane, Missouri

The Prince of the Power of the Air and the Last Days
Satanology - History - Prophecy - Technology
by Jeffrey W. Mardis

Copyright © 2022, Jeffrey W. Mardis.

All rights reserved. No part of this book may be reproduced or used in print, online, or video without the copyright owner's prior written permission.

First Edition 2022

PUBLISHER'S NOTE:
All Scripture quotations are taken from the Final Authority of the *Authorized King James Version of the Holy Bible* (1611), without apology. Any other deviations therefrom are not intentional. All-caps are added for emphasis and do not represent an alteration of the text. Some of the works referenced in this material were cited from the internet and were current at the time of publication. Neither the publisher nor the author is responsible for dead web links, or any inaccessible sources cited online. If you wish to use any part of this book beyond brief quotations in articles and reviews, you must ask permission. You may contact the author at swordinhandpub@gmail.com.

ISBN - 13: 978-1-948014-64-9

Cover design and interior layout by Jeffrey W. Mardis

Interior images and illustrations are licensed through Adobe Stock or iStock. Unless noted otherwise, all other images are in the public domain or are used under fair-use copyright laws.

A CIP catalogue record of this book is available from the Library of Congress.

Printed in the United States of America

Defender Publishing
Crane, MO 65633
www.skywatchtvstore.com

Contact the author at:
www.swordinhandpub.com

*"For we wrestle not against flesh and blood,
but against principalities, against powers,
against the rulers of the darkness of this world,
against spiritual wickedness in high places."
Ephesians 6:12*

CONTENTS

PART I - LIGHT ON THE DARKNESS | 11
- Facing Reality, Facing the Devil | 13
- Prince Charmer | 17

PART II - FOWL AND FOUL SPIRITS | 21
- Spirit in the Sky | 23
- Demons of a Feather | 25
- A Murmuring of Birds | 28
- Speed Demons | 32
- Baalzebub, Baalze-bird | 33
- Wrong with the Wind | 34
- Omen of the Owl | 37

PART III - WONDERS SEEN AND UNSEEN | 43
- Entertaining Devils Unawares | 46
- When the Laws of Nature are Nullified | 50
- Hidden in Plain Sight | 52

PART IV - EVIL RIDES THE WIND | 61
- An Ill Wind that Bloweth No Good | 63
- The Tornado & the Butterfly People | 71
- The Day of Euroclydon | 73
- The Storm & the Spirits of the Gadarenes | 75
- Alien Tornado | 77

- The Tempest that Swallows the Earth | 78
- Prince of Pestilence | 80

PART V - MARVELOUS MACHINES | 85
- The First Aero-vessel in Time & History | 78
- The Prince of the Power of the Aircraft | 91

PART VI – AN IMPARTATION OF KNOWLEDGE | 97
- Evil Imaginations | 99
- A Word to the Wise | 104
- Noah's Ark: The First Super-Tech | 107
- The Timing of the Technology | 116
- Knowledge Forbidden, Knowledge Allowed | 118
- It's a Bird, It's a Plane | 122
- The Riddle of Similtaneous Invention | 123
- Is a Spirit Driving Innovation? | 131

PART VII – THE GOD OF FORCES | 137
- Dawn of the Mad Scientist | 139
- A Baffling, Unexplained Connection | 145
- Blinded by the Light | 149
- The Mystery of Electricity | 155
- What You Were Never Told About Lightning | 164
- Something Unknown is in the Air | 181
- Demon in the Thunderbolt | 207

PART VIII – UNCLEAN SPIRITS IN OUR DAY | 211
- Age of Electric, Age of Demons | 213
- Spirit of the Twenty-First-Century | 225

PART IX – THE CITY WITH NO NIGHT | 229
- Cities of Light in a Fallen World | 231
- Cities of Men, Cities of Death | 234

PART X – WHAT HATH THE DEVIL WROUGHT | 243
- The Secret of Crystals | 245
- Like Living Stones | 250
- The Future is Counterfeit | 256

PART XI – LAST DAYS WEB OF SATAN | 259
- The Numbering of People | 261
- A Byte from a Fruit | 263
- What You Never Knew About the Internet | 266
- Behold, a Voice Out of the Cloud | 272
- Life in a Web | 277
- Building an Electric Eternity | 280
- The Problem with Technology is Sin | 284

PART XII – SUMMARY AND CLOSING COMMENTS | 289

Appendix | 303

Index | 311

Bibliography | 329

About the Author | 333

PART I

LIGHT ON THE DARKNESS

Satanology - History - Prophecy - Technology

"... For this purpose the Son of God was manifested, that he might destroy the works of the devil."   *1 John 3:8*

FACING REALITY, FACING THE DEVIL

IN AN AGE where the reality of the Devil is regularly mocked, scoffed, and laughed at, *The Prince of the Power of the Air and the Last Days* attempts to face this issue head-on. As scripture declares, *"...I am not ashamed of the gospel of Christ: for it is the power of God unto salvation to every one that believeth..."* (Rom. 1:16). The existence of the Devil certainly is a factor in the sinner's need for Christ and the gospel. Satan is the source of sin. But in looking at the reality of the Devil, not only does the Holy Bible never argue for the existence of the Creator (the fact is taken as granted –– *"In the beginning God..."* Gen 1:1) it also NEVER QUESTIONS the reality of the Adversary. The Final Authority need not weigh any pros or cons when it has all the answers. It is the Great Arbiter which shall outlast heaven and earth (Mt. 24:35). The Bible's job is to simply provide truth, all that's required on our part is belief.

In today's world, the Devil is little more than a joke. Even many professing Christians shy away from the subject for fear of appearing the fool if he's taken too seriously. Evidently, it's okay to "believe" in the Devil so long as he's a mythical do-nothing. But the problems begin when you dredge him up and stick him ACTIVELY IN MAN'S EVERDAY LIFE––past, present, and future. That's when many begin to get nervous. But that's exactly where he's at and the Bible has never taught otherwise. One astute saint from the mid-1800s made the following scathing indictment regarding this:

> "We are fully aware of the fact that the personal existence of Satan is admitted by nearly all those who bear the Christian name. It is at least among the articles of their faith. But by the great majority of professing Christians of the present day, it is so feebly realized, and so superficially regarded, that their faith is, in a great degree, inoperative, and the fact of his existence, and influence upon the minds of the people, is virtually disbelieved." [1]

One of the objectives of this book is to give the reader an opportunity to shed any "feeble" beliefs they may have about Satan. You might even say that this study will be doing an "about face," and traveling one hundred and eighty degrees in the opposite direction. Scripture doesn't present any sort of weak presence on the part of this enemy, so we have no excuse to hold beliefs reflective of such error.

To say that man has UNDERESTIMATED THE DEVIL is a commentary as old as history itself. It's an ancient story that hasn't changed in six thousand years. Satan's relationship with man BEGAN AS A DECEIVER (Gen. 3), and it will end the same (Rev. 20:7-8). To believe that anything different is going on now (in the twenty-first-century) in regards to this enemy is simply evidence that you're exactly where he wants you. The entire history of man upon this earth (Genesis to Revelation), is the history of a people under the thumb of a fallen, sinful, wicked, rebellious, unholy, creature. The Devil was here when the Lord first placed man upon this earth (Gen. 3:1), he'll be here after the millennial reign of the Lord Jesus Christ (Rev. 20:7), and he's been active in all ages in between (Eph. 2:2). If such a thing bothers you, then close this book now, because the very purpose of this study is to investigate the extent of the Devil's involvement with the air, and how this relates to our current age and the end-times.

---

[1] Ramsey, William. *Spiritualism, a Satanic Delusion and a Sign of the Times.* (H. L. Hastings: Peace Dale, RI, 1856), p. 11

Facing Reality, Facing the Devil | 15

As a result of both God and Satan, the Bible leaves no room for doubt that we live in a reality profoundly impacted by the SUPERNATURAL. In God, *"...the high and lofty One that inhabiteth eternity..."* (Isa. 57:15), such a condition far transcends the confines of the known universe. The existence of so-called "smartphones," "smart cars," or "smart cities" will do nothing to change this. In today's world, this truth is rejected in favor of "science." Should Christians follow this lead, or should we follow the lead of scripture? Since the word of God knows the beginning from the end, and man does not, the Bible's knowledge of the future indicates that SCIENCE CAN DECEIVE US (especially false sciences). Faith in God's word is the more sure measure of truth (2Ptr. 1:19). The great heroes of the faith proved this (Abel, Enoch, Noah, Abraham, Sarah, Moses, Samson, David, etc. – Heb. 11):

Today, the Devil is often seen in pop culture. Here, he's cutesified into the character "Hot Stuff" by Harvey Comics (c. 1957). Many other variations of this kind continue today. Devil-themed products are hot sellers. This is the kind of "devil" people like to believe in, not what's in the Bible.

> *"By faith Noah, being WARNED OF GOD OF THINGS NOT SEEN as yet, moved with fear, prepared an ark to the saving of his house; BY THE WHICH HE CONDEMNED THE WORLD, and became heir of the righteousness which is by faith."*   Heb. 11:7

The Lord, today, through scripture is continuing to warn us of *"things not seen."* In fact, nowhere in the Bible do we find God exalting science, or lauding it as something we should live by or constantly seek for guidance. The faith of the born-again, Bible-believer is to be placed in the words and *"power of God,"* not *"the wisdom of men"* (2Cor. 2:5). When it comes to science, IT IS POWERLESS in regard to these things. And why wouldn't it be? Scripture says:

> *"But THE NATURAL MAN receiveth not the things of the Spirit of God: for THEY ARE FOOLISHNESS UNTO HIM: NEITHER CAN HE KNOWN THEM, because they are SPIRITUALLY DISCERNED."* 1Co 2:14

While man's wisdom can certainly bring with it many technological wonders, in the hands of lost sinners, it will also bring about Satan's will without them even knowing it. This is why the nineteenth century largely laid the foundation for the Global Age. A worldwide setup that will eventually culminate with the Prince of the Devils being exalted as "God." We are in the midst of the building of this now, and have been moving full steam ahead for about the last 200-or-so years.

The Lord Jesus Christ died, was buried, and then resurrected under his own power by raising himself from the dead. He is our Anchor to the SUPERNATURAL. Through this truth, we realize that there is much more to reality than what we can detect with our five senses. To fully understand what's going on in this world, it is required that this realm which science cannot pierce be taken into account. This means that all the "laws" that science swears by go out the window. After all, God created the laws, and he can overrule them. God is the Law. The Creator is not bound by his creation.

The intent of this book is to help the Christian establish a more Bible-centric view of what's going on around us. This view puts SCRIPTURE AND THE SUPERNATURAL back at the center of our minds. The Lord Jesus Christ is our Anchor to these kinds of wonders, and it is through these phenomenal truths that we are warned about... THE PRINCE OF THE POWER OF THE AIR!

PRINCE CHARMER

Why is Satan called *"the prince of the power of the air"* (Eph. 2:2)? Have you ever thought about this? How does the Devil relate to the air? To what, exactly, is this "power of the air" referring? Is it about THINGS THAT ARE CAUSED BY THE AIR (like blowing, forming storms, etc.)? Or is the phrase exclusive to THINGS THAT TAKE PLACE IN THE AIR (like flying, lightning bolts and flashes, sky-based phenomena)? Or, perhaps, the name is characteristic of both? Would scripture label Satan with such a title just to project an intimidating, eight-word-long name, or are there legitimate, substantive reasons? The Bible's not in the business of using frivolous words (2 Tim. 3:16-17). In examining this, we should not only consider the meaning of the title, but also scriptural instances where the Devil is acting in the air or having some effect upon it. This will help provide a more complete answer.

In regards to the name, the Prince of the Power of the Air, the first thing to note about this particular title is that it identifies the Devil as a "PRINCE" concerning the air. Unlike today, the Bible's use of the word *"prince"* is not about the son of a king, like a parallel to the word "princess." The word is more demonstrative of a "king," denoting a RULER, SOVEREIGN, OR AUTHORITY. The Lord Jesus Christ refers to Satan as *"the prince of this world"* on three occasions (Jn. 12:31, 14:30, & 16:11). The Devil is also called *"the prince of the devils"* three times (Mt. 9:34, 12:24, & Mk. 3:22). This shows that Satan's no stranger to the *"prince"* title. In contrast, Christ also holds the title of prince with respect to several things (Dan. 8:25, Acts 3:15, Rev. 1:5, Isa. 9:6, etc.). The point is, that the labeling of Satan as a *"prince"* regarding the power of the air has not been done arbitrarily. It's not some random name pulled out of a hat. There's an important reason and purpose for him having been called this. The designation points to the fact that SATAN HAS BEEN GRANTED SOME KIND OF EXCLUSIVE RELATIONSHIP TO THE AIR, or has some kind of AUTHORITY OVER THE AIR, that angels, men, and animals do not.

The apostle Paul tells us that one of the primary battlegrounds for the Christian is found in wrestling "...against PRINCIPALITIES, against POWERS, against THE RULERS OF THE DARKNESS of this world, against SPIRITUAL WICKEDNESS IN HIGH PLACES" (Eph. 6:12). This reflects our circumstances exactly. Note the word "principalities" (there's the prince), the word "powers" (there's his power), and the phrase "in high places" (there's the air or atmosphere of the Earth). And while Ephesians 6:12 entails much more than this, it certainly encompasses our subject at hand. As we explore this further, it will be discovered that this particular satanic ability may be referring to a variety of air-related traits or characteristics. This is because AIR, and THE POWER OF THE AIR, are indicative of and related to many different things. And since scripture defines the Devil as "the prince" of this element, then it should not be a stretch to surmise that he has authority over many different facets of it.

In beginning this study, one of the first important things the reader should note, is how the Devil's various titles of "prince" parallel each other and collectively reveal THE FAR-REACHING EXTENT OF HIS POWER. Each separate title encompasses an abundance of particulars and details that scripture doesn't necessarily address. It's kind of like when a man is called "the President of the United States." How much power and authority does such a title include? Have you ever thought about that? How many separate things and responsibilities does such a name involve? To say that it's a lot would be an understatement. But it's much easier to simply call a man by the title of "President of the United States," than to call him by the separate names of every little thing the office entails. This same principle applies to the Devil in his capacity as a prince:

> 1.) As **THE PRINCE OF THE DEVILS**, Satan has command and authority over THE ENTIRE DEMONIC REALM.
>
> 2.) As **THE PRINCE OF THIS WORLD**, Satan has command and authority over THE WHOLE WORLD.

3.) As **THE PRINCE OF THE POWER OF THE AIR**, Satan has command and authority over THE IMMEDIATE HEAVENS WHICH SURROUND THE EARTH.

The fact that one title of "prince" encompasses a tremendous range of power means the others do as well. In this respect, each name sheds light on the other. The conclusion is that Satan is a prince over (1) a SPIRIT REALM (devils), (2) an EARTHLY REALM (the kingdoms of this world), and (3) a HEAVENLY REALM (the atmosphere of the earth). The other characteristic they all share is that the Bible does not go into detail on any of the particulars of these names. All we can really surmise at this point is that all three titles are significant. The purpose of this book is to try and flesh out the importance of the title of the Prince of the Power of the Air. The various aspects of this ability will be addressed as we progress. Before we get too much into this, however, I want to make clear right at the outset that just because something may happen in the air, with the air, or as a result of the air, doesn't necessarily mean "the Devil did it." Maybe he did, but maybe he didn't. The Bible shows that aerial phenomena can result from several different things. We'll talk more about this later. The important thing to take away from our introduction is that THE DEVIL OCCUPIES AN ELITE POSITION IN THIS AREA. While he certainly doesn't influence the air at every given second, to ignore him to the extent that most do today (he's practically nonexistent in the minds of most), is to grossly distort reality. This book has been written to help put the Bible-believing Christian in mind of this. The sections that follow will break down the title and examine the various implications and scriptural evidence of the name. It will also delve into the modern age and look at how this infernal prince could be manipulating it, via his authority over the air, to bring about his eventual world enthronement. Some of the fascinating subjects we'll explore include: Birds, Earth's atmosphere, cherubim, air, wind, storms, tornados, lightning, electricity, wisdom, knowledge, technology, aviation, demon activity, demon possession, serial killers, unexplained aerial phenomena, the supernatural and more.

PART II

FOWL AND FOUL SPIRITS

Satanology - History - Prophecy - Technology

"... Babylon the great is fallen, is fallen, and is become the habitation of devils, and the hold of every foul spirit, and a cage of every unclean and hateful bird."
Revelation 18:2

SPIRIT IN THE SKY

IN MAKING some initial headway into our study of the Prince of the Power of the Air, we're first going to compare scripture with scripture to discover the meaning of the phrase "*of the air.*" When the wording first appears in the Bible, it shows up with animals called "*fowl,*" also known as "birds" (see Gen. 1:26-30, 2:16-20, etc.) Understanding why birds are described as being "*of the air*" will help us understand at least one reason why the phrase applies to Satan.

Concerning birds being labeled as "*of the air,*" consider that they can also be found in trees, but scripture doesn't address them as "fowl of the trees." Birds can also be found on the ground, but neither are they addressed as "of the ground." Some birds can even be found on water, but the Bible never calls them "of the water." Despite all these other bird facts, why does scripture always accentuate their connection to the air? As obvious as it may be, the phrase is pointing to the primary location where these creatures have A SPECIAL ABILITY TO CONVEY THEMSELVES. Beasts "*of the field*" can't do this, nor can fish "*of the sea.*" The phrase is pointing to WHERE BIRDS FLY. The Bible calls this place "*heaven*" (Gen. 1:20). While scripture may also call outer space "*heaven*" (Gen. 1:14 & 17) and the place of God's Throne, "*heaven*" (1Kg. 8:30, 39, 43 &49), birds fly in neither of these other two places designated with this same name. The reason for this is that "*heaven*" is comprised of three separate regions, with only one being A PATHWAY FOR FOWL. The greatest height any modern bird is known to fly is about 37,000 feet or about seven miles above sea level. Because the movement of birds is restricted to this zone, we can

As "*the prince of the power of the air*," the Devil has tremendous authority over the immediate heavens which surround this world. He is the spirit of the sky.

now understand that the Bible's expression "*of the air*" is a reference to THE ATMOSPHERE AROUND THE EARTH. A domain existing from earth's ground level all the way up to the maximum height of where fowl fly. This is not to say that the Devil "only" has power and influence in this area, but rather, special power and influence.

Having now compared the Bible with itself, to define Satan as "*the prince of the power of the air*," is to address him as THE PRINCE OF THE POWER OF EARTH'S ATMOSPHERE. Such a title accredits a substantial ability to the Devil. What this infers is that anything that happens as a result of the air, or takes place in the air, has the potential of being a consequence of SATANIC AUTHORITY. Earth's atmosphere is responsible for many different things. Air can carry water, dirt, dust, sand, pollen, and soot. Air can travel slowly or very fast. It can be lite or forceful. It can move minimally with a short breeze or travel for long distances. It can even press down upon the earth as "pressure," or reshape the earth's surface through erosion or the creation of dunes. One of its primary features is the weather. Air can do all these things and more. Thus, Satan's name as the "prince" of this region relates to us that he must have some kind of mastery over many of these same things.

DEMONS OF A FEATHER

The Bible uses the three-word phrase "*of the air*" exactly 30 times. Twenty-nine of these references are to FOWL. The linking of birds with Satan's "*power of the air*" is no coincidence, because FOWL ARE ALSO USED BY SCRIPTURE TO PICTURE SPIRITS. The fact that spirits are often presented as BIRDS naturally imparts to spirits THE POWER OF FLIGHT. Sometimes a bird is used to picture the Holy Spirit (like the dove, Lk. 3:22, etc.), but the bird is also used to typify UNCLEAN SPIRITS (Mt. 13:32, Lk. 13:19, Rev. 18:2, etc.). Because of this, we find:

> "*Curse not the king, no not IN THY THOUGHT; and curse not the rich IN THY BEDCHAMBER: for A BIRD OF THE AIR SHALL CARRY THE VOICE, and that which hath wings shall TELL THE MATTER.*"
> Ecc. 10:20

A man writing what a bird tells him.

Here, scripture presents a special kind of "*bird*" that can carry a man's voice through the air and tell of the man's thoughts or spoken words. This is no natural bird. Real birds can't convey sound or man's ideas. But, according to this verse, there are certain kinds of flying things that can.[2] Believe it or not, scripture gives us an example of the Lord's Spirit doing this very thing. While the king of Syria was in his bedroom, a flying thing (in this case, the Holy Spirit) carried away the king's voice and told it to Elisha. Note:

> *"...Elisha, the prophet that is in Israel, telleth the king of Israel the words that thou [the king of Syria] speakest in thy bedchamber."*   2Kgs. 6:8-12

When scripture talks of a "bird of the air" carrying a man's voice, it's speaking of THE ABILITY OF SPIRITS TO SPREAD OR REPORT MAN'S WORDS OR THOUGHTS. Have you ever heard of the phrase, "a little bird told me"? Now you know where the expression comes from. While the example in Second Kings shows the spirit of God doing this, such action of "birds" is not limited to the Holy Spirit. The Bible shows that birds often typify DEVILS. The parable of the sower and the seed is especially demonstrative of this:

> "[2] A*nd he taught them many things by parables, and said unto them in his doctrine,* [3] *Hearken; Behold, there went out a sower to sow:* [4] *And it came to pass, as he sowed, some fell by the way side, and* THE FOWLS OF THE AIR CAME AND DEVOURED IT UP. ... [14] *The sower soweth the word.* [15] *And these are they by the way side, where the word is sown; but when they have heard,* SATAN COMETH IMMEDIATELY, AND TAKETH AWAY THE WORD *that was sown in their hearts."* Mk. 4:2-4 & 14-15

Satan as bird-like demon sowing tares (c.1510)

---

[2] FOOTNOTE FROM PREVIOUS PAGE: The phrase *"that which has wings"* doesn't necessarily imply physical wings. On occasion, the Bible ascribes "wings" to both the Lord and the wind, but neither of these have literal wings. In such verses, the word *"wings"* concerns the ability to travel through the air or to move quickly (see Ruth. 2:12, Psa. 18:10, 104:3, etc.).

Devils as fowl flocking to the seed.

"[4] *And when much people were gathered together, and were come to him out of every city, he spake by a parable:* [5] *A sower went out to sow his seed: and as he sowed, some fell by the way side; and it was trodden down, and THE FOWLS OF THE AIR DEVOURED IT. ...* [11] *Now the parable is this: The seed is the word of God.* [12] *Those by the way side are they that hear; THEN COMETH THE DEVIL, AND TAKETH AWAY THE WORD out of their hearts, lest they should believe and be saved."* — Lk. 8:4-5 & 11-12

Here, "fowl" clearly represent DEVIL SPIRITS. And that's not all, if the reader will look closely, these verses in Mark and Luke also help illustrate how and why the Devil is referred to as *"the spirit that now worketh in the children of disobedience"* (Eph. 2:2). The parable initially states that *"fowls"* (plural) come and steal away the seed. But the Lord's explanation simply says *"Satan"* (singular), or *"the devil"* (singular). Do you see that? So, why does the parable flip-flop from depicting a plurality of perpetrators (fowls) to a single perpetrator (Satan)? Because these scriptures are also showing the

Devil's authority over other unclean spirits. We're getting a window into why Satan is called THE PRINCE OF THE DEVILS. Note also how Ephesians links the title of *"the prince of the power of the air"* with Satan's ability to control masses of humanity:

> "[1] *And you hath he quickened, who were dead in trespasses and sins;* [2] *Wherein in time past ye walked according to THE COURSE OF THIS WORLD, according to THE PRINCE OF THE POWER OF THE AIR, THE SPIRIT that now worketh in THE CHILDREN of disobedience:"*   Eph. 2:1-2

These verses show A LONE SPIRIT working in A PLURALITY OF PEOPLE. Did you see that? It is of little doubt that this peculiar "spirit," which operates in every unsaved rebel against God, is not the Devil singularly, but includes his infernal SPIRIT HORDE which likewise helps facilitate, or at least exacerbates, the sinner's disobedience towards God. Satan is not omnipresent. He's not God. He cannot be in more than one place at a time. But by this power of the air he nearly appears to be so, due to THE MULTITUDE OF EVIL SPIRITS AT HIS DISPOSAL. This is why he's not only known as *"the prince of the power of THE AIR,"* but also *"the prince of THE DEVILS."* See how the titles correlate? Like birds, devils are things *"of the air."* This is why fowl often typify spirits. And since Satan is *"the prince of the power of the air,"* he is the primary controlling factor behind these things. Unclean spirits do his bidding. This is why the parable of the sower and the seed shows a multiplicity of *"fowls"* taking away the seed, and yet Christ says it's the work of THE DEVIL. When scripture states that Christ was manifest to *"destroy the works of the devil,"* no doubt Satan's command over these forces is included in the things which Christ will eventually eradicate (1Jn. 3:6).

A MURMURING OF BIRDS

Have you ever witnessed a mass of birds moving together through the sky? They often appear as an ominous, morphing, black cloud.

One particular documentary put out by the Public Broadcasting System states of this mystery:

> "When birds assemble, something extraordinary happens. They act like a super-organism, traveling with a single purpose." [3]

This is an astounding statement. Note the words "extraordinary," "super-organism" and "single purpose." This indicates that since birds typify unclean spirits, this is one of the behavioral characteristics of devils when in the air. The parallel suggests that devils often traverse the sky, like a swarm of darkness, moving as a unified consciousness under Satan's command. [4]

But while birds can be observed traveling in this manner, evil spirits cannot. Fowl, especially when they're in flight, help pull back the veil on the invisible world (Rom. 1:20). If this hive-like mentality sounds unreasonable, consider the demoniacs of the Gadarenes and what they said to the Lord about the foul spirits within them – these devils traveled as an army, a solitary unit consisting of individuals:

> *"My name is LEGION: for WE ARE MANY."* Mk. 5:9

---

[3] *The Gathering Swarms*, PBS, 2014, 9:01

[4] FOOTNOTE: A Bible typology shows a parallel between two subjects (like birds and spirits). While typologies can sometimes be complex in their layers, generally, they reveal that the physical world and spiritual world mirror each other in some way. The *King James Bible* uses seven words to describe this teaching method, namely: the PARABLE, the PATTERN, the ALLEGORY, the EXAMPLE, the FIGURE, the SHADOW, and the SIMILITUDE. The book of Hebrews says of the *"shadow"* that it is an *"example"* of something else, but *"not the very image"* of it (Heb. 8:5, 10:1). This means that no biblical typology can be applied a hundred percent because no typology matches its type in every aspect. It's not *"the very image."* It only represents the real thing in part. For example, Christ is called *"the Lamb of God,"* but he doesn't have four hoofed feet or wool. The *"Lamb of God"* title speaks to the Lord's obedience, humility, purity, and innocence (Isa. 53:7, Phil. 2:8, etc.), not his physical appearance. This partial picture is true of all typologies.

This means the PBS video on birds described these spirits precisely: "They act like a super-organism, traveling with a single purpose."

Starlings, blackbirds, and grackles can often be found flying in large flocks called "murmurations" which can number in the thousands. Interestingly, according to the Bible, the word "murmur" or "murmuring" generally always entails A SIN COMMITTED AGAINST THE LORD. This is why scripture connects murmuring with evil:

> *"How long shall I bear with this EVIL CONGREGATION, which MURMUR against me? I have heard the MURMURINGS of the children of Israel, which they MURMUR AGAINST ME."* Num. 14:27 (see also Ex. 16:7-8, Psa. 106:25, 1Cor. 10:10, etc.)

Hitchcock's 1963 film, *The Birds*, has the aerial beasts behaving in unison like one, giant, demon-possessed monster.

Certainly, the Bible's word "murmur" is not addressing a swarm of birds in its context. Yet, the scriptures foreseeing (Gal. 3:8) that the word would eventually apply to the movement of such, provides us a stunning revelation. A "murmuration of birds" shows in type something that's WORKING AGAINST GOD or is OPPOSED TO GOD. Isaiah even parallels murmuring to one who has A SPIRIT OF ERROR (Isa. 29:24). Do murmurations of birds teach us about the reality of devils? Do they disclose that evil spirits can carry with them an error, a lie, to feed to the masses? I wouldn't be too quick to dismiss the idea.

In a "murmuration," fowl move in a black, shadowy, cloud-like formation as if under the control of a single mind. With insects, this type of behavior is sometimes called the "hive mind" or "hive mentality."

In looking at this particular fowl behavior, we find that some of the world's largest avian flocks are often dense enough to block out the light of the sun or, at least, dilute it. The Red-Billed Quelea of Africa can travel in swarms of millions (they also happen to be Africa's most hated bird and the world's most destructive bird). One source estimates that yield losses due to the Quelea have been estimated at "over 1 million tons of grain" per year. [5]

Bats are also found in swarms (Bats are unclean animals – Lev. 11:13-19). Some flying insects also travel en masse. Bees, hornets, gnats, mayflies, and cicadas are common examples. But the largest flying swarmer, by far, is the LOCUST. A locust swarm, which can number into the tens of billions of individual grasshoppers, is technically called a "plague" by entomologists (bug scientists). Surprisingly, scripture ties both the first and last mentions of

---

[5] Muimba-Kankolongo, Ambayeba. Food Crop Production by Smallholder Farmers in Southern Africa (Academic Press: San Diego, CA, 2018), p. 90-96]

"locusts" to plagues. While swarms and flocks of fowl can restrict the sun's light, foul spirits can block the Son's Light (Mk. 4:4, Lk. 8:5). They work against God's word, the seed, and either steal it outright or pollute it like leaven in a lump (Mt. 13:32-33, 1Cor. 5:6-8). This is why scripture, when speaking of the kingdom of heaven (which contains both good and bad – see Mt. 13:38 & 48, etc.), compares it to birds lighting in a tree:

> "...*the birds of the air come and lodge in the branches thereof.*" Mt. 13:32

These particular birds are indicative of something bad. They picture unclean spirits at work.

SPEED DEMONS

When we think of the fastest animals in the world we often think of large cats like the Cheetah. Cheetahs can reach speeds of 70 to 80 miles per hour. But this pales in comparison to the true fastest animals. The fastest animals in the world are BIRDS. The peregrine falcon, when in a dive, can fly at speeds of over 240 miles per hour. That's three times the speed of the fastest land animals. Does the fact that birds are the quickest creatures in the world teach us anything about

Peregrine Falcon

the spirit realm? Certainly. The implication is that the Devil's aerial armies are some of the fastest-moving things on earth.

BAALZEBUB, BAALZE-BIRD

Scripture identifies birds as *"fowls"* (Gen. 1:20, etc.), classifies bats *"among the fowls"* (Lev. 11:13-19), and declares flying insects as *"fowls that creep"*, or *"flying creeping things"* (Lev. 11:20-21)

The Bible also shows that FLYING INSECTS (like locusts, beetles, grasshoppers, etc.) are known as *"flying creeping things,"* or *"fowls that creep,"* and are thus classified as A KIND OF FOWL (see Gen. 6:20 & Lev. 11:20-23). "Fowl" is a general word primarily for the bird, the roots of which are of Dutch and Germanic origin, "vogel," which means "to fly." Although the word "fowl" is most often speaking of the feathered kind, in scripture, it may also be used as a catch-all term for any earth-based life form that flies or has literal wings.

Satan's name of *"Baalzebub"* (or Beelzebub – Mt. 12:24, etc.), which casts him as the lord of the flies, can certainly be seen as a parallel to his title as *"the prince of the power of the air."* Flies, or flying things, be they birds or bugs, are all denizens of the air. The implications of this are that, in conjunction with birds, CERTAIN INSECTS MAY PICTURE DEMON SPIRITS. The book of Revelation speaks of a future outbreak of mongrelized monsters called "locusts." Clearly, these things are not the familiar bug-type of locusts. Led by a fallen angel, there's no doubt that this airborne armada is an army of flying demons. The fact that real locusts are the most devastating creatures to fly in swarms, speaks to the severity of the torment of these future monsters (Rev. 9:1-11). The Bible reports of the event:

> *"And the rest of the men which were not killed by THESE PLAGUES yet repented not of the works of their hands, that they should not worship devils, and idols of gold, and silver, and brass, and stone, and of wood: which neither can see, nor hear, nor walk:"* Rev 9:20

WRONG WITH THE WIND

Scripture not only uses flying creatures like birds and insects to teach us about spirits, but a common atmospheric event often typifies spirits as well:

FOOTNOTE: The Bible's system of classifying life forms is different than modern science. And since God is the Creator of life, I don't have to guess which classification is correct. Two major differences may be found between these systems of categorization (God vs. Man): (1.) Unlike the man-made system, the Creator does not group mankind with the "animal" class; and (2.) All flying things are considered "fowl" – regular BIRDS are fowl, BATS are fowl, and FLYING INSECTS are fowl. The book of Leviticus speaks of certain insects as "fowls that creep, going upon all four" (Lev. 11:20-21). While man says that these tiny creatures have six legs, scripture says they have "four." The Creator does this because their two remaining limbs are counted as "hands" (Prov. 30:28). Four legs, plus two hands, equals six limbs. In another instance, the Bible mentions "feathered fowl," as if to distinguish them from fowl which are not feathered (Ezk. 39:17). The word "bug" or "insect" is not used by the Bible, nor does it bother with differentiating so-called "mammals," like the bat, from other animals. When a bat creeps across the ground, it moves with its folded wings and feet *"going upon all four."*

"THE WIND BLOWETH WHERE IT LISTETH, and thou hearest the sound thereof, but CANST NOT TELL WHENCE IT COMETH, AND WHITHER IT GOETH: so is every one that is born of the SPIRIT." Jn. 3:8

Air is made up of tiny, floating particles and molecules in the region around the earth. Differences in pressure, generally caused by the heat of the sun, causes these aerial gasses to move from one location to another. This movement of the air is called "wind." While scripture shows that wind can travel in *"circuits"* (Ecc. 1:6), these God-ordained ordinances are not always responsible for moving the air. God can intervene, Satan can intervene, angels can intervene, and man can affect the wind through technology. In regard to Satan being THE PRINCE OF THE POWER OF THE AIR, this certainly expands his authority and bestows upon him a substantial amount of influence. The ramifications of this means that NEARLY ANY TYPE OF ATMOSPHERIC PHENOMENA INVOLVING THE MOVEMENT OF AIR IS A POTENTIAL CANDIDATE FOR SATANIC MANIPULATION.

The fact that wind cannot be seen, but only heard and felt, speaks to the INVISIBLE EARTHLY PRESENCE of spirts. This is not a earth-shatteringing revelation until one considers how much of an impact wind has on us. It's practically a daily occurrence and impossible to escape. If wind typifies demons, what does this teach us? Are they sparse and rare, or plentiful and numerous? Since wind events take place on a regular basis, I think it's safe to conclude that evil spirits are in no short supply. In getting a little more insight on this, the prophet Zachariah comments on the Millennium:

"...I will cause...the UNCLEAN SPIRITS TO PASS OUT OF THE LAND." Zech 13:2

What does this mean? It indicates that during the thousand-year reign of Christ that, not only will Satan be locked in the Pit (Rev. 20), but unclean spirits will be put away as well. They will vacate all areas which they normally occupy. Until that time, however, they remain in the earth, and in our lives, working the Devil's wiles.

Lewis Spence, an early twentieth-century authority on the occult, made the following interesting comment about air:

> "It was formerly believed by some authorities that a ghost was wrapped in air, by which means it became visible. Thus a spectre might appear wherever there was air." [6]

While the quotation above is not biblical, it is interesting in the fact that it does draw a parallel between air and the spirit realm.

Hollywood unknowingly takes advantage of this truth regularly. In many films, the blowing of the wind, especially at night, is indicative of evil or something ominous. We often see tree leaves turning, maybe paper trash tumbling down the street, or curtains waving in the wind. The message being communicated is that something bad, yet invisible, is at hand. In fact, in movie history, there have been several productions simply titled *The Wind* (1928, 1986, 2018). Two of the three are horror films, with the latest installment being a story about DEMONS. The Bible knows what it's talking about. It's always a million years ahead of science and Hollywood. We'll say more about the wind in the pages ahead.

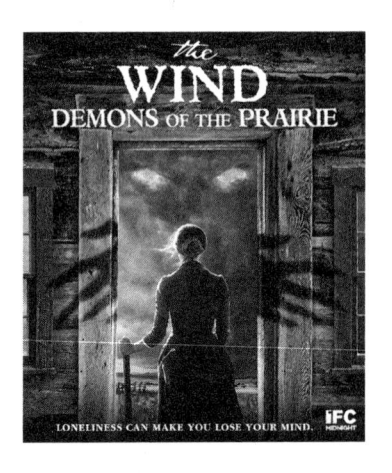

---

[6] Spence, Lewis. *An Encyclopedia of Occultism.* (Citadel Press & Carol Publishing Group: Secaucus, NJ, 1996) p. 7

OMEN OF THE OWL

Owls are some of the most interesting fowl depicted in both the Bible and the world. Scripture shows the owl as an UNCLEAN BIRD (Lev. 11:13-17). In type, this pictures the UNCLEAN SPIRIT (Rev. 18:2, etc.). Owls operate at night and have the ability to see in TOTAL DARKNESS (this is also true of another unclean fowl, the bat – Lev. 11:19, Deut. 14:18). This suggests that "the rulers of the darkness" also have some sort of heightened ability to function in the dark (Eph. 2:2). As birds of stealth, owls can move and fly silently without making a sound. They have large wings relative to their body which allows them to fly in very slow, precise, controlled movements. This makes them subtle creatures (Gen. 3:1). Scripture also uses the owl to depict a thing on the receiving end of God's wrath, a being destined for ETERNAL DAMNATION. Because of this, the Bible often mentions OWLS in conjunction with DRAGONS (see Job 30:29, 13:21, 34:13, Isa. 34:13, 43:20, Mic. 1:5-8, etc.). The dragon pictures Satan (Rev. 12:3). Are owls, then, directly analogous with demons? If not, why do we often find imagery of owls and devils sharing the same themes like witchcraft, magic, Halloween, evil, etc.?

The owl is also often used as a symbol for "wisdom," but the Bible never shows the bird as depicting this. While the world may use this bird to represent a form of higher knowledge, unbeknownst to them, it's not the wisdom of God (Jam. 3:15). The Greek goddess, Athena (named in honor of the city of Athens) was often depicted by an owl, or accompanied by an owl. Athena was the goddess of WISDOM and CRAFTSMANSHIP (invention). In the Bible, Paul visits Athens

38 | Omen of the Owl

This "DEVIL IN ME" owl-themed t-shirt is used to promote Antichristism. Note the inverted crosses.

Halloween card: *"When the Owl & Witch together are seen, there's mischief brewing on Halloween."*

and finds it a place "superstitious" and "wholly given to idolatry" (Acts 17:15-34). Ironically, scores of witnesses have reported seeing owls in locations related to encounters with the "paranormal" or "unexplained." Whether it be sightings of ghosts, strange humanoid creatures, or mysterious lights in the sky, according to author Mike Clelland, such birds have often been reported to make an appearance:

> "I have AMASSED A WEALTH OF REPORTS where people describe what seem to be REAL OWLS right around the time of a UFO sighting." [7]

Concerning this, some have suggested that sightings of the so-called "Mothman" (West Virginia, 1966, etc.) may have been

---

[7] Clelland, Mike. *The Messengers*. (Richard Dolan Press: Los Angeles, CA, 2020) p. 73

From an ancient coin (c. 450-400 BC) showing the Goddess "Athena" as an owl. Athena was the false god (demon) of wisdom and invention. Much more will be said about these two subjects later in the book.

A Devil mask packaged in an owl box from the iconic costume manufacturer, Ben Cooper (c. 1950-1970).

encounters with a large owl. Not only are people meeting owls while experiencing these strange cases, but doubters alike are promoting the creature as an answer for sightings of many unexplained beings. Clelland continues:

> "There are more examples of skeptics using the owl as a convenient scapegoat for an outright dismissal of anything unusual. The Flatwoods Monster (also known as the Braxton County Monster) from 1952 was shrugged off as a bunch of confused witnesses seeing a great gray owl. The 1955 Kelly-Hopkinsville encounter where two families saw odd lights in the sky and weird entities in rural Kentucky, were blamed on nothing more than people seeing owls. These are two classic cases from the beginning of the modern UFO era. Both accounts have flying craft seen by multiple witnesses

in conjunction with entities on the ground... It seems that in the case of Point Pleasant [the West Virginia Mothman phenomenon] and elsewhere, the skeptics are eager to use owls as a stand-in for aliens." [8]

Whether the sightings of any of these strange creatures were actual encounters with owls, I don't know. Most of the witnesses who've run into these entities say that such birds do not meet all the criteria of what they've seen. But be that as it may, it is interesting that the "owl" is sometimes suggested as an "explanation" for these mysteries. It's just another example of THE OWL BEING TIED TO THE DEMONIC.

Considering these things, perhaps the classic image of owls perched outside haunted houses is not so far off the mark. Especially when one understands that owls, as unclean birds, are representatives of demons. All devils are destined to spend eternity in the Lake of Fire. It's their appointed time of torment, and they're terrified of it (Mt. 8:29). This is why scripture pictures the owl as dwelling with dragons, and one day in a place of *"brimstone"* and *"burning pitch"*:

> "[8] *...it is the day of the LORD'S vengeance...* [9] *And the streams thereof shall be TURNED INTO PITCH, and the dust thereof INTO BRIMSTONE, and the land thereof shall become BURNING PITCH.* [10] *It shall not be quenched night nor day; the smoke thereof shall go up for ever: from generation to generation it shall lie waste; none shall pass through it for ever and ever.* [11] *But the cormorant* [a bird] *and the bittern* [a bird] *shall possess it; THE OWL* [a bird] *also and THE RAVEN* [a bird] *SHALL DWELL IN IT...* [13] *...and it shall be AN HABITATION OF DRAGONS, and A COURT FOR OWLS."*   Isa. 34:8-11 & 13

---

[8] Clelland, Mike. *The Messengers.* (Richard Dolan Press: Los Angeles, CA, 2020) p. 211

Right here is a good place to stop and remind the reader that literal owls are no more real demons than a literal lamb is the Lord Jesus Christ (Jn. 1:36, etc.). What we're dealing with here are TYPOLOGIES, PARABLES, SHADOWS, and FIGURES. What we're dealing with here is how the Bible teaches us about the spirit realm by using physical, visible things. Fowl teach us about spirits (both holy and unholy). Fowl are not spirits themselves. If you shoot an owl, you haven't shot a demon, you've simply killed a bird. The point is, that Christians are not to confuse the figure with the real thing. Owls are a figure, they're not evil spirits. The reason real owls show up in some of these strange situations is because God specifically created this bird to show us things about the invisible realm. It's the owl's job to be in such places. In this sense, in certain situations the owl can truly be an OMEN. A portent telling us that something about a person, place, thing or event is contrary to God. The owl is telling us, "Hey, this is of the Devil." Some animals can even become devil-possessed (Mk. 5:13, Lk. 8:33), but the animal itself is not a devil, whether it be a bird or anything else. Does owl imagery sometimes appear in conjunction with witches or witchcraft? It's because witchcraft is of the Devil. Do owls, real or imagined, sometimes manifest in conjunction with humanoid-type creatures (Mothman, aliens, Bigfoot, etc.)? It's because these monsters are of the Devil. Do owls show up from time to time with the appearance of unidentified aerial lights? It's because much of this phenomenon is of the Devil. Do owls occasionally show up in connection to "haunted houses"? It's because such strangeness is of the Devil.

Depiction of an ancient demon known as "Aamon" that was part serpent, part wolf, and part owl. Beware of owls!

PART III

WONDERS SEEN AND UNSEEN

Satanology - History - Prophecy - Technology

"For the invisible things of him from the creation of the world are clearly seen, being understood by the things that are made..."   *Romans 1:20*

ENTERTAINING DEVILS UNAWARES

IF YOU GET nothing else from this book, at least try and get ahold of the information contained in this section. It will go far in helping the Christian in matters of discernment. This cannot be emphasized strong enough. If you're unable to grasp what's being presented here, you're going to miss out on the "how" of a lot of the things being perpetrated today by *"the rulers of the darkness of this world"* (Eph. 6:12).

Wind, as we've already discovered, can picture in type the silent movement of spirits, be they good or evil. But this is not the only thing scripture teaches us about the wind. In fact, according to the Bible, the literal wind is one of the most profound aspects of the Earth's atmosphere over which the Devil can have control. This means that not only can the movement of wind typify devils in motion, but its very movement is also often influenced by the Devil. When the Bible declares Satan as *"the prince of the power of the air,"* his ability to MANIPULATE AND DIRECT AIR is one of the more outstanding reasons why he's been given this name. There's no need to doubt this because scripture gives us a blatant example:

> "[12] *And THE LORD SAID UNTO SATAN, Behold, all that he* [Job] *hath IS IN THY POWER; only upon himself put not forth THINE HAND. So SATAN WENT FORTH from the presence of the LORD. ...* [14] *And*

> *there came a messenger unto Job, and said, ... [16] ... The FIRE of God is fallen FROM HEAVEN and hath burned up the sheep, and the servants,... [18] While he was yet speaking, there came also another, and said, Thy sons and thy daughters were eating and drinking wine in their eldest brother's house:* [19] *And, behold, THERE CAME A GREAT WIND from the wilderness, and SMOTE THE FOUR CORNERS OF THE HOUSE, and it fell upon the young men, and they are dead; and I only am escaped alone to tell thee."*
>
> Job 1:12, 14, 16, 18 & 19

In the book of Job, we find the Lord lifting his hedge of protection from around this godly servant. As a result, Job is exposed to the raw forces of Satan. Note that the verses cited explicitly identify the "power" and "hand" of Satan as being responsible for (1) KILLER FIRE FROM THE SKY and (2) DEADLY WINDS strong enough to decimate a house. These two actions speak volumes concerning the actual potential of the Devil in influencing Earth's atmosphere. In quantifying this potential, God's word labels Satan as a "prince" over this power. We've already addressed the meaning and importance of the title of "prince." It indicates, not a casual involvement in a thing, but AN AUTHORITY OR RULER OVER IT. Thus, when God relinquished Job into the hands of the Prince of the Power of the Air, we find Satan turning these very forces against Job.

In looking closer at these events, more profound things are discovered. When the survivors of these calamities ran to inform Job, not a single servant mentions the Devil. Not one. Did you get that? Job's servants say nothing about the Devil because THEY HAD NO IDEA THAT SATAN WAS RESPONSIBLE. From all outward appearances, these disasters were all individual, UNRELATED EVENTS. Job's servants were completely ignorant of the fact that the Sabeans and Chaldeans were moved by the Devil; the fire from heaven was caused by the Devil, and the tornadic winds were brought by the Devil. In other words, without the revelation of scripture, there would be no way to know that these disasters were the moving of Satan's hand. And had God not revealed these things to us, we would be just as blind and dumb as Job's servants. Remember earlier we said that God warned Noah of *"things not seen"* (Heb. 11:7)? Well, here the scriptures are warning us of the powers of Satan in a similar manner. Certain aspects of this power we may be able to observe. But what our eyes actually see, many not fully disclose what's happening. If modern science were to have investigated the tragedies which befell Job, their conclusions would be no different than they are today. Science would announce that all these things were "coincidences" or "accidents of nature." This is an extremely important lesson for the Bible-believer to get. Because if you don't

When Job's servants brought evil tidings, none of them were aware that they were witnessing the moving of the hand of Satan. One servant even professed to be seeing an act of "God" (Job 1:16), but he was grossly mistaken.

get it, you're going to have the wool pulled over your eyes again, and again, and again. What's unfolding here is one of the primary reasons why *"the wisdom of this world is foolishness with God"* (1 Cor. 3:19). The reports that Job's servants gave to Job teach us that MANY SUPERNATURAL EVENTS CAN OUTWARDLY APPEAR AS NATURAL EVENTS. SUPERNATURALISM CAN BE HIDDEN BEHIND THE APPEARANCE OF NATURALISM. A thing can look natural, or of its own accord (like robbers and cutthroats stealing property or murdering people; or fireballs falling from the sky; or winds blowing a house down), but in reality, it may very well be THE HAND OF SATAN. None of the events in Job had any outward supernatural markers, but they were all SUPERNATURAL. They were all the result of principalities, powers, and the rulers of the darkness of this world (Eph. 6:12). People have the misconception that an event that's "supernatural" must always outwardly appear contrary to nature. But this is not what the Bible reveals. While all supernatural events most certainly are contrary to nature, they don't always manifest this way. This is so because what you may see with your literal eyes, may not always be what is so. The events in Job are a prime example of this, but there are many others. The scriptures tell us:

> *"Be not forgetful to entertain strangers: for thereby some have entertained angels UNAWARES."* Heb 13:2

This verse from the book of Hebrews is addressing the reality of supernatural beings in our midst (angels of God). It's telling us that we are mostly "unaware" of these creatures. But not because they're physically invisible (although this can sometimes be the case), but because angels can outwardly appear exactly as human men, albeit "strangers." Did you ever read over there about Samson's parents who were caught off guard by one of the Lord's holy messengers? They mistook him for a normal human man until he *"ascended in the flame"* (Jdg. 13:1-20). In other words, until this being did something BLATANTLY AGAINST NATURE, those who were visibly and physically in his company were completely clueless about their involvement with a paranormal event. Had the angel never gone up in the fire, Manoah and his wife would've remained ignorant of their angelic encounter. This is what happened with the servants of Job. When Satan worked against Job, he did not indicate that the things he did were the result of anything outside of nature. Many supernatural occurrences happen exactly like this. While Samson's father and mother were unaware of ANGELIC ACTIVITY, Jobs's servants were unaware of DEMONIC ACTIVITY. What this all means is that there are TWO KINDS OF SUPERNATURALISM found in scripture: OVERT and COVERT. While the word "supernatural" appears nowhere in the Bible, I'm sure that no one would argue the fact that things and events indicative of the word are easily found there. The circumstances surrounding Job and Manoah have helped

The encounter of Samson's father and mother with an angel is an outstanding case of COVERT SUPERNATURALISM. Manoah and his wife were both under the impression that this being was nothing more than "a man of God" (Jud. 13:6). It wasn't until they witnessed OVERT SUPERNATUALISM that they realized their eyes had deceived them –– the man was more than just a man.

introduce us to this truth. The following segments will further outline and define these two supernatural classifications while giving more scriptural examples.

WHEN THE LAWS OF NATURE ARE NULLIFIED

The word "overt" refers to something that is out in the open, apparent, or public. Thus, "Overt Supernaturalism" can be defined as a thing or event, that when witnessed, IT IS IMMEDIATELY OBVIOUS that something out of the ordinary or unnatural is taking place. Here, viewers observe established laws of nature being counteracted, broken, or bent. The Bible often refers to these kinds of blatant events as signs, wonders, tokens, or miracles. While many examples of this can be found in scripture, here are some of the most outstanding:

> **1.) THE BURNING BUSH** (Ex. 3:2) – When witnessing a bush burning with fire that wasn't being consumed, Moses knew immediately that it was not an event of nature.
>
> **2.) AARON'S ROD** (Ex. 7:10, etc.) – At the very moment Aaron's rod was transformed into a serpent, all those who saw the event were instantly without doubt that such a thing was supernatural. Even Pharaoh knew that this feat couldn't be duplicated naturally, this is why he called his "sorcerers" and "magicians" to come to his aid (Ex. 7:11).
>
> **3.) THE PARTING OF THE RED SEA** (Ex. 14:21) – When the waters of the Red Sea were parted into two walls and congealed, not a single person who crossed

over on the dusty ground considered the happening an act of nature.

4.) FLYING HORSES OF FIRE (2 Kgs. 2:11-12) – When Elijah and Elisha witnessed fiery horses descending from the sky, they knew right away that such beasts were not of this earth.

5.) CHRIST WALKING ON THE SEA (Mt. 14:25, Mk. 6:45-51) – The walking of the Lord Jesus on the sea of Galilee is one of the most well-known overt acts of the supernatural in all of the Bible. Christ's disciples literally saw this happen. And not only did the Lord walk upon the water, but the wind was raging and creating great, *"boisterous"* waves, in so much that the disciples were unable to properly row their boat. But, not only did the water have no effect on the walking of the Lord, neither did the wind. He walked ON THE WATER and THROUGH THE TEMPESTUOUS AIR without hindrance of any kind. The laws of physics and nature were completely nullified.

6.) CHRIST ASCENDING INTO HEAVEN (Acts 1:10) The ascension of the Lord Jesus Christ into heaven was another shocking sight with many witnesses. The movement of a man up into the air, without wings, or any mechanical or man-made assistance, had to have been a jaw-dropping sight.

The paranormal aspects of all the cases above were OUTWARDLY MANIFEST. Meaning, all instances have witnesses which can testify that these were events BEYOND THE NATURAL. When people think of "the supernatural" it is always THESE KINDS OF SELF-EVIDENT EVENTS that they think of. When Christ healed the blind, deaf, maimed, and crippled, this is the exact kind of supernaturalism

52 | Hidden in Plain Sight

Christ's walking upon the stormy sea is one of the greatest displays in the Bible of OVERT SUPERNATURALISM.

the people witnessed. They saw the laws of nature being violated, publicly, out in the open. However, unbeknownst to the average person (and many Christians), many other Bible instances of nature-breaking phenomena do not happen this way. Instead of being open and obvious (overt), they are hidden and secret (covert). This is a very important truth for the Bible-believer to grasp.

HIDDEN IN PLAIN SIGHT

The word "covert" means the opposite of "overt." In contrast to a thing that's exposed, "covert" refers to something that is covered or hidden. "Covert Supernaturalism" may be defined as a thing or event, that when witnessed, IS NOT IMMEDIATELY OBVIOUS that something out of the ordinary or supernatural is taking place. It outwardly appears as something happening of its own accord, naturally, without intervention from forces outside of nature. The scriptures below help demonstrate this:

1.) JONAH SWALLOWED BY A WHALE - When Jonah was swallowed by the fish, there was no way for him, nor the men who threw him overboard, to know that this creature had been *"prepared"* by God (Jon. 1:17). It outwardly appeared as simply a fish swallowing down its next meal. No one was aware of the fact that the whale was controlled by forces higher than nature.

2.) THE RAIDER ATTACKS ON JOB – These events have already been addressed, but they are paramount examples of the supernatural taking place covertly. When the Sabeans and Chaldeans invaded Job's land, stole his cattle, and murdered his servants, nothing about these things appeared out of the ordinary. Superficially, it simply seemed to be evil men doing the things that evil men do. But the Bible clearly delineates Satan's *"power"* as the moving force behind it (Job 1:12). This helps give us a clear window into how the Devil directly uses fallen man. The profound thing about Job chapters 1 and 2, is that nearly all the events, on the surface, appear to be manifestations of the NATURAL, when in fact, THEY ARE SUPERNATURAL.

3.) ANGELIC MANIFESTATION – Angels can also manifest overtly and covertly. In some instances, it's obvious to the viewer that what's being witnessed is an "angel" (Lk. 2:6-14, etc.). In other cases, however, the viewer is completely unaware. We've already talked about this and it happens over and over in the Bible.

4.) THE MURDER OF CHRIST – The whole reason Christ was crucified was because of covert supernaturalism. God was right there in their midst, but they didn't believe it. Most of the witnesses who looked at the Lord Jesus, outwardly, were not convinced that he was the Creator of the universe. He simply appeared to be a man, and this is exactly what many believed, his working of miracles notwithstanding. Covert supernaturalism hid the truth that he was God "*manifest in the flesh...*" 1 Tim. 3:16

"*The Jews answered him, saying, For a good work we stone thee not* [miracles of healing, etc.]; *but for blasphemy; and BECAUSE THAT THOU, BEING A MAN, MAKEST THYSELF GOD.*" Jn. 10:33

God Himself came unto man in the form of a man, and this is what most people were (and are) ignorant of:

"[5] *...Christ Jesus:* [6] *Who, BEING IN THE FORM OF GOD, thought it not robbery to be EQUAL WITH GOD:* [7] *But made himself of no reputation, and TOOK UPON HIM THE FORM OF A SERVANT, and was MADE IN THE LIKENESS OF MEN:* [8] *And BEING FOUND IN FASHION AS A MAN, he humbled himself, and became obedient unto death, even the death of the cross.*"
Phil. 2:5-8

The whole concept of God being manifest in the flesh is the ultimate form of COVERT SUPERNATURALISM. In fact, the whole notion appears to be a paradox. How can a "man" be "God"? Well, a normal, human, earth-born man can't be God. The only way for such a thing to occur is if God willingly takes on the form of a man himself. And this is exactly what God did when he was born of a virgin. When such a thing happened, God was forcing us not to believe what we're SEEING, but to believe what He's SAYING. This is why the words of God are so important. God often teases man with works of OVERT SUPERNATURALISM (healings, walking on water, ascending into heaven, etc.), because this is what man always demands of him (Mt. 12:38, etc.). But, the Lord wants our faith placed in HIS WORDS, not in OUR EYES:

"Now faith is the substance of things hoped for, the evidence of THINGS NOT SEEN." Heb 11:1

"Jesus saith unto him, Thomas, BECAUSE THOU HAST SEEN ME, thou hast believed: blessed are THEY THAT HAVE NOT SEEN, AND YET HAVE BELIEVED." John 20:29

Surprisingly, devil-possession (the indwelling of an unclean spirit in the body of a human host) can also manifest similarly in both overt and covert forms. One form of demonic possession, the more overt, makes it obvious that something is not right with the host in whom the foul spirit dwells. Scripture shows that this kind of possession can manifest openly in individuals as inappropriate nakedness (Mk. 5:15, etc.); superhuman strength (Mk. 5:4, etc.); affinity for death, dead things, or locations of such (like tombs, cemeteries, and graveyards, etc. – Mt. 8:28-32, Lk. 8:27, etc.); chronic depression (Mt. 4:4-6, etc.); self-mutilation or self-torture (Mk. 5:5, etc.); suicidal thoughts and fulfillment (Mk. 9:17-22, Mt. 27:5, etc.); chronic illness; and deafness, muteness, or blindness (Lk. 13:16, Mk. 9:25, Mt. 9:32-33, Mt. 12:22, etc.). And this is also in spite of the fact that nearly all of these things can happen to a person without that person being demonically "possessed."

On the other hand, in the more covert or hidden form of devil-possession, no such outward signs are on display. THE POSSESSED INDIVIDUAL OUTWARDLY APPEARS NO DIFFERENT THAN ANY NORMAL PERSON. Examples of this may be found in Satan's possession of Judas Iscariot. A case in which the possessed was not running around naked, mutilating himself, nor had an affinity for the dead. He was acting like a saint – a disciple – one who took part in the ministry of the apostleship (Acts 1:25). In other words, Judas was COMPLETELY INVISIBLE as far as being detected as one being moved and used by the Devil. This is so much the case, that when the Lord announced that one of the disciples would betray him, none of them had any idea to whom Christ was referring:

"[20] Now when the even was come, he sat down with the twelve. [21] And as they did eat, he said, Verily I say unto you, that ONE OF YOU SHALL BETRAY ME. [22] And they were exceeding sorrowful, and BEGAN EVERY ONE OF THEM TO SAY unto him, LORD, IS IT I?"
Matt. 26:20-22

"[27] And after the sop SATAN ENTERED INTO HIM [Judas]. Then said Jesus unto him [Judas], That thou doest, do quickly. [28] Now NO MAN AT THE TABLE KNEW for what intent he spake this unto him."
John 13:27-28

This type of hidden demonic infestation continues today:

"[13] For such are false apostles, deceitful workers, transforming themselves into the apostles of Christ. [14] And no marvel; for Satan himself is transformed into an angel of light. [15] Therefore IT IS NO GREAT THING if his ministers also be TRANSFORMED AS THE MINISTERS OF RIGHTEOUSNESS; whose end shall be according to their works." 2Cor. 11:13-15

Another case of this is seen in the *"damsel possessed with a spirit of divination,"* who displayed none of the signs indicative of one being inhabited by an evil spirit. This is even though the very account openly states that the woman was *"possessed"* (Acts 16:16). Witches, wizards, sorcerers, and other practitioners of occult arts, can also fall into this category of being possessed, without exhibiting any apparent signs of it. Scripture identifies these individuals as those that *"have"* familiar spirits; *"consulters"* with familiar spirits; *"workers"* with familiar spirits; and those that *"dealt"* with familiar spirits (see Lev. 19:31, 20:27, Deut. 18:11, etc.). The Witch of Endor, of whom King Saul inquired, was not running around like a mindless demoniac when the king sought her (1 Sam. 28:6-25); nor were Pharaoh's magicians when approached by Moses and Aaron (Ex. 7, etc.); neither was

Hidden in Plain Sight | 57

The possession of Judas Iscariot is a great example of demon activity in covert operation. What could possibly be more deceptive than appearing as *"one of the twelve"* while alerting no one (Jn. 6:71, etc.)? See Revelation 13:3 for a good example.

"Elymas the sorcerer," when encountered by Paul (Acts 13:6-12). Yet, in all these cases, according to scripture, such individuals dealt with, worked with, and were possessed regularly by unclean spirits. Don't be deceived by the fact that some demonized people are associated with "wisdom." Scripture doesn't deny this. Some people will use this fact to draw others into it (this is how many witches recruit followers by appealing to ones desire to gain knowledge). But, mere "wisdom" is not the issue. The issue is WHAT KIND OF WISDOM because not all forms of wisdom are equal. There's GODLY WISDOM and UNGODLY WISDOM. There's THE WISDOM OF THIS WORLD and THE WISDOM OF GOD. The question is WHICH WISDOM IS BEING ACQUIRED. The Bible's clear that witches, wizards, magicians, and such do not possess the wisdom of God:

> *"Regard not them that have familiar spirits, neither seek after wizards, TO BE DEFILED BY THEM: I am the LORD your God."* Lev. 19:31

> "And the soul that turneth after SUCH AS HAVE FAMILIAR SPIRITS, and after wizards, to go a whoring after them, I will even set my face against that soul, and will cut him off from among his people." Lev. 20:6

> "[10] There shall not be found among you any one that maketh his son or his daughter to pass through the fire, or that useth divination, or an observer of times, or an enchanter, or a witch, [11] Or a charmer, or a consulter with familiar spirits, or a wizard, or a necromancer. [12] For ALL THAT DO THESE THINGS ARE AN ABOMINATION UNTO THE LORD: and because of these abominations the LORD thy God doth drive them out from before thee." Deut. 18:10-12

And by the way, I'm not picking on magicians, witches, and wizards to shoehorn all false, ungodly wisdom to people who are only involved in such things. SATANIC WISDOM EXISTS AT LEVELS MUCH DEEPER THAN THIS (2 Cor. 11:14-15). These types of practitioners are simply listed TO DEMONSTRATE THAT SUCH FORMS OF FALSE WISDOM DO EXIST AND CAN BE LEARNED, it's just that the Lord forbids it. If you care about God, truth, and your own soul, you'll heed God's warnings.

A wizard

Normally, people expect devil-possession to exhibit signs similar to lunacy or being mentally unstable. There's just cause for thinking this way. But, as a result of certain covert-like forms of demonization, some instances of devil-possession or influence are not limited to public, crazy-type behavior. Some diabolic individuals may come across as HIGHLY INTELLIGENT (more on this later). This is why we find the titles of "witch," "wizard" and "magician," all having etymological ties to a form of "wisdom." But this should come as no surprise since Satan himself is described as *"full of wisdom"* (Ezk. 28:12). Lucifer's fall didn't turn him into a blabbering imbecile, it merely corrupted the wisdom that was in his once-perfect mind:

"...thou hast CORRUPTED THY WISDOM..." Ezk. 28:17

One of the easiest ways to demonstrate covert supernaturalism is for you to go look in the mirror and stand there a few seconds while staring yourself in the eyes. Do you see that spirit behind there? The spirit behind your eyes? Do you see it? No, you don't. Well, now you can congratulate yourself because YOU'VE JUST WITNESSED COVERT SUPERNATURALISM in action. According to the Final Authority, every man, woman, boy, girl, and animal on this planet has a SUPERNATURAL ASPECT closer to them than their own beating hearts – a spirit. But science has never recognized this. And make no mistake, such grand lapses in scientific circles are still going on today, and probably to a greater extent. Recognizing the reality of veiled incidences of the supernatural can be a huge game-changer when it comes to the discernment of supernatural events. Science really has no way of getting its foot in the door on these things. When such mysteries take place, nothing out of the ordinary is suspected. The events occur in plain sight, but the supernatural characteristics are hidden (just like the satanic events of Job 1 and 2). One outstanding example in the Bible of this, as we've already addressed, declares that witnesses of such happenings are left "unawares" (Heb 13:2).

Although modern science believes it, the universe is not built or guided by "nature" (mindless blind chance, chaos, and accidents) where microscopes, telescopes, and computers will eventually figure everything out. THE UNIVERSE WAS BUILT AND IS GUIDED BY THE SUPERNATURAL. The Bible tells us *"In the Beginning, God..."* (Gen. 1:1). Both God and Satan play a major role in history in this current fallen world. Not only thousands of years ago but also in the twenty-first-century. But most of those today who are in charge of our teaching are completely ignorant of this (take any public school or university). Understanding this helps lay a foundation on HOW THE DEVIL CAN WORK THROUGH NATURE WITHOUT MANKIND BEING AWARE OF HIM. His role as *"the prince of the power of the air"* can manifest in exactly this manner. This means any aerial phenomena is fair game for his manipulation, whether it be storms, tornados, hurricanes, fireballs, lightning, or other occurrences. While the incident in Job (1:19) represents the Bible's only outright example of Satan manipulating the air, this does not imply in any way, that this was the only time such power was exercised. Such a conclusion would be highly naive. The Devil's title of "prince" over the air expels this notion. As Bible-believers, we are to take the example in Job and apply it to real-world situations. This way, scripture becomes a light to our path, illuminating the world around us. These truths help us avoid being ignorant of the Adversary's many devices (2 Cor. 2:11).

What's been covered in this section, I believe, is one of the most important lessons the Christian can learn. This knowledge (the reality of overt and covert forms of the supernatural) opens up a whole new avenue of spiritual discernment. Read this section over as many times as you need. The bottom line is to let this information sink down into your brain, because it's too important to ignore. Due to thee things, I'm reminded of words the Lord once spoke to Israel:

"My people are destroyed for lack of knowledge…" Hos 4:6

The first three parts of this book have laid a foundation for what's to be addressed hereafter.

PART IV

EVIL RIDES THE WIND

Satanology - History - Prophecy - Technology

"Terrors are turned upon me: they pursue my soul as the wind: and my welfare passeth away as a cloud."
Job 15:30

AN ILL WIND THAT BLOWETH NO GOOD

THE WORD "storm" is defined as a strong, turbulent wind. Storms happen all around the world nearly every second of every day. According to the National Oceanic and Atmospheric Administration (NOAA) and the National Weather Service:

> "It is estimated that there are as many as 40,000 thunderstorm occurrences each day worldwide. This translates into an astounding 14.6 million occurrences annually!" [9]

This estimate indicates that there are approximately 1,666 storms every hour or a storm forming every two seconds. To call the earth a "storm planet," would not be an understatement.

It is the VIOLENT MOVEMENT OF AIR that causes a weather front to be labeled as a "storm." Without intense airflow, there is no storm. Storms can come in a variety of forms: Thunderstorms (also called electrical storms), windstorms, tornados, tropical storms, and hurricanes (cyclones, typhoons). There are also storms of hail, ice, and snow (Psa. 148:9).

---

[9] "Introduction to Thunderstorms" (National Weather Service: US Department of Commerce), https://www.weather.gov/jetstream/tstorms_intro

One of the most volatile and dangerous kinds of storms is the TORNADO. Sometimes called a "twister," a tornado is a spinning column of air attached to a giant storm cloud (called a "supercell" by meteorologists). Scripture calls it a "whirlwind" (Job 38:1, Jer. 23:19, Ezk. 1, Nah. 1:3, etc.) When a tornado forms and touches down a whole array of things are taking place including changes in air pressure, moisture, electromagnetic discharges, atmospheric turbulence, and fluctuating rotational wind speeds. Because they're comprised of rotating air, ALL TORNADIC VORTICES ARE INVISIBLE. But, their positions may be given away due to the formation of ground-level dust and debris clouds. Tornados carry the strongest winds on earth, with speeds varying between 65 to 300-plus miles per hour. Often, tornados are on the ground for only a few minutes, but they can remain grounded for over three hours and travel for hundreds of miles. Tornados classified at EF4 or EF5 strength contain more power than a nuclear detonation. It's not unheard of for these monster windstorms to mangle, maim, impale, decapitate, or kill their victims. Meteorologist, Matthew Cappucci writes:

> "Tornados are the definition of meteorological caprice. They can obliterate one home while leaving the neighboring household untouched. They can drive blades of straw through a two-by-four but spare flowers in the garden with petals unruffled. Some funnels — perhaps the width of a school bus — can ravage a narrow path, while others can grow to mile-wide buzz saws." [10]

Throughout history, it has been reported by witnesses that these vortices often bring with them an ominous sense of THE PRESENCE OF EVIL. Instead of a storm being simply a violent tempest, many report the incident as feeling more like AN ENCOUNTER WITH A

---

[10] Cappucci, Matthew. "A house blown onto a street, an untouched cake and photos carried 100 miles: Tornados leave bizarre scenes in their wake" (The Washington Post. 14, April, 2020), www.washingtonpost.com/weather/2020/04/14/house-street-an-untouched-cake-debris-carried-100-miles-deadly-tornados-leave-bizarre-scenes-amid-destruction/.

An Ill Wind that Bloweth No Good | 65

A "tornado" is an invisible vortex which produces violent and deadly rotational winds. Tornaods become visible with the formation of debris clouds. They are the most powerful storms on earth.

LIVING BEING. Peter J. Thuesen, Professor of Religious Studies at IUPUI, writes of the reports of frequent tornado victims:

> "... Like apparitions from another world, tornados loom with a LIFELIKE PRESENCE, often causing witnesses to feel pursued, as if by a MALEVOLENT SPIRIT. Despite vastly improved radar and warning systems...why it obliterates one house but leaves a neighboring one untouched--defies prediction. ... Recent scientific advances have only increased the sense that NATURALISTIC EXPLANATIONS CANNOT CAPTURE THE FULL COMPLEXITY OF A TORNADO." [11]

Thuesen then adds that tornados "...prove the existence of mysteries beyond what is scientifically discoverable and measurable." [12]

---

[11] Thuesen, Peter J. "Question & Answer with Peter Thuesen about Tornado God" (Peter J. Thusesen), https://www.peterthuesen.com/question-and-answer-on-tornado-god
[12] Ibid.

Former Chicago Tribune columnist, John Kass, experienced a tornado firsthand in 1967. Upon the storm's approach, Mr. Kass reported that he had eerie feelings of "nature as evil, nature with a mind, predatory, nature intent on hunting us down." As the monstrous rotation overtook him, he said it sounded like a "freight train of DEMONS." [13]

The idea of ascribing awareness or intelligence to violent storms is certainly unsettling. But why do many victims do this? Does man's sense of mortality and awe in the face of such dangerous and frightening power make him delusional, or is there more to these feelings? Is it all just supposed "primeval superstition" that can be explained away psychologically or is there something unknown going on – something science never considers? As we've already discussed, the existence of a guiding, thinking mind behind supposed "natural weather" events is not beyond the scope of reality. In fact, some storms may involve exactly this, according to the Bible. This means that not all atmospheric phenomena are a thing of mere climate cycles. Scripture shows that aerial events can result from several different things:

> 1.) Some aerial phenomena result from the ordinances and laws which the Lord has put in place to regulate it (modern man calls this "nature" – Job 38:33-35, Psa. 119:90-91).

> 2.) Some aerial phenomena may be the result of the direct Hand of God (Ex. 14:21, Psa. 107:25, Psa. 135:6-7, Isa. 29:6, Nah. 1:3, etc.).

> 3.) Some aerial phenomena may be the result of angelic interaction (Lk. 2:9, Rev. 16:17-21, etc.).

---

[13] LaFrance, Adrienne. "Supercomputers, Tornados, and the Biggest Unsolved Mystery in Weather Technology" (The Atlantic: The Atlantic Monthly Group, 23, November, 2015), https://www.theatlantic.com/technology/archive/2015/11/tornados-hard-predict/417213/

4.) Some aerial phenomena may be the result of the direct hand of the Devil (Job 1:12, 16 & 19, etc.).

Because of these various particulars, distinguishing which of these is actually affecting the air at any given moment is not possible most of the time. We only know that GOD'S WORD DRAWS DISTINCTIONS. Failure to recognize these differences can lead to error. All must be taken into account.

Since mankind's awareness of tornados, such atmospheric events have left anomalous, unexplainable phenomena in their wake. "No one has ventured to call tornados 'inquisitive,'" writes scientist and author, William Corliss, "and 'prankish' seems too mild a term for such deadly storms. Yet the tales of tornado freaks are legion and devilishly hard to account for." [14]

In 2019, a powerful twister struck the community of Harris County, Georgia. Woodland which surrounded one family was all felled or uprooted, yet their house was left virtually unscathed. "It's mind-blowing," said the resident who heard his trees cracking and splintering, "an EF4 tornado comes across and destroys everything around you, except your house, and you and your family... We were just completely overwhelmed. It can't be explained." [15]

The Associated Press affirms: "While hurricanes, floods, and blizzards create broad swaths of damage, tornados seem to have tiny fingers that can reach into small areas and cause some weird mischief. Some say tornados have their own personalities." [16]

---

[14] Corliss, William R. *Handbook of Unusual Natural Phenomena*. Avenel, NJ: Gramercy Books & Random House, 1977) p. 217

[15] *The Unexplained*, S1 E13, Extreme Weather Mysteries, First aired: Saturday, March 28, 2020.

[16] Wolf, Jeffrey. "WEIRD: Toilet paper unwinds and rewinds during tornado" (9news: KUSA-TV, 2, June. 2008), www.9news.com/article/news/weird/toilet-paper-unwinds-and-rewinds-during-tornado/73-342689553

The 2019 Harris County, Georgia tornado aftermath and the house that mysteriously survived. [photo ©2019, Matt Gillespie]

What we're dealing with here is precise, surgical-like activity BY AIR. Sometimes these storms appear to "play" with their targets, the results of which are often disturbingly uncanny, especially for a weather event known for its destructive power. The words "play" and "destruction," generally don't go together. But such things are certainly baffling when supernatural involvement is ignored.

In 1977, scientist and author William R. Corliss wrote:

> "Meteorologists, in fact, do not really understand the genesis of atmospheric vortices. …no other atmospheric phenomena can generate wind velocities of several hundred miles per hour [300-plus mph], suggesting that SOMETHING BESIDES AERODYNAMIC FORCES IS AT WORK." [17]

If you're thinking the above statement is outdated, you're wrong. In 2016, tornado experts at the Weather Channel admitted:

---

[17] Corliss, William R. *Handbook of Unusual Natural Phenomena*. Avenel, NJ: Gramercy Books & Random House, 1977) p. 213

"Tornado genesis, discovering the specifics of what triggers a tornado is considered the Holy Grail for many storm scientists." [18]

"...tornados have consistently defied scientists' efforts to unlock their secrets. Meteorologists now acknowledge that even the most powerful computers will likely never be able to predict a tornado's precise path." [19]

The Storm Prediction Center at the National Oceanic and Atmospheric Administration asks and answers its own question:

"How do tornados form? The classic answer—'warm moist Gulf air meets cold Canadian air and dry air from the Rockies'—IS A GROSS OVERSIMPLIFICATION. Most thunderstorms that form under those conditions (near warm fronts, cold fronts and drylines respectively) NEVER MAKE TORNADOS. Even when the large-scale environment is extremely favorable for tornadic thunderstorms, as in an SPC 'High Risk' outlook, not every thunderstorm spawns a tornado. THE TRUTH IS THAT WE DON'T FULLY UNDERSTAND." [20]

In so many words, science will often put out a bite of information for public consumption that makes it seem like they know what's fully going on, when in truth, they don't.

In 2018, Florida State University's Department of Geography released a report stating that there "is a clear upward trend in tornado power over the past few decades that amounts to 5.5% per

---

[18] *Top Ten Weather Mysteries*, First aired: September 78, 2016.

[19] Thuesen, Peter J. "Tornado God: American Religion and Violent Weather" (Peter J. Thuesen), https://www.peterthuesen.com/tornado-god

[20] Edwards, Roger. "The Online Tornado FAQ" (Storm Prediction Center, US Dept of Commerce), https://www.spc.noaa.gov/faq/tornado/index.html

year..." The study concluded that THE POWER OF TORNADOS IS INCREASING, year by year, in the United States. They're becoming more powerful.[21] Not only are these things getting more powerful, they're also becoming more frequent. A study from 1975 reported:

> "The recorded annual incidences of tornados in the United States has increased steadily and dramatically in the past four decades, by at least a factor of six." [22]

In relation to this, many aspects of hurricanes are also mysterious. Sometimes they can explode in power with no meteorological explanation, whatever. In 2004, hurricane "Charley" did exactly this. Punta Gorda, Florida was under evacuation as it prepared for a "moderate Category 1" storm. However, Charley suddenly and mysteriously erupted into a monstrous "Category 4" – a hurricane capable of inflicting 250-times more damage than the initial manifestation. Hurricane expert, Michael Lowry, reports:

> "Sometimes ocean conditions and atmosphere is just absolutely perfect, and a storm doesn't strengthen. But in other instances, it's sort of marginally favorable, and a hurricane will spin up [*snaps fingers*] just like that, and we just don't know why." [23]

The important thing to take away from this is that it's unwise for the Christian to ignore the Devil's involvement in such things. Sometimes the reactions of victims in the face of these powerful forces show hints of something greater at work. While this in no way implies that such aerial events, or severe weather events, are always "of the Devil," I'll guarantee that Satan is responsible for more than

---

[21] *The Unexplained*, S1 E13, Extreme Wether Mysteries, First aired: Saturday, March 28, 2020.

[22] Corliss, William R. *Handbook of Unusual Natural Phenomena*. Avenel, NJ: Gramercy Books & Random House, 1977) p. 217

[23] *Top Ten Weather Mysteries*, First aired: September 78, 2016.

the weatherman gives him credit. If what the Bible says is true (Jn. 17:17), I would guess that Satan is extremely under-appreciated in this department.

THE TORNADO & THE BUTTERFLY PEOPLE

On May 22, 2011, Joplin, Missouri was hit by one of the most devastating tornados to ever strike the United States. When the dust finally settled, over 158 people lay dead in the aftermath. Shortly after the catastrophe, stories began to emerge that strange, humanoid-like flying things were reportedly observed by several victims during the disaster. Most of the witnesses were children who "didn't know each other," but some of the observers were parents, including one Red Cross volunteer. According to eyewitnesses, the mysterious, winged phantoms, now called "Butterfly People," seemed to be "descending down from the sky and covering them [the tornado victims] with wings" or "carrying other kids and adults up into the heavens".[24] The various accounts were so stunning and similar that two books have been written about the phenomenon, the first of which is *Butterflies at the Window: A Story*

Strange flying things were witnessed in this skies above Joplin, Missouri during one of the worst tornados in US history.

---

[24] Rowland, Stephen. "Stephen Rowland: 'Butterfly people' a testament to things seen and unseen." (Columbia Daily Herald, The Daily Herald, 27, April, 2021), https://www.columbiadailyherald.com/story/opinion/2021/04/28/stephen-rowland-butterfly-people/4852703001

The official butterfly mural of Jopin, Missouri was erected as a symbol of community recovery and as a memorial to survivors and to those who witnessed the strange, aerial, winged, humanoids during the 2011 tornado.

of Butterfly People and Miracles in the Storm. The city of Joplin later built a historical marker dedicated to testimonies associated with the sightings. Because of this, when the community began to rebuild, the butterfly became their symbol of recovery. Most Joplinians interpreted the beings as "angels." Although it's a widely held belief that "angles have wings," this is a myth. There is no scripture to support the idea. I don't necessarily doubt that these strange events took place, or that witnesses actually saw something. But if the said creatures were heavenly servants of God, they were mistakenly identified as having wings, or they were something other than "angels" (Isa. 8:20). Never let your experiences override scripture or interpret it, no matter how real, convincing or miraculous they may be (1Th. 5:21, 1Jn. 4:1 Acts 17:11, etc.). Unclean spirits are not beyond the capacity of working miracles (Rev. 16:13-14).

FOOTNOTE: Satan can use catastrophes like tornados to turn people against God. This is an important point for Christians to remember, because this is exactly what he was trying to do in Job's case (Job 1:11 & 2:5). But unlike Job, who would not *"curse God"* (Job 2:9), many people who are shallow in their faith, or have no faith at all, certainly don't think twice about snubbing their nose at their Maker.

As addressed in Part III, *Wonders Seen & Unseen*, the first example in the Bible of Satan demonstrating his power of the air is revealed when the Devil kills Jobs children by use of *"a great wind"* (Job 1:19). The verse shows that wind struck *"the four corners of the house,"* causing it to fall. This is comparable to tornadic activity or "straight-line winds" and should leave the Bible-believer no room for doubt as to Satan's potential in this area. Air currents strong enough to flatten a house are generally around 100 to 200 miles per hour, but gusts of over 300 mph are not unheard of. While the example in Job is the only one in the Bible which mentions the Devil outright in conjunction with such wind power, could he possibly be tied to other storm accounts without being named explicitly? Knowing that Satan is the prince over the earth's atmosphere, to think otherwise would be negligent. The next sections will examine a couple of potential cases regarding this.

THE DAY OF EUROCLYDON

The longest-lasting storm in the Bible (over two weeks) is actually given a name: "EUROCLYDON" (Act 27:14). So, what are we to make of this? Was this a storm brought by the Devil? Possibly, especially when we consider several Bible facts. First, even before the tempest appears, the ships which bring Paul to Rome (there are two) are FIGHTING AGAINST THE WIND. The winds first become *"contrary,"* just after departing Sidon (Acts 27:1-4). Later, more difficulty in sailing is encountered near Cnidus (Acts 27:5-7). Once Paul reaches the Fair Havens at Crete, he warns his captors:

> *"I perceive that this voyage will be with hurt and much damage, not only of the lading and ship, but also of our lives."* Acts 27:11

What caused Paul to *"perceive"* that the remainder of his trip would be wrought with peril? Was this some kind of premonition on Paul's part or was it something more? I believe the answer to this is revealed later in the account. In any case, before departing Crete, the sea appears to settle down. This lull prompts the master of the ship to journey onward. It is then that EUROCLYDON APPEARS (Acts 27:12-14). Clearly, the arrival of this monster storm is the danger of which Paul warned his shipmates. And true to his forewarning, once caught by the gale, all hell breaks loose. After being *"exceedingly tossed with a tempest,"* and that being *"no small tempest,"* the ravages of Euroclydon, with its dark and blackened skies, brings Paul's companions to a state of forlorn and hopelessness. This looked like the end (Acts 27:12-14). And yet, in spite of all this, Paul announces:

> [22] *And now I exhort you to BE OF GOOD CHEER: for THERE SHALL BE NO LOSS OF ANY MAN'S LIFE among you, but of the ship.*
> [23] *For there stood by me this night THE ANGEL OF GOD, whose I am, and WHOM I SERVE,*
> [24] *Saying, Fear not, Paul; thou must be brought before Caesar* [to Rome]: *and, lo, GOD HATH GIVEN THEE ALL THEM THAT SAIL WITH THEE.*
> [25] *Wherefore, sirs, be of good cheer: for I BELIEVE GOD, that IT SHALL BE EVEN AS IT WAS TOLD ME.*
>
> Acts 27:22-25

The fact that Paul is now told that the Lord is protecting him and his companions from Euroclydon, indicates that this thing was probably not a product of the Lord's hand. Euroclydon, and verily all the contrary winds from the very start, likely resulted from the Prince of the Power of the Air. Paul's escape from this storm finally comes once he reaches the isle of Melita (Acts 28:1). If the Devil was responsible for Euroclydon, what purpose would it have served in preventing Paul from reaching Rome? Paul's presence in Rome was part of his commission from God that he would be sent *"far hence unto the Gentiles"* (Acts 9:15, 22:21). From all outward appearances, Paul was on his way to Rome to simply stand before Caesar (Acts 25:10-12), but it was the Lord who was bringing him there TO SPREAD THE GOSPEL TO THE GENTILES. Thus, who would benefit the

Paul and his shipmates after being hit by the monster tempest Euroclydon.

most by preventing Paul from reaching Rome, God or the Devil? I don't believe the appearance of Euroclydon was a coincidence, nor was it a mere act of nature, especially since the storm is recorded in scripture. Greater forces were at work. Consider that even before this incident, in Paul's early writings, he mentions SATAN HINDERING HIM in the spreading of the gospel (1Thess. 2). Satan and his minions knew Paul, personally, and what he was doing for the Lord. One devil is even recorded as saying, "...*Jesus I know, and Paul I know...*" (Acts 19:15). If there was ever any man in this world that the Devil was going to attack, it would've been Paul. There's no reason to believe that such satanic obstructions would've abated on Paul's voyage to Rome. In all likelihood, "Euroclydon" was the Devil incognito.

THE STORM & THE SPIRITS OF THE GADARENES

In the books of Matthew, Mark, and Luke, we find another curious occurrence surrounding the manifestation of a storm. All three books give corresponding records of the event. Here, Christ and his disciples are found crossing the Sea of Galilee to the eastern shore. Upon their arrival to the country of the Gadarenes (a.k.a. Gergesa), they encounter two men inhabited by THE LARGEST CONCENTRATION OF DEVIL SPIRITS mentioned anywhere in the Bible – *"Legion"* (Mk. 5:9, Lk. 8:30). The interesting thing about this, is that just before this meeting, the Lord and the disciples ARE FACED WITH A VIOLENT WIND. All three books give testimony to this:

> *"And, behold, THERE AROSE A GREAT TEMPEST IN THE SEA, insomuch that the ship was covered with the waves..."* Mt. 8:24

> *"And THERE AROSE A GREAT STORM OF WIND, and the waves beat into the ship, so that it was now full."* Mk. 4:37

> *"...THERE CAME DOWN A STORM OF WIND on the lake; and they were filled with water, and were in jeopardy."* Lk. 8:23

This storm is so strong, and erupts so fast, that its waves immediately fill the boat with water. Recognizing that their lives are in danger, the disciples are terrified and cry out to the Lord. Christ then speaks to the foul wind, whereupon it instantly dissipates. Is this another supposed "coincidence," like the appearance of Euroclydon with Paul, or is there a connection between this great wind and the demon-infested lands next door? Knowing the demon of the empire of the air, I think it would be naive to assume that these two things (the storm and the Legion) were completely independent of each other. I believe that once Jesus and his disciples entered their ship and headed towards the Gadarenes, the Devil may have attempted to protect a demonic stronghold. He did this by raising a storm. This is not beyond the realm of possibility. The Legion, likewise, attempted to turn Christ away by asking him:

Immediately following a powerful storm at sea, Jesus encounters Legion.

> *"...What have we to do with thee, Jesus, thou Son of God? art thou come hither to torment us BEFORE THE TIME?"*
>
> Mt. 8:29

The devils knew that they had an appointed *"time"* (Rev. 20:10). They also knew that this was not it. But their question did not deter the Lord from rebuking them. He had the power to send them away, even though this was not their appointed time of judgment. And this is exactly what he did. Christ then casts the Legion into a herd of swine. The possessed host then departs into the very waters over which the recent tempest arose (Mt. 8:32, Mk. 5:13, Lk. 8:33).

Euroclydon and the fierce storm adjoining Gergesa, both contain compelling circumstantial evidence that they may have been wrought by the Prince of the Power of the Air. If this is the case, then they're also good examples of COVERT SUPERNATURALISM.

ALIEN TORNADO

In the 2012, made-for-tv film, *Alien Tornado* (also called *Alien Storm* and *Tornado Warning*), unseen intelligences from beyond earth are found creating severe, electrical, storm activity as a way to conquer the world. Does this sound like an original idea? It's not. Satan really can control such things. The movie simply replaces demons with "space aliens" for its storyline. That's how the Devil does it. He often shows what he's doing in movies. And then, when a Christian brings up the issue, someone says; "You got that from a science fiction movie!" No, I got it from the Bible. The filmmaker got it from the Devil. The Bible is always lightyears ahead of science (and science fiction). And Satan's ahead of Hollywood (or *the* head of Hollywood). There's *"no new thing under the sun"* (Ecc. 1:9).

THE TEMPEST THAT SWALLOWS THE EARTH

The largest and oldest storm in the known universe is not found on Earth, but the planet Jupiter. Having been mysteriously sustained for at least the last 340 years, Jupiter's cyclonic behemoth is easily

---

FOOTNOTE: To read more about so-called "aliens" and how Satan uses science fiction, see the book *What Dwells Beyond*.

big enough to engulf the whole Earth. At one time, the hurricane-like vortex was said to be large enough to immerse three worlds of the Earth's size. With outer wind speeds, according to NASA, estimated at around 400 mph, it takes the monster about seven days to make one complete rotation. A whole list of unknowns surround this thing:

1.) Science doesn't know when the storm began. Its longevity can't be explained.
2.) Science doesn't know when it will stop, or if it will stop.
3.) Science has no idea what makes the thing red.
4.) Science can't explain how the storm's speed fluctuates so much and so drastically.

Does this alien cyclone have any connection to the Prince of the Power of the Air? Maybe. Perhaps it's worth considering that the official name of this Jovian tempest is: "The Great Red Spot." In scripture, the word "spot" is nearly always in reference to a blemish or imperfection. The word "spot" first appears in conjunction with LEPROSY which always TYPIFIES SIN (Lev. 13:2, see also Eph. 5:27, Heb. 9:14, etc.). According to the Bible, when a spot in the skin appears *"reddish"* (like Jupiter's storm) it's indicative of an UNCLEAN THING (Lev. 13:18-51, etc.). Christ, the Lamb of God, because he's sinless is said to be *"without blemish and WITHOUT SPOT"* (1Ptr. 1:19). And finally, the first creature that sinned and brought sin to man, is now also called a *"Great Red"* something (Rev. 12:3). So, what do these scriptures imply about the largest storm known to man? Like leprosy, the giant storm is reddish. Like leprosy, the giant storm is called a "spot." In certain ways, Jupiter's GREAT RED SPOT seems emblematic of that GREAT RED DRAGON. The Devil, after all, is the great red spot that mars the universe with sin. This is why he must be destroyed (1Jn. 3:8). And just as *"the god of this world"* will eventually rule the world, so too, is Jupiter's great spot large enough to engulf our planet. Note what the Bible says about Nebuchadnezzar, who often pictured the Devil:

"Nebuchadrezzar the king of Babylon hath devoured me, he hath crushed me, he hath made me an empty vessel, he hath SWALLOWED ME UP LIKE A DRAGON..." Jer 51:34

Interestingly, apart from the Earth, Jupiter is the only other planet the Bible explicitly mentions by name (Acts 19:35). In this reference is found a record of something falling to earth from Jupiter. Is this foreshadowing the day when the Great Red Sinner is finally cast out of the heavens and down to the Earth? Like the arrival of a monstrous tempest, this marks the time when the world goes into chaos and tribulation. A time when Satan will unleash his powers of the air upon this world, unfettered. Perhaps the day that Jupiter's giant storm dissipates and finally comes to an end will coincide with this catastrophic event?

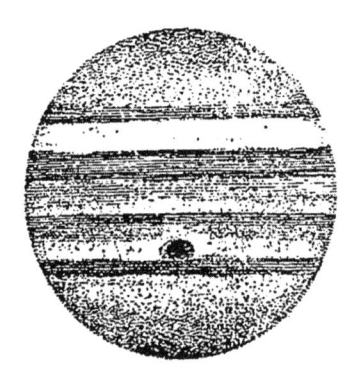

An early sketch of Jupiter's "Great Red Spot" (c.1667)

"Therefore rejoice, ye heavens, and ye that dwell in them. WOE TO THE INHABITERS OF THE EARTH and of the sea! FOR THE DEVIL IS COME DOWN unto you, having great wrath, because he knoweth that he hath but a short time." Rev. 12:12

PRINCE OF PESTILENCE

Another pertinent matter related to Satan and the air is sickness, disease, and pestilence. Again, this is not to say that the Devil is responsible for every single case of these types of things, but he certainly has more involvement than modern science credits him.

Disease and sickness are innate in fallen man, as well as animals, and pollutants in the environment. This is due to the curse of sin upon the universe. This means that we can be born with infirmities (Jn. 9:2), as well as acquire them at any time throughout our lives. In addition to this, however, these things can also be inflicted by God, angles, or devils. The first time any sort of disease shows up in the Bible, it appears in connection with the plagues of Egypt. These plagues consisted of massive outbreaks of frogs, lice, flies, and locusts, along with aerial phenomena like hail, fire, and preternatural darkness. With these things also came, blains, boils, and a *"destroyer,"* a bringer of death, which was likely the Devil himself (Ex. 12:23, 1 Cor. 10:10, etc.).

Satan, no doubt, can inflict any sort of infirmity. The Lord Jesus Christ once healed a woman *"which had a SPIRIT OF INFIRMITY eighteen years, and was bowed together... whom SATAN HATH BOUND ..."* (Lk. 13:10-17). Paul was also afflicted with a specific infirmity which he described as *"a thorn in the flesh, THE MESSENGER OF SATAN"* (2Cor. 12:7). Giving an affliction a title like *"the messenger"* implies that Paul's blemish was more than something physical, but some kind of unclean spirit. Since many illnesses are airborne, and communicable by the air, it's easy to see how the Prince of the Power of the Air can impact the outcome of disease. His command over atmospheric phenomena gives him license to control such things as the common cold, the flu, chicken pox, measles, mumps, whooping cough, tuberculosis, diphtheria, anthrax, SARS, and a whole host of other airborne afflictions we know nothing about. Birds and certain flying insects are also known to be carriers of disease. Of course, the Devil's not limited to the control of airborne viruses, but his princeship over the air certainly gives him an advantage. In the context of "plagues," the Psalmist writes of *"the pestilence that walketh in darkness,"* which may very well be the Devil, or a description of some kind of active, malefic spirit (Psa. 91:6).

Author and scientist, Dr. Mike Baillie, has said about one of mankind's worst pestilence encounters:

> "We have discovered that...THIS COULD HAVE BEEN AN EXTRA-TERRESTRIAL IMPACT. This would have CAUSED A CORRUPTION IN THE ATMOSPHERE... which made the population highly susceptible to disease. The 1348 plague really was in a league of its own, killing a third to half of the population." [25]

Dr. Baillie's "extraterrestrial" object was not an "alien" of any kind, but reportedly a COMET which interacted with the earth's atmosphere. Plainly speaking, it may have been an astronimical event, A FIREBALL IN THE SKY, that brought one of the world's most deadly diseases -- the Black Plague. There are actual reports from witnesses of the time which substantiate this theory, as well as modern tree-ring studies and ice core data. [26] Johannes Nohl, a twentieth-century authority on the "Great Mortality", wrote in his comprehensive examination of the subject:

> "Comets were regarded as particular instigators and precursors of all plagues, and in the centuries when these epidemics were most prevalent, they were extraordinarily frequent." [27]

---

[25] Rao, Nathan. "'Black Death was 'triggered by ASTEROID impact and could reoccur TODAY', scientist claims" (Express: Express Newspapers, 21, February, 2015), https://www.express.co.uk/news/history/559714/Black-Death-trigger-asteroid-impact-scientists

[26] FOOTNOTE: See the book *New Light on the Black Death: The Cosmic Connection*, by Mike Baillie

[27] Nohl, Johannes. *The Black Death*. Hassell Street Press: A reprint of the original 1924 edition. p. 34

Interestingly, the word "influenza" (from which we get the word "flu"—a highly contagious viral infection inhaled FROM THE AIR) originates with the word "influence." According to Webster, the word "influence" means:

> "Literally, a flowing in, into or on, and referring to SUBSTANCES SPIRITUAL or TOO SUBTLE TO BE VISIBLE... In a general sense, INFLUENCE DENOTES POWER WHOSE OPERATION IS INVISIBLE and known only by its effects, or A POWER WHOSE CAUSE AND OPERATION ARE UNSEEN."

Ancient peoples often pointed to the stars as being these agents of influence. This sometimes manifested as astrological beliefs. Although astrology is a false practice, it did, nevertheless, point to the "influences" as being something celestial, aerial or atmospheric. Several modern researchers have demonstrated that plagues were often preceded by reports of SKY-BASED PHENOMENA, like strange rains, comets, fireballs, electrical activity, blasts of hot wind, and the like. Remember what a certain "influential power" did to Job before he was smitten with boils? (Job 1:16-19, 2:7)

A fifteenth-century comet

Up to this point, we've looked at the scriptural perspective of the three-word phrase *"of the air"* and discovered that it's primarily linked to birds. In this capacity, the wording refers to the atmosphere around the earth where fowl have THE ABILITY TO FLY. This unique power of aeronautics parallels a prime characteristic of spirits, both clean and unclean. Secondly, we've noted that the Devil's *"power of the air,"* not only involves flight but parlays over into the actual control of this invisible element. Wind, storms, tornados, hurricanes, pestilence, disease, and other related phenomena (some of which we have yet to address) are all potential outcomes of this power.

In moving forward with this study, we will next attempt to go a little deeper and see how the Devil's authority over the air, and knowledge of the air, in conjunction with his ability to control, manipulate, and deceive man, can have a direct effect on man's TECHNICAL KNOWLEDGE. Before doing this, however, a little groundwork must be laid.

PART V

MARVELOUS MACHINES

Satanology - History - Prophecy - Technology

"And the cherubims lifted up their wings, and mounted up from the earth in my sight..." Ezekiel 10:19

THE FIRST AERO-VESSEL IN TIME AND HISTORY

THE DEVIL'S pre-fallen name was *"Lucifer,"* a designation that generally indicates a "bearer of light." This is exactly what we find in regards to the cherubim as outlined by the prophet Ezekiel. Before the Devil sinned and became the Devil, he was not an "angel" as many suppose, but an *"anointed cherub"* (Ezk. 28:14). Although scripture recognizes both cherubim and angels as "heavenly hosts," cherubim are not angels, but a completely different type of being. Unlike angels, a perusal of scripture will show that one of the primary jobs of cherubim is to ferry the Throne of God. In this capacity, as transporters of the Lord's Chariot, cherubim are literally "lux-fer," light ferrymen, or BEARERS OF THE LIGHT. [28] We see this same job mirrored by the Kohathites who were charged with bearing the Ark of the Covenant:

> *"[4] This shall be the service of the sons of Kohath in the tabernacle of the congregation, about the most holy things: [5] And WHEN THE CAMP SETTETH FORWARD, Aaron shall come, and his sons, and they shall take down the covering vail, and cover THE ARK... [15] ...the sons of Kohath SHALL COME TO BEAR IT..."* Num. 4:1-15 [29]

---

[28] FOOTNOTE: The word "chariot" is the root of our modern word for "car" – a wheeled vehicle.

[29] FOOTNOTE: See also Numbers 3:29-31, 7:9 and 10:21

Cherubim were typologically represented by the Kohathites who were assigned to bear the Ark of the Covenant whenever it was in transit – four cherubim, four Kohathites. The "Mercy Seat" of God was upon the Ark, between the cherubim, and this is where the Lord "sat" when he met with Israel (Ex. 25:17-22).

In that the Kohathites ported the Lord's "mercy seat," this not only typified the moving of God's throne from one place to another but also movement through the air by cherubim.[30]

> [7] *In my distress I called upon the LORD...* [11] *And HE RODE UPON A CHERUB, AND DID FLY: and he was seen UPON THE WINGS OF THE WIND."*
> 2 Sam. 22:7-11 (see also Psa. 18:6-10)

---

[30] FOOTNOTE: In regard to these things, someone may be asking, "Why does God need a flying throne?" The answer to that is, "He doesn't." But as far as that goes, God doesn't "need" angels, men, heaven, or earth, but he made them anyway. The only thing that God's ever "needed" is when Lucifer's rebellion brought sin – God needed to get rid of both him (Satan) and it (sin).

Many ancient cultures carried their dignitaries or "gods" in a seat called a "sedan." They're all counterfeits of the Lord's throne and light-bearers, even those that preceded Israel. Roman Catholics can often be found carrying their images of "Mary" in this same manner.

Note in one of the quoted verses how that flying cherubim are likened to the movement of *"wind."* Does the wind have "wings"? Not literally, but cherubim do. This riding of God *"upon a cherub"* is the exact thing the prophet Ezekiel is found describing:

> "[1] *Then I looked, and, behold, in the firmament that was above the head of THE CHERUBIMS there appeared over them as it were a sapphire stone, as the appearance of the likeness of A THRONE. ... [20] This is the living creature that I saw UNDER THE GOD OF ISRAEL by the river of Chebar; and I KNEW THAT THEY WERE THE CHERUBIMS."*
>
> Ezk. 10:1 & 20, etc.

Another scripture refers to this flying thing as *"the chariot of the cherubims"* (1Ch 28:18).

So what does all of this have to do with the Devil being *"the prince of the power of the air"*? Well, the important thing about this is that we see the role of cherubim tied to A HOLY, CELESTIAL, VESSEL THAT TRAVELS THROUGH THE AIR as *"the wind"* (2 Sam. 22:11). Not only are cherubim themselves winged, but they're

The prophet Ezekiel is privilidged to have witnessed the flying Chariot of the Lord. This first aerial machine in time and history is described in detail in the first and tenth chapters of the book of Ezekiel. The vision was not "symbolic," but literal, and it was not a "flying saucer" from another planet.

also the first aviators in time and history. This device, however, is not powered by a combustion engine (like conventional aircraft), but by THE SPIRITS OF THE CHERUBIM themselves. According to the words of God, the spirits of these four creatures literally interfaced with some type of *"wheels"* (Ezk. 1:16-21, 3:13, 10:2, etc.). This is what gave the machine lift and movement. When in motion, this thing appeared as a glowing, whirling, or rotating wind that emitted some form of electrical energy (Ezk. 1:4). The Bible identifies this energy as *"lightning"* (Ezk. 1:13-14). While this airborne device didn't transport people or freight as modern machines of the air, it did port the Lord God. This is why cherubim were placed on either side of the Ark of the Covenant upon which was added the Mercy Seat (Ex. 25:18, etc.). The ark not only pictured this heavenly flying machine, the centerpiece of the tabernacle, but also depicted cherubim as "lux-fer," literal bearers of the Light of God.[31] The Devil's link to this astounding, flying craft should give the reader room for pause, especially when considering man and the birth of modern aviation (1903). Because the spirits of the cherubim were the means of locomotion behind this device (Ezk. 1:19-20), Satan, who was once a cherub himself, no doubt HAS DEEP KNOWLEDGE OF FLYING CRAFT. Such wisdom falls perfectly in line with one of his princely titles.

THE PRINCE OF THE POWER OF THE AIRCRAFT

Man's first baby steps in harnessing the air for travel came from creating power from the air by heating it. This hot air was then directed into a balloon to create lift. While the invention of the first manned hot-air balloon (1783) didn't do a whole lot as far as giving man the ability for mass transportation, it did help point his attention skyward.

---

[31] FOOTNOTE: The name "Lucifer" is derived from the Latin words "lux," light, and "fer," to bear, ferry or carry.

Wilbur Wright at the controls of the Wright Flyer after a landing (December 14, 1903, Kitty Hawk, North Carolina).

Balloons, planes, jets, and helicopters have only existed for a tiny fraction of man's history. In 1967, NASA created the first Saturn V rocket. Built to take man to the moon, this vehicle could reach speeds of 18,000 miles per hour. That's nine times faster than the average rifle bullet. I think it's fair to say that such feats of locomotion, an ability once reserved to only birds and angels, had been brought to our very doorstep. Only 64 years separate the first motorized, piloted, heavier-than-air craft from the invention of the Saturn V (1903 to 1967). Yet, even at this, the sophistication behind the first generation of powered flying vehicles advanced slowly. From the 1900s through the 1920s, planes were little more than glorified kites with motors (fabric stretched around wooden box frames with a small engine attached). *The Timechart History of Aviation* reports:

> "The Wright Flyer and its successors were FLIMSY affairs, light enough to be manhandled on the ground." [32]

---

[32] *The Timechart History of Aviation*.(Lowe & B. Hould Publishers: Ann Arbor, MI, 2001), p. 9

Wernher von Braun, designer of the massive Saturn V launch vehicle, poses with this state-of-the-art technology as it was in 1969. The facing page shows the most sophisticated form of aviation as it was a mere 66 years prior. One technology is "flmsy," the other "mind-boggling," even by today's standards.

While the first all-metal plane appeared in 1915, this was the exception. According to newspapers at the time, Germany had designed an all-aluminum, "almost bullet-proof" airplane during World War I, but the vehicles never had the chance to see frontline action.[33] Standardization of all-metal craft, worldwide, didn't happen until the early 1930s. But, the "Jet Age" shrinks this window even smaller. Only thirty years separate the world's first jet plane (the Heinkel He178) from the moon rocket. That is mind-blowing to think about. And even more mind-boggling, is that the integration of computer-based avionics systems were not standardized in aircraft until after man went to the moon. Today, man is over half a century removed from the first lunar landing (April, 1969). People don't think about theses things. But when considering such an astounding jump forward in AVIATION TECHNOLOGY, this minuscule blip of time is practically imperceptible when viewing the history of man on the whole. In many ways, IT IS THE AIRCRAFT which prompts modern man to identify himself as an "advanced civilization." This is equally why the UFO phenomenon is disturbing for many, because AIR TECHNOLOGY IS SYNONYMOUS WITH HIGHER KNOWLEDGE. So, why is such technical knowledge of the air appearing with man at this time? Why not a hundred, thousand, or five thousand years ago?

The Bible tells us that the last days will be a time of *"ever learning"* accompanied by a rise in evil, wickedness, and demon activity (2Tim. 3:1, 7 & 13, 1Tim. 4:1). One of the most outstanding hallmarks of this time, according to the prophet Daniel, will be the advancement in man's ability to *"run to and fro"*––the same thing the book of Job says the Devil is currently doing (Job 1:7 & 2:2). Ironically, history shows that man's technical knowledge of moving "to and fro" advanced most significantly with THE INVENTION OF MACHINES THAT UTILIZE THE AIR FOR TRAVEL. Once mechanized aviation was realized, IT ADVANCED FASTER THAN ANY OTHER FORM OF TECHNOLOGY IN THE HISTORY OF THE WORLD. One of the significant things flying craft accomplished was it helped shrink the world. Many of the major technological advances of the past 175 years could rightly be classified as "world-shrinking" technologies (telegraph, telephone, radio) a trend that continues today (cell phones,

---

[33] *The Daily Morning Oasis*. (Nogales, AZ, May 03, 1919), p. 2

internet, etc.). International travel was soon to become an everyday thing. The Lord's scattering of man at Babel was being undone:

> *"And the LORD said, Behold, the people is one, and they have all one language; and this they begin to do: and now nothing will be restrained from them, which they have imagined to do."* Gen. 11:6

Today, people tend to take air travel for granted. Despite this, if the birth of aviation doesn't qualify to meet the prophet Daniel's prediction of knowledge increasing at a time when *"many shall run to and fro,"* then nothing ever will. In the modern era, *"many"* are doing exactly this. About 14,000 craft, and 500,000 people, are moving through the air AT ANY GIVEN SECOND of the average day. According to the International Air Transport Association, over four billion passengers were carried by airlines in 2017 (that's more than double the world population at the time of the Wright brothers). Can there be any doubt that we're in the midst of a time when the Prince of the Power of the Air is influencing the world more than ever before?

When scripture speaks of man *"ever learning"* but *"never able to come to the knowledge of the truth"* (2Tim. 3:7), one of the outcomes of this is that the end times age may indeed proliferate with technical gadgets, but IT WILL HAVE NO DISCERNMENT IN SPIRITUAL MATTERS. Mankind will be learning, but essential information will be missing. Discernment comes by way of Bible study and Bible belief (Heb. 5:13-14, 1Thess. 2:13), but the last generations will hate the word of God (2Tm. 3:1-5). This means, in spite of the millions of schools, colleges, and universities around the globe, spiritual ignorance will reign. And despite it being a supposed time of enlightenment, it will actually be a form of DARK AGE – an age oblivious to the workings of God and the Devil.

Because many Christians fail to tie the everyday workings of history to the Bible, I think it's only naivety that omits the hand of Satan from such a quick onslaught of inventions dependent upon the air (airplanes, jets, helicopters, rockets, etc.). And this goes equally so for such things as radio, television, satellites, electromagnetic transmissions, etc. COULD MODERN SCIENCE UNKNOWINGLY BE WORKING IN CONJUNCTION WITH DEMONS? How? Were the Sabeans and Chaldeans working in conjunction with the Devil when they attacked Job? Yes (Job 1:13-17). Did they know it? No, they didn't. What's preventing Satan from doing the same thing today?

Although we've already briefly touched on the concept that the wisdom of the last generations will be corrupt, there's much more that can be said about this. To better understand how aviation is linked to the Devil, and indeed much of the inventions of the end times, one must understand what the Bible reveals about THE DISSEMINATION OF KNOWLEDGE AND TECHNOLOGY. From where does man get his ideas? Why does certain kinds of information appear in specific generations and not the generations prior? Are all such thoughts of man coincidental? With God being actively involved in man's history, and the Devil being actively involved in man's history, you can be assured that when it comes to the sudden appearance of knowledge, there's more to it than what appears superficially. We'll talk more about this in the sections that follow.

PART VI

AN IMPARTATION OF KNOWLEDGE

Satanology - History - Prophecy - Technology

"Why do the heathen rage, and the people imagine a vain thing?"
Psalm 2:1

EVIL IMAGINATIONS

WHEN YOU BEGIN talking about things like the Bible and technology, right at the outset other things must be addressed. Since technology deals with knowledge and the application of it, then the subjects of knowledge, and man's acquisition of it, are pertinent matters to talk about. Such a study includes subjects like MAN'S HEART, MIND, IMAGINATION, AND WISDOM, all of which are important things in scripture. We've already said a little bit about this in addressing the two kinds of wisdom found in the Bible (see "wisdom" on pages 58-59), but this can be elaborated upon. Take the word *"imagination(s),"* for example. This word is found twenty times in the *King James Bible*. All mentions of it as it relates to man are NEGATIVE, except for two, which lean more neutral (1Chr. 28:9 & 29:18). Nine of the twenty are paired with the phrase *"evil heart,"* which accounts for nearly half of all references. Two more are linked to either a *"proud heart"* or a *"foolish heart."* What this is saying is that man's imagination, generally speaking, is a thing that WORKS AGAINST GOD (such thinking birthed the literary and movie entertainment worlds of "science fiction"). Note the Bible's very first mention of the word:

> *"And GOD saw that THE WICKEDNESS OF MAN WAS GREAT IN THE EARTH, and that EVERY IMAGINATION OF THE THOUGHTS OF HIS HEART WAS ONLY EVIL CONTINUALLY."* Gen. 6:5

One of the things that's interesting about this first appearance is that the word *"imagination"* is not only joined with *"evil,"* but it also shows up with the days of Noah. Scripture predicts *"the days of Noe"* to return (Mt. 24:37, Lk. 17:26). Does this mean that the imaginations of man's heart will again be *"only evil continually"*? That sure seems to be the case.

The last time the Bible uses the word, it's in the context of thoughts being exalted against God:

> *"CASTING DOWN IMAGINATIONS, and EVERY HIGH THING THAT EXALTETH ITSELF AGAINST THE KNOWLEDGE OF GOD, and BRINGING INTO CAPTIVITY EVERY THOUGHT to the obedience of Christ;"*   2Co 10:5

Man's own opinion of his imagination is normally in contrast to this. The agnostic, liberal, socialist, A-bomb architect, and world-government advocate, Albert Einstein, is quoted as saying:

> "The true sign of intelligence is not knowledge but imagination. ... Imagination is more important than knowledge. Knowledge is limited. Imagination encircles the world."

Famous American writer, John Steinbeck, who authored *The Grapes of Wrath* and *Of Mice and Men* and over 30 other works, was more honest in his opinion when he said:

> "My imagination will get me a passport to Hell one day."

Two famous children's books authors have also said some things about imagination. J.K. Rowling, author of the *Harry Potter* series has stated:

> "Imagination is...the uniquely human capacity to envision that which is not, and, therefore, the foundation of all invention and innovation."

L. Frank Baum (1856–1919), creator of the Oz fantasy series, did not believe in a personal Devil. He did, however, have strong interests in certain occult sciences and believed in a "...spirit realm and proposed to replace Christianity with the then-popular quasi-spiritualist doctrine of Theosophy..." 34

According to an opinion piece published in *The New York Times*:

"Although raised in a strict Methodist family, Baum early rejected the Christian teachings of his childhood. ...Baum and his wife, Maud, joined the Theosophists in 1896, held seances in their home and consulted with clairvoyants and astrologers. They both believed in the transmigration of souls and were certain that they had been together in past lives and would be in future ones." 35

Of imagination the author of *The Wonderful Wizard of Oz* has stated:

"Imagination has brought mankind through the Dark Ages to its present state of civilization. Imagination led Columbus to discover America. Imagination led Franklin to discover electricity. Imagination has given us the steam engine, the telephone, the talking-machine and the automobile, for these things had to be dreamed of before they became realities. So I believe that dreams – day dreams, you know, with your eyes wide open and your brain-machinery whizzing – are likely to lead to the betterment of the world."

The Bible shows that when man's imagination becomes corrupt, it has a direct effect on his wisdom:

> "[21] *Because that, when they knew God, they glorified him not as God, neither were thankful; but BECAME VAIN IN THEIR IMAGINATIONS, and their foolish HEART WAS DARKENED. [22] PROFESSING THEMSELVES TO BE WISE, THEY BECAME FOOLS...*" Rom. 1:21-22

---

[34] "Baum, L. Frank" (Freethought Trail), https://freethought-trail.org/profiles/profile:baum-l-frank/
[35] Hearn, Micheal Patrick. The New York Times, No Mysticism in Oz, Just the Populist Credo. December 20, 1991, Section A, p. 34

In other words, what modern education describes as the "Age of Enlightenment," actually marks the beginning of an age of "endarken-ment" – a global darkening of man's heart due to his vain imaginations. The so-called "Age of Enlightenment" or "Age of Reason," appeared just prior to the rise of A WORLDWIDE EXPLOSION IN TECHNOLOGY consisting of several industrial revolutions (c. 1820s - 1890s). The Age of Enlightenment generally dates from about the mid-to-late 1600s to the early 1800s and encompassed 150-or-so years. All of these things laid the groundwork for the technological world we live in today. This age of "ever learning" began with the casting-off of God.

The "Age of Reason" was anything but. The Bible tells us *"Come now, and let us REASON together, saith the LORD..."* (Isa 1:18). Genuine "reason" doesn't exempt God. The heavens declare his glory (Psa. 19:1). Those who refuse to see this are said to be *"vain in their imaginations"* and *"without excuse"* (Rom. 1:20). To be vain in your imaginations can infer two things. One form of vanity connotes a thing that's worthless, fruitless, or ineffectual (1Cor. 15:58). Another form infers excessive pride in oneself, conceit, arrogance, narcissism, and egotism. It's easy to see how professing atheists fall into this trap. Since they refuse to acknowledge God, they become their own gods. This results in a man who's *"highminded,"* a hallmark of the attitude of man in the last days (2Tim. 3:1-4). This is why you never find the Bible attempting to prove the reality of the Creator. It simply takes the Lord's existence as granted. This is so because knowledge begets knowledge. A thinking mind cannot spring from nothing. Information begets information, thus man had a Creator. Any modern scientist who's honest knows this. Just ask any of them who are attempting to bring about "artificial intelligence." Will AI come into reality on its own, or will THINKING MINDS be the reason behind it? Artificial intelligence will not spontaneously manifest. The so-called "Age of Reason," which laid the foundation for both the first and second Industrial Revolutions, was simply the rise of ATHEISM, AGNOSTICISM, MATERIALISM, HUMANISM, and HEDONISM. All are overt efforts to rid the world of BELIEF IN

THE SUPERNATURAL – belief in God and the Devil. By and large, the scientific community of today is a direct offspring of this (public schools, colleges, universities, the National Education Association, etc.).

Some readers may be wondering if the Age of Enlightenment was a negative thing, why has much of the world reaped such prosperity from the fruits of it and the industrial revolutions which followed?[36] The answer is that, much like the rich man who awoke to find himself in Hell, the unsaved man of today is getting his rewards now, rather than later. Just because much of the world today appears outwardly "rich," due to advances in technology, doesn't mean the world's rich spiritually. Today's man is "gaining the whole world," while losing his soul. Scripture reminds us that we are not to confuse gain with godliness (1Tim. 6:5). Just because a thing may become rich and prosperous, doesn't necessarily imply God's involvement or blessing. The bottom line is that our modern technical age is a man-made counterfeit of what God has ultimately promised to those that trust and believe in Him. This explains why much of technology is geared towards "making life easier," and why facets of science today are working towards life-extending technologies to ultimately provide to man ARTIFICIAL IMMORTALITY (we'll talk more about these things later in the book). But this man-made era is doomed to failure. Much like Israel who REJECTED GOD and demanded themselves a king (1Sam 8:5 & 20, etc.), God gave them the desire of their hearts, but REJECTING GOD CAME WITH A PRICE. Israel's first human king, Saul, was a demon-possessed maniac (1Sam. 18 - 31). In other words, when society rejects God, they get the Devil. And this is exactly what's happened with Friedrich Nietzsche's "God is dead" generation (1800s) and the industrial revolutions – the godless knowledge they

---

[36] FOOTNOTE: Technologies that supposedly make life easier are not the only fruits of the Age of Enlightenment and the Industrial Revolutions. In 1945 the world reaped the atomic bomb. So much for "science helping the world," eh? Today, some nuclear weapons are 3000 times more powerful than those of the first generation of nuclear weapons. Neither has science solved world hunger, disease, death, the problem of evil, etc. In many ways has caused these things.

sowed reaped the Devil. So too is the humanistic, atheistic, science-run world of today. The Lord is stepping back and leaving mankind to his own devices – devices which will eventually destroy him:

> "Behold, I know your thoughts, and THE DEVICES WHICH YE WRONGFULLY IMAGINE AGAINST ME."
> Job 21:27

> "Therefore shall they EAT OF THE FRUIT OF THEIR OWN WAY, and be FILLED WITH THEIR OWN DEVICES."
> Pro. 1:31

A WORD TO THE WISE

Scripture emphasizes the acquiring of both wisdom and knowledge:

> [5] *GET WISDOM, GET UNDERSTANDING: forget it not; neither decline from THE WORDS OF MY MOUTH.*
> [6] *Forsake her not, and she shall preserve thee: LOVE HER, and she shall keep thee.*
> [7] *WISDOM IS THE PRINCIPAL THING; therefore GET WISDOM: and WITH ALL THEY GETTING GET UNDERSTANDING.*
> [8] *Exalt her, and she shall promote thee: she shall bring thee to honour, when thou dost embrace her.*
> Prov. 4:5-8

However, as briefly mentioned earlier in the book, there are certain kinds of wisdom which the Lord warns us against. The verses above which stress *"get wisdom: and with all thy getting get understanding"* are not talking about enrolling your child in public school, or signing up for courses at your local college. Absolutely not. Scripture doesn't emphasize *"wisdom"* simply for the sake of sounding "positive." The Bible's specific in its instructions. And just because someone may be getting "wisdom," doesn't necessarily mean the Lord approves of it. The kind of wisdom that the Bible is encouraging is the embracing of GOD'S WORDS (see verse 5). With a love of the words of God (the Holy Bible)) come "*the knowledge of the holy,*" "*the fear of the Lord,*" and "*the knowledge of the truth*" (Pro. 30:3, Job 28:28, Psa. 11:10, Pro. 1:7, 1:29, 2Tim. 3:7, etc.). Look at those three things. Have you ever seen anything that's more needed today than that? What we need today is not more love for our fellow man. Putting the love of man before the love of God, especially on a planet full of God-haters, creates HUMANISM. What we need today is the fear of the Lord, the knowledge of the Holy, and the knowledge of the truth. Unfortunately, however, most modern men have filled their brains with none of these things. In fact, I think it can be said that with the alternate comes the despising of the Lord (Rom. 1:30), knowledge of the unholy (1Ti. 1:9), and the embracing of lies (2Th. 2:11, 1Ti. 4:2, Rev. 22:15). Clearly, this other kind of wisdom is not from God. James describes it as "*not from above, but is EARTHLY, SENSUAL, DEVILISH*" (Jam. 3:15). It is "*the wisdom of this world,*" and the wisdom of "*the princes of this world*" (1Cor. 2:6). Of this other wisdom the Bible says:

AUTHORIZED VERSION

> [19] ...*I will DESTROY THE WISDOM OF THE WISE, and will BRING TO NOTHING THE UNDERSTANDING of the prudent.*
> [20] *Where is the wise? where is the scribe? where is the disputer of this world* [arguer, debater, skeptic, scoffer]?

> *hath not GOD MADE FOOLISH THE WISDOM OF THIS WORLD? [21] For after that in the wisdom of God THE WORLD BY WISDOM KNEW NOT GOD...*   1Co 1:19-21

The Bible shows one of the leading spirits of the age to be a SADDUCAICAL SPIRIT. This is a very important point for the reader to get. Because, if you don't get it, you're going to be in a world of hurt – a world of deceit. Note the words of the author of the book of Acts:

> "*For* THE SADDUCEES SAY THAT THERE IS NO RESURRECTION, NEITHER ANGEL, NOR SPIRIT: *but the Pharisees confess both.*"   Acts 23:8

The essence of the Sadducee was that THEY DENIED THE SUPERNATURAL. Today's academia, at its heart, pushes this same ideology making it A MODERN CULT OF SADDUCEES, a cult of skeptics. And by the very thing it brags about (its wisdom), it's missed the most important component of reality – GOD IS A SPIRIT (Jn. 4:24). The words from Acts are plain and clear, and the Lord Jesus Christ warned us to avoid the doctrines of these spiritually blind fanatics:

> "*[6] Then Jesus said unto them, TAKE HEED AND BEWARE of the leaven of...the Sadducees. ... [12] Then understood they how that he bade them not beware of the leaven of bread, but of THE DOCTRINE OF...THE SADDUCEES.*"   Mt. 16:6 & 12

This is the reality that today's Christians must face to better understand what's truly going on within our mainstream "scientific" age. THE FALSE DOCTRINES AND TEACHINGS OF TWENTY-FIRST-CENTURY EDUCATION ARE HIDING SOMETHING FROM US. Their Sadducaical ties tells us exactly what's being covered up (we'll talk more about this as our study advances). Some modern educators may be aware of this deception, but most are not. No matter how "smart" man may get, nor how intelligent he may seem, the Bible-believer must always remember that *"the wisdom of this world is foolishness with God"* (compare Psa. 111:10, etc., with 1Cor. 2:6, 1:20, & 3:19). Taking this to heart helps the Christian understand that, despite how much man thinks he knows about it, there could easily be MORE GOING ON WITH THE EARTH'S ATMOSPHERE than anyone in the mainstream realizes. The reality and implications of COVERT SUPERNATURALISM are pivotal in grasping this. While God never praises the wisdom of man, he does recognize its potential (Gen. 11:6). He also knows its limits (2Tim. 3:1-7).

So, by these things, the reader now hopefully realizes that there are TWO PRIMARY KINDS OF WISDOM. One form of wisdom God instructs us to *"get,"* the other form is foolish and leads man away from his Creator. This is why we find the Bible contrasting *"the words which man's wisdom teacheth"* against the wisdom *"which the Holy Ghost teacheth"* (1Cor. 2:13).

Now that we've briefly addressed what scripture says about man's imagination, and talked about an alternate kind of wisdom, it's time to move forward and address how all these things IMPACT TECHNOLOGY.

NOAH'S ARK: THE FIRST SUPER-TECH

The English word "technology" is rooted in the Greek word "tekhne" (meaning art, craft, belonging to or pertaining to the arts). One of the earliest examples in the Bible of technology comes from the word "artificer," found in an early chapter of Genesis. Webster says:

> "ARTIF'ICER, n. [L. artifex, from ars, and facio.] 1. An artist; a mechanic or manufacturer; one whose occupation requires skill or knowledge of a particular kind; as a silversmith..."

It is from the word "artificer" that we get our words "artifact" (an object made by a human being) and "artificial" (made or contrived by art, or by human skill and labor, in opposition to natural -- as in "artificial intelligence"). A bedfellow to the word "artificer" is the word "craftsman," as well as its associates "craft," "crafty," and "craftiness." A "craft" reflects one's skill or trade.

Specifically, the artificers found in Genesis highlight technologies resulting from working with metals (Gen. 4:22). The interesting thing about this is that it completely skips man's use of wood and stone. Meaning, that early man had a general-to-advanced knowledge of metallurgy and smithing right from the start. There are no "cave men" or sub-human "apes" experimenting with anything. In fact, before the Bible even mentions these metal workers, it demonstrates that early man had immediate knowledge of gardening (Adam, Gen. 2:8); farming, agriculture, animal husbandry (Cain and Abel, Gen. 4:2), and city-building -- which necessarily included knowledge of design, mathematics, and architecture (Cain, Gen. 4:17). By the time of Noah's birth, mankind had accumulated several hundred years of knowledge and technology. But the five-hundredth year of Noah's life brings with it a special point in time -- the Bible's first mention of SUPER TECHNOLOGY.

Noah's ark is one of the earliest forms of super technology. At first, this wood-built vessel may not seem like super science. But many scientists today, in their arrogance, scoff at the idea, because modern technology is unable to duplicate it. Twenty-first-century man cannot build a wooden, seaworthy, vessel of this size. Could a man who lived over 6,000 years ago possibly be smarter than today's PhDs? Citing things like material strength (the longer a boat, the stronger the need for internal structure), the modern "scholar" says that such a feat was unlikely, if not, impossible.

The largest known wooden sea vessel in the modern world was the Wyoming (1909–1924). Completed in Bath, Maine, in 1909, the deck of this giant was 350 feet long and 50 feet wide (100 feet shorter than Noah's ark, and 25 feet less wide). Due to its large size, and its wooden frame, however, the boat was plagued throughout its life with constant flexing, bending, twisting, and buckling. This resulted in continuous leakage. Eventually, the boat sank at sea with the loss of all hands on deck. Because man can't build a functioning wooden ship of the Ark's size today, the assumption is that it could not have been done thousands of years ago:

> "Only when ships were made of steel, in the last hundred years or so, we are told, has man been able to build a ship approaching the biblical dimensions of Noah's ark, (450 feet long, 75 feet wide, and 45 feet high)." [37]

> "The experience of the Wyoming shows what a challenge the eight people on the Ark would have faced. The flexibility of wood made the long hull of the Wyoming twist and hog [bend upward] in the slightest seas. This caused separation between the hull planks that no caulking could ever fully seal, so the ship had to be pumped out constantly during its 14-year career." [38]

One of the major problems with modern man attempting to build a sea vessel equivalent to Noah's ark is that science assumes that the world of today is no different than the Antediluvian Age, but they are severely mistaken. First of all, Noah and the generations of his forefathers all lived nearly a thousand years (Noah died when he was 950 years old, Gen. 9:29). After the flood, life expectancy began to drastically drop off (Gen. 11:10-32, etc.). How could the men of Noah's day have lived so long? Because today, in the twenty-first century, the curse of sin has had five thousand more years to work its death and decay. So, what does this mean regarding Noah's ark? It

---

[37] Pierce, Larry. "The Large Ships of Antiquity." (Answers In Genesis. 1, June, 2000), https://answersingenesis.org/noahs-ark/the-large-ships-of-antiquity.

[38] McDorr, Zac. "Noah's ark or the Wyoming." (*The Times Record*, Press Herald. 10, December, 2018), https://www.pressherald.com/2017/07/27/noahs-ark-or-the-wyoming/.

indicates that the tensile strength of wood could've easily been much stronger then, regardless of what kind of wood was used in the ark's construction. And in that case, boats made of wood could've been much larger than they are today. Secondly, no one today even knows exactly what *"gopher wood"* was, the material which Noah and his sons used to build the ark. The interesting thing about this fact is that the verse which mentions this timber is THE ONLY REFERENCE OF IT ANYWHERE IN THE BIBLE (Gen. 6:14). Thus, it may very well indicate that *"gopher woo*d," was exclusive to the pre-flood era. Some may doubt this, but if men back then were drastically different (they were much smarter and lived much longer), and animals back then were drastically different (all animals were herbivores, and none were afraid of man), then there's no reason to scoff at the idea of differences in plants and trees as well. Men have tried to interpret the meaning of *"gopher,"* but have had little luck. Generally, it's categorized as some type of "cypress" or "pine," but this is just a guess. But why the need to interpret? It is what it is.

"...yea, let God be true, but every man a liar..." Rom. 3:4

Noah and his sons were not marine engineers. And even if they were, the ark was unlike anything that had ever been made on earth before or since. It wasn't a boat. It was more akin to a giant floating animal warehouse or bank vault. Unlike a boat, it had no mast, mainsail, rudder, or ship's wheel. It didn't need these things because it wasn't designed to be driven. Instead, it was intended to be A PLACE OF REFUGE DURING A GLOBAL CATASTROPHE. It was not created to be a VEHICLE, like normal vessels on the sea, but simply a STORM SHELTER made to float on top of the water. This is why the ark typifies Christ as the Shelter from God's wrath. The men of Noah's day had no idea what Noah was building. It was one-of-a-kind. [29] I've also often pictured in my mind that the ark, at the time of its building, was landlocked, with no body of water anywhere in sight. In other words, Noah didn't have to drag the ship into the ocean to float it, the rising floodwaters simply lifted it up once the rain began to accumulate. At least, that's my idea. If this was the case,

Noah's Ark: The First Super-Tech | 111

One of the things that makes Noah's ark a form of "super technology" is that modern man cannot duplicate it.

[39] FOOTNOTE: The word "ark" (also spelled "arc") in its ancient form refers to a "box" or "chest" (like a treasure chest), a thing designed to hold or keep something precious or safe inside. The Ark of the Covenant was designed for the same purpose. The word "arcane" is related to this which means secret, hidden, to enclose, or to shut up. This is exactly what God did with Noah at the time of the Great Flood – *"And they that went in, went in male and female of all flesh, as God had commanded him: and THE LORD SHUT HIM IN."* Gen 7:16

it would've made the giant vessel appear even more "crazy" in the eyes of those who witnessed its construction. The great faith which Noah placed in the words of God in the need to build such a thing, was accounted unto him for righteousness:

> "By faith Noah, being WARNED OF GOD OF THINGS NOT SEEN AS YET, moved with fear, PREPARED AN ARK to the saving of his house; by the which he condemned the world, and BECAME HEIR OF THE RIGHTEOUSNESS WHICH IS BY FAITH." Heb. 11:7

In any case, this begs the question:

"Where did Noah and his sons get the knowledge to build the ark?"

From where did they get this information? Did they go to school to learn it? Did they read books about it? Did they have any prior experience with it? Were the eggheads of today around to tell them how to do it (or that they couldn't do it)? How did they do it? Scripture is clear that the knowledge to build the ark came directly from the Lord (Gen. 6:14-22). It was KNOWLEDGE DISSEMINATED SUPERNATURALLY. Modern science hates this kind of answer but it is what it is. The ignorance, denials, and hard-heartedness of the modern, know-it-all cult of Sadducees (public school teachers, scientists, college professors, etc.) don't change the truth (Acts 23:8). So, unlike the statement of *The Times Record* in the footnote on page 109 which suggests that Noah and his sons faced a "challenge," I'm here to tell you they didn't. Nothing is a "challenge," when the Lord feeds you with the wisdom to do it.

No one knows the exact state of technology before the Great Flood. But since the world began with a man whose wisdom was instilled directly from his Maker, it is certain that the TECHNICAL KNOWLEDGE of that era was higher than the scientists of today give credit. [40] Adam, a man who named all the animals (Gen. 2:19), had to have had a tremendous mind. One comparable to a supercomputer.

Noah's Ark: The First Super-Tech | 113

In his book, *The Puzzle of Ancient Man*, lecturer and college professor, Dr. Donald E. Chittick reports:

> "With the possible exception of the amazing developments of the past one hundred years, the further we go into the past, the higher was the level of science and technology as reflected by human artifacts." [41]

While there's no way to know how similar Noah's ark was compared to other technologies of its day, there's one thing we can know for sure: MODERN SCIENCE CAN'T DUPLICATE IT. And based on this fact alone, many today discredit it. But who's the real dummy? Even in the twenty-first-century, there is much that's UNKNOWN about ancient technology. Some examples of technologies lost to time that currently cannot be duplicated include: (1) Greek Fire (a powerful, seventh-century incendiary weapon); (2) Damascus Steel (a 12th-to-18th-century super-steel formula); (3) the Giza Pyramids; and (4), believe it or not, the ability to go to the moon, just as man did on July 20, 1969, is impossible. According to Robert Frost, Instructor and Flight Controller at NASA:

> "If we, today, said - 'Let us build another Saturn V rocket and Apollo CSM/LEM and go to the moon!' it would not

---

[40] FOOTNOTE: The knowledge of the Antediluvian Age, eventually, also included the advanced knowledge of the fallen "sons of God" (fallen angels – Gen. 6:4). The tales of lost super-civilizations, like the legendary continent of "Atlantis" or "Mu," which supposedly sank beneath the sea, were possibly due to the existence of the superior intellect of this era. When people think of advanced technology, they generally think of "computers" or "jets" similar to what we have today. But this isn't the only way to think of technology. Antediluvian tech could've been something completely different, even more advanced than the current century. Things that, by today's standards, would appear as "magic." A possibility even more pronounced once the fallen sons of God arrived. Angels, including the fallen ones, have all kinds of supernatural abilities beyond the understanding of science.

[41] Chittick, Donald E. *The Puzzle of Ancient Man*. (Creation Compass: Newberg, OR. 1997), p. 1

be a simple task of pulling out the blueprints and bending and cutting metal. We don't have the factories or tools. We don't have the materials. We don't have the expertise to understand how the real vehicle differed from the drawings. We don't have the expertise to operate the vehicle. We would have to substitute modern materials. That changes the vehicle. It changes the mass, it changes the stresses and strains, it changes the interactions. It changes the possible malfunctions. It changes the capabilities of the vehicle. We would have to spend a few years re-developing the expertise. We would have to conduct new tests and simulations. We would have to draft new flight rules and procedures. We would have to certify new flight controllers and crew. WE WOULD ESSENTIALLY BE BUILDING A NEW VEHICLE." [42]

In short, what Mr. Frost is saying is that the technology that took man to the moon in 1969 is no longer around (Oba. 1:4). Greek Fire, Damascus Steel, the Giza Pyramids, and the Apollo 11 Lunar Landing Module all represent forms of lost technology. Does modern science deny the reality of all these things too? Take Egypt's pyramids, for example. The great pyramids of Egypt have long been a wonder of the world (both ancient and modern). Yet, Egypt is not the only pyramid-building culture. In spite of this, there is no evidence of exploratory pyramid-building in Egypt, or anywhere else. One well-known author comments on the technical skills of the ancients:

> "The archeological evidence suggests that rather than developing slowly and painfully, as is normal with human societies, the civilization of Ancient Egypt, like that of the Olmecs, emerged all at once and fully formed. Indeed, the period of transformation from primitive to advanced

---

[42] "How We Lost The Ability To Travel To The Moon." (Forbes, Forbes Media, 11, December, 2015), https://www.forbes.com/sites/quora/2015/12/11/how-we-lost-the-ability-to-travel-to-the-moon/?sh=1a81145a1f4

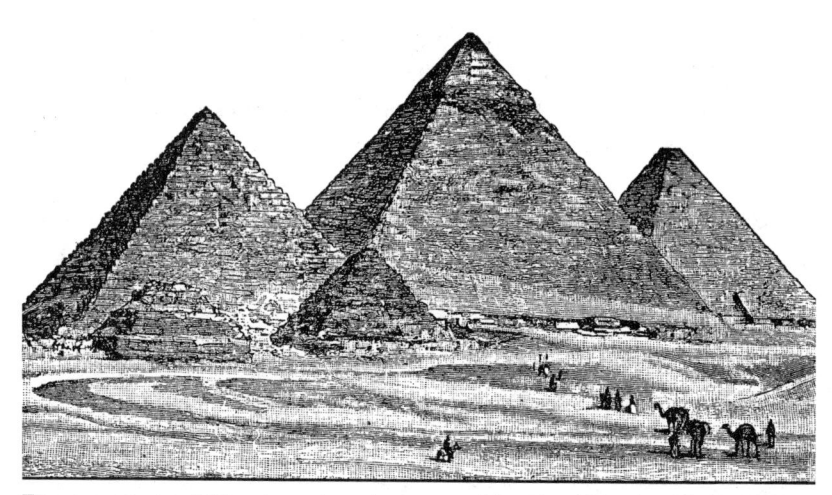

The pyraminds of Giza have long been concidered a "Wonder of the World." Interestingly, there is no evidence of a gradual knowledge of pyramid-building for any civilization. The knowledge seems to have developed without precedent.

society appears to have been so short that it makes no kind of historical sense. TECHNOLOGICAL SKILLS that should have taken hundreds of years or even thousands of years to evolve were BROUGHT INTO USE ALMOST OVERNIGHT – and with no apparent antecedents whatever." [43]

What's being said here is that, even though there's evidence of advanced pyramid-building from cultures worldwide, there is no evidence of the evolution of pyramid-building. Man's knowledge to do these things seems to have HAPPENED ALL AT ONCE. Like much of modern technology, which has appeared abruptly in society, so too do many ancient technologies.

Late Christian author, Dr. Emil Gaverluk, observed:

"There are many science mysteries in the ancient world. Why? Intelligence and science were on a very high order

---

[43] Hancock, Graham. Fingerprints of the Gods. (Three Rivers Press: New York, NY, 1995), p. 135

in the past. We have underestimated the Ancients' capabilities. Even with our technology today it would be difficult to duplicate some of the astounding engineering of the Ancients." [44]

Astounding engineering like Noah's ark? Absolutely. And before we leave this matter, there's still one very important point the Christian reader needs to be made aware of.

THE TIMING OF THE TECHNOLOGY

Another significant thing we can learn from Noah's ark is THE TIMING OF THE TECHNOLOGY. This is an EXTREMELY IMPORTANT thing for the Christian to recognize. Note that Noah and his sons did not always have this knowledge, but only acquire it upon God's timetable. Were Noah and his sons born with aspirations to build floating storm shelters? No. Was this a goal Noah had worked towards all his life? No. The Lord only first mentions it after the birth of Shem, Ham, and Japheth, after Noah is 500 years old (Gen. 6:9-22). Essentially, Noah's knowledge and desire to build this thing CAME SUDDENLY, AND OUT OF NOWHERE. What this illustrates, is that CERTAIN KINDS OF KNOWLEDGE may only be acquired by man AT CERTAIN TIMES. In other words, it was no accident that a man with the knowledge to build an ark appeared AT THAT PRECISE PERIOD IN HISTORY (approx. 2444 BC). Had it not, the world as we know it would not exist today. Of course, in hindsight, we know why this is so -- God gave Noah the knowledge to build this super-structure AT THE VERY TIME IT WAS NEEDED. But the men of Noah's day didn't know this. From the outside, the building of this strange craft seemed like an arbitrary thing. In like manner, modern science sees technology as simply an unguided process. Supposedly, technology

---

[44] Gaverluk, Emil, *Did Genesis Man Conquer Space?* (Thomas Nelson Inc. Publishers: Nashville, TN, 1974). p. 55

Was it by mere chance that the knowledge needed to build a floating shelter appeared in the days of Noah? In hindsight, and Bible-sight, it's easy to realize that this technology did not manifest by accident. What about the tech of today?

is nothing more than an evolution of ideas. A thing that runs and builds on its own with no real reason why certain technologies and inventions APPEAR AT CERTAIN PERIODS IN HISTORY AND NOT OTHERS. We know that knowledge builds upon itself, but WHAT TRIGGERS IT TO BEGIN AND TO GROW IN ONE AGE AND NOT AN ALTERNATE ONE? Could it be that technology, on the whole, like Noah's ark, IS NOT ARBITRARY IN ITS TIMING? What if, like the ark, knowledge appears at specific times in history for specific reasons? This is what Noah and his son's acquiring the knowledge to build the ark suggests. Secular historians are oblivious to the idea that the appearance of knowledge at certain periods may do so for a reason. Modern man knows nothing about this. To them, like the creation of the world itself, EVERYTHING IS A COINCIDENCE OR AN ACCIDENT. But if there's a God in heaven, and a Devil running loose, then there's much more to history, knowledge, and technology than most realize. This is a very important thing for the reader to grasp. For neither God nor Satan, are personalities afar off. They have always had direct influence over what's going on in man's world.

God puts a stop to the building of a city and tower in Shinar (approx. 2130 BC)

KNOWLEDGE FORBIDDEN, KNOWLEDGE ALLOWED

Believe it or not, history is peppered with out-of-place artifacts (called OOPArts) and "lost technologies." These indicate that certain similar-to-modern (or more advanced) devices were on the verge in certain ages, as well as the possible existence of science-fiction-like exotic technologies, but for reasons unknown, they vanished. These inventions never saw widespread use, at least not beyond the immediate circles in which they were derived. It's almost as if certain advanced technologies attempted to rise and proliferate in certain eras, but couldn't. Why? Could it be that it was not the Lord's intent to allow those ideas freedom at the time, and because of this, the knowledge died? Some may scoff at this idea, but scripture gives us a great example of this. The only reason many Christians haven't noticed it, is because they don't think of the verse in an "advancement of technology" context. Note:

> [4] *And they said, Go to, let us BUILD US A CITY AND A TOWER, whose top may reach unto heaven; and let us make us a name, lest we be scattered abroad upon the face of the whole earth.*
> [5] *And the LORD came down to see the city and the tower, which THE CHILDREN OF MEN BUILDED.*
> [6] *And the LORD said, Behold, THE PEOPLE IS ONE, and THEY HAVE ALL ONE LANGUAGE; and this they begin to do: and NOTHING WILL BE RESTRAINED FROM THEM, WHICH THEY HAVE IMAGINED TO DO.*
> [7] *Go to, let us go down, and there confound their language, that they may not understand one another's speech.*
> [8] *So the LORD scattered them abroad from thence upon the face of all the earth: and THEY LEFT OFF TO BUILD THE CITY.*
> [9] *Therefore is the name of it called Babel; because the LORD did there confound the language of all the earth: and from thence did the LORD scatter them abroad upon the face of all the earth.* Gen. 11:4-9

In this incident, God acknowledges the unfettered potential of the wisdom of fallen man (vs 6). Yet in man's attempt to build a one-people, one-language world, God steps in and stops it. The profound thing about the Lord putting an end to this is that GOD WILL ALLOW A WORLD ORDER RUN BY FALLEN MAN, EVENTUALLY. Did you get that? But the reset button is hit on this attempt because THE ANCIENT TOWER OF BABEL WAS NOT THE RIGHT TIME OR PLACE. This example then begs the question:

> What if, like Noah's ark, man acquires technical knowledge in certain periods only because God allows it or allows its freedom?

This goes back to our point made regarding the timing of the tech. If true, it would mean that the appearance of certain knowledge at certain times is no accident. For better or for worse, it's serving some higher purpose. And like the ark, that purpose is unknown to the vast majority of men. The technology invested in Noah's ark was designed to save Noah, his family, and the world's animals, but other technologies have their own end goals. Neither is the Lord always the source of inspiration. If things do start to appear that are not in alignment with the Lord's plan, like the Tower of Babel, God ends it. In many ways, MAN-MADE HIGH TECHNOLOGY CREATES THE ILLUSION THAT MAN IS ESCAPING GOD or no longer needs God, or that God does not exist, but this is in no way the truth:

> *"There are many devices in a man's heart; nevertheless the counsel of the LORD, that shall stand."* Pro 19:21

In further addressing history's out-of-place artifacts, what if the reason these things vanished, is because God doesn't allow the proliferation of certain kinds of knowledge? He forbids it from the minds of men because he knows that AS SOON AS IT'S ALLOWED ON A WIDER BASIS, fallen man being what he is, it will begin a "Tower of Babel" scenario all over again (Gen. 11). And with modern technology, this is exactly what's happening. The only difference between this generation, and generations past, is that the Creator has allowed today's generations to acquire and grow the knowledge while

In 2007, the world's first language-learning app was created. As if to mock God, designers dubbed it "Babel," a play on the ancient city of "Babel." Today, it is the best-selling language app and removes the communication barriers created by 14 leading world languages. The Bible says: *"Grant not, O LORD, the desires of the wicked: further not his wicked devices; lest they exalt themselves. Selah."* Psa. 140:8

Knowledge Forbidden, Knowledge Allowed | 121

> EUROPE:
> MANY
> TONGUES,
> ONE VOICE
>
> CONSEIL DE LA COOPÉRATION CULTURELLE
> COUNCIL FOR CULTURAL CO-OPERATION
>
> COUNCIL OF EUROPE ★ CONSEIL DE L'EUROPE

hiding it from the past. National conglomerates of the day (like the UN and EU) are no longer hiding the fact that they're pushing for the creation of a twenty-first-century "Babel." A poster from 1992 leaves no room for doubt (see above) -- and the building continues today.

The 1889 discovery of a wooden, airplane-like model in Egypt has lead some researchers to speculate that north Africa may have had some type of knowledge of aviation as far back as 2,200 BC.

IT'S A BIRD, IT'S A PLANE

In 1898, a 6x7-inch, bird-like wooden model was discovered in a tomb in Saqqara, Egypt. The structure was dated to about 2,200 BC. Later, with the advent of airplanes and jets, researchers were stunned at how closely the thing resembled such machines. Some speculated that the Saqqara bird was evidence that ancient Egypt may have known of flying craft:

> "This ancient model is a glaring challenge to our ideas about the development of technology. And it is only one of innumerable oddities and enigmas that fuel speculation about the scientific knowledge and engineering skill of our ancestors." [45]

But whether the plane-like bird is proof of such knowledge or not, the point is, if the ancient Egyptians were beginning to grasp, or had already grasped, the concept of artificial flight, it was lost before

[45] *Mysteries of Mind, Space & Time.* (Websters Unified H.S. Stuttman, Inc: NY, 1992). p. 153

it had a chance to advance. Had it not been, the airplane would've appeared in 2200 BC and not 1903 AD. The possibility exists that every generation since man's beginning (Gen. 1) may have had the ability to grasp aviation. But the birth of such technology was not yet in alignment with the Lord's timing, so its growth and spread (like the tower built at Babel) were halted.

In concluding our investigation on how man can sometimes acquire knowledge, and how it is disseminated to man, the next sections will present to the reader some stunning facts.

THE RIDDLE OF SIMULTANEOUS INVENTION

Believe it or not, with the advent of the Industrial Revolutions (1760-1915), the sudden blast of numerous technological ideas on the world scene presents a great mystery to historians. They have no idea how or why it happened. Where did all of these ideas come from all of a sudden? There are theories, of course, but no one understands why it all occurred at the time it did, and in many ways is continuing today. One of the big puzzles in this knowledge eruption was the birthing of unique ideas and decivess by multiple strangers, in diverse places, all at the same time. The general belief is that new inventions are the product of a sole creator. This is often the case. But throughout the last 200 or so years, many new devices have come to fruition, more than once, through multiple, unrelated inventors. The end-times rise in technology is replete with simultaneous discoveries and inventions, where all parties involved are ignorant of the other:

> "...The phenomenon of two people inventing or discovering the same thing in two different locations without any contact, called MULTIPLE DISCOVERY, HAS DOGGED THE SCIENTIFIC COMMUNITY FOR HUNDREDS OF YEARS. ... It's not just about who gets credit.

Unravelling HOW NEW IDEAS ENTER THE HUMAN CONSCIOUSNESS could be a holy grail for anticipating the future, and shape how we invent new technology." [46]

"Synchronicity is not just a phenomenon of the past, when communication was poor, but very much part of the present." [47]

Anthropologist, Alfred Kroeber, who studied the social and physical development of man has stated:

"The whole history of inventions is one endless chain of parallel instances." [48]

"Alexander Bell and Elisha Gray both applied to patent the telephone on the same day, February 14, 1876. This improbable simultaneity (Gray applied three hours before Bell) led to mutual accusations of espionage, plagiarism, bribery, and fraud. Gray was ill advised by his patent attorney to drop his claim for priority because the telephone 'was not worth serious attention.' ...at least three other tinkerers besides Gray had made working models of phones years earlier. In fact, Antonio Meucci had patented his 'teletrofono' more than a decade earlier, in 1860, ..." [49]

How do you get a SINGLE IDEA, or a very similar idea, SPREAD TO THE MINDS OF MULTIPLE PEOPLE of the same era at nearly

---

[46] "Quartz - Simultaneous invention: When genius strikes twice" (Quartz Weekly Obsession, December, 2018), https://qz.com/emails/quartz-obsession/1482596/?utm_source=email&utm_medium=quartz-obsession

[47] Kelly, Kevin. *What Technology Wants*. (Penguin Group: New York, NY, 2011), p. 134

[48] Ibid. p. 135

[49] Ibid. p. 132

the same time? What are the chances of TWO INDEPENDENT PEOPLE inventing or discovering a thing within a short amount of time of each other, or at the same time? What about three people or four? Do we dare estimate the chances of five, six, seven, eight, or nine? Impossible! Perhaps. But this has happened more times than modern science would like to admit. And it has become a great riddle which they've chalked up to mere chance.

> "It is a singular fact, that not an electrical invention of any importance has been made but that the honor of its origin has been claimed by more than one person." 50

In an article stunningly titled "In the Air," Malcolm Gladwel of *The New Yorker* writes:

> "One of the first comprehensive lists of MULTIPLES was put together by William Ogburn and Dorothy Thomas, in 1922, and THEY FOUND A HUNDRED AN FOURTY-EIGHT MAJOR SCIENTIFIC DISCOVERIES that fit the multiple pattern. ... There seem to have been at least SIX DIFFERENT INVENTORS of the THERMOMETER and no less than NINE CLAIMANTS of the invention of THE TELESCOPE. Typewriting machines were invented simultaneously in England and in America by SEVERAL INDIVIDUALS in these countries. ... For Ogburn and Thomas, the sheer number of multiples could mean only one thing: scientific discoveries must, in some sense, be inevitable. They must be IN THE AIR, products of the intellectual climate of a specific time and place." 51

---

[50] Park, Benjamin. *The Age of Electricity From Amber-Soul to Telephone.* (Berwick & Smith: Boston, MA, 1886), p. iii

[51] Gladwell, Malcolm. "In the Air: Who says big ideas are rare?" (*The New Yorker*, 12 ,May, 2018), https://www.newyorker.com/magazine/2008/05/12/in-the-air

Ogburn and Thomas theorized that ideas of invention are merely products of the "intellectual climate." They then add that THIS KNOWLEDGE IS FLOATING IN THE AIR at the time, evidently, and ripe for anyone to pluck. What these researchers are ignorant of, however, is that their tongue-in-cheek comment about knowledge being "in the air," may not be as symbolic as they'd like to believe. The Bible has something to say about this. Just as the universe was not created by chance, so too are many of these ideas not born by chance. Nor are they simply floating around like mindless balloons waiting for someone to catch. All of this is easy to understand when one's aware of THE OPERATION OF UNCLEAN SPIRITS AND THEIR ABILITY TO IMPART KNOWLEDGE:

> "[19] ...*I saw the LORD sitting on his throne, and all the host of heaven standing by him on his right hand and on his left.* [20] *And the LORD said, WHO SHALL PERSUADE AHAB, that he may go up and fall at Ramothgilead? And one said on this manner, and another said on that manner.* [21] *AND THERE CAME FORTH A LYING SPIRIT, AND STOOD BEFORE THE LORD, and said, I WILL PERSUADE HIM.* [22] *And the LORD said unto him, Wherewith? And he said, I WILL GO FORTH, and I WILL BE A LYING SPIRIT IN THE MOUTH OF ALL HIS PROPHETS. And he said, Thou shalt persuade him, and prevail also: go forth, and do so."* 1Kgs. 22:19-22

So, how many prophets were able to persuade Ahab to go up to battle? One, two, three, four? No, *"about four hundred"* (1Kgs. 22:6, 2Ch 18:5). And all four hundred men enticed the king with THE SAME IDEAS AT THE SAME TIME. While this example does not show various men becoming inventors of the same things, it does provide the Christian a window into how unclean spirits can impart the same information to multiple subjects simultaneously. In other words, the spread of the idea for Ahab to go to Ramothgilead, had nothing to do with the political or "intellectual climate" of the time. It had to do with THE DEMONIC DISSEMINATION OF INFORMATION (a lying

The Riddle of Simultaneous Invention | 127

Diagram illustrating how devil spirits can impart information to multiple subjects.
"I will go forth and be a spirit of wisdom in the hearts of all these inventors"

spirit), which God permitted because the subject (Ahab) refused to obey or listen to the Lord. Incidentally, all the early inventors that are outright named in scripture (the first city-builder, the first tent-maker, the first artificer of musical instruments, the first metal smith) are ALL DESCENDANTS OF CAIN (Gen. 4:16-22). A man who, before these things, had *"went out from the presence of the LORD "* (Gen. 4:16) being *"of that wicked one."* (1Jn. 3:12) You can draw whatever conclusions you want to regarding this, but facts can be stubborn.

To illustrate this, what follows is a short list of simultaneous, independent inventions. The word "simultaneous" means "at the same time or nearly the same time." The word "independent" suggests that no inventor was aware of anyone else working on the same project. This is a very short list. There are many more examples:

1.) Invented the Lightning Rod – Benjamin Franklin (1749), Prokop Divis (1754).

2.) Invented Chloroform – Samuel Guthrie (1831), Eugène Soubeiran (1831), Justus von Liebig (1831).

3.) Invented the Telegraph — Charles Wheatstone (1837), Samuel F.B. Morse (1837).

4.) Invented the Telephone – Elisha Gray (1876), Alexander Graham Bell (1876). Both men filed a patent on the telephone the same day.

5.) Invented the Record Player / Phonograph – Charles Cros (1877), Thomas Edison (1878).

6.) Invented the Radio – Nikola Tesla (1893), Aleksandr Popov (1895), Guglielmo Marconi (1896).

7.) Invented the Airplane – Gustave Whitehead (1901), Wright brothers (1903), there are also others that claim this invention.

8.) Invented the Television – Charles Jenkins (1922), Vladimir Zworykin (1923), John Logie Baird (1926), Philo Fansworth (1927).

9.) Invented the Jet Engine – Hans von Ohain (1939), Secondo Campini (1940), Frank Whittle (1941).

10.) Invented the Microchip – Jack Kilby (1958), Robert Noyce (1959).

WISDOM, INVENTION, ENVY & STRIFE

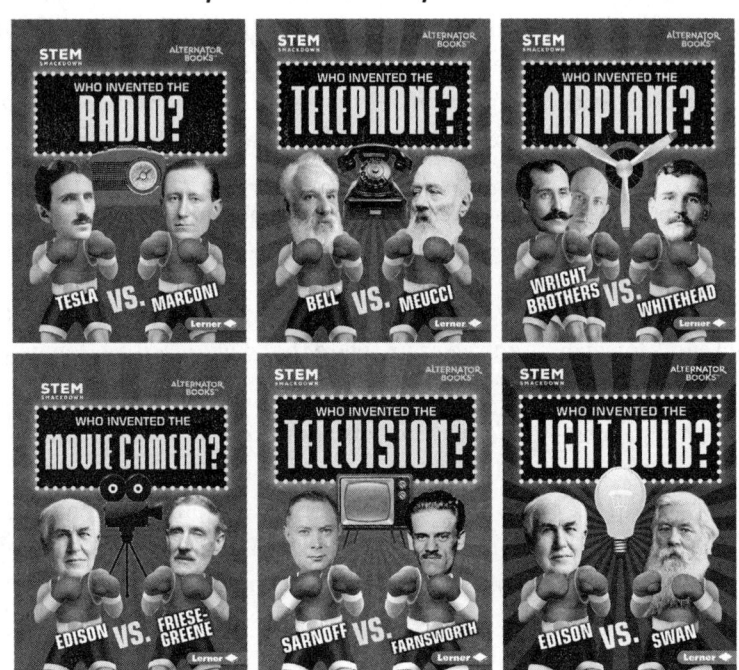

Who Invented the **RADIO?** TESLA VS. MARCONI

Who Invented the **TELEPHONE?** BELL VS. MEUCCI

Who Invented the **AIRPLANE?** WRIGHT BROTHERS VS. WHITEHEAD

Who Invented the **MOVIE CAMERA?** EDISON VS. FRIESE-GREENE

Who Invented the **TELEVISION?** SARNOFF VS. FARNSWORTH

Who Invented the **LIGHT BULB?** EDISON VS. SWAN

"This wisdom descendeth not from above, but is earthly, sensual, devilish. For where envying and strife is, there is confusion and every evil work." Jn. 3:15-16

Confusion, envy and strife followed in the wake of many inventors. As a businessman, Thomas Edison was ruthless. Many of his "inventions" were simply ideas that already existed that he (or one of his assistances) improved upon. This is not to say that he didn't have any original ideas, but according to the Library of Congress, "…Edison's life, and legal battles over various patents and corporations were continuous." [52]

[52] "Inventing Entertainment: The Early Motion Pictures and Sound Recordings of the Edison Companies" (Library of Congress), https://www.loc.gov/collections/edison-company-motion-pictures-and-sound-recordings/articles-and-essays/biography/life-of-thomas-alva-edison/

In plainer words, in cases of abrupt "simultaneous invention," scripture shows it can easily be the outcome of spirit activity. Just as the Bible shows God imparting technical knowledge to certain people (like Noah, Shem, Ham and Japheth with the ark, or Bezaleel and Aholiab with the tabernacle – see Gen. 6:13-16 & Ex. 31:2-6, etc.), so too can the unclean spirit impart knowledge. Modern science claims that the "holy grail" for predicting the future is in understanding "how new ideas enter" the minds of men. The Bible reveals the answer, but do you think modern man is ready to face these things? Will he believe it?

With the worldwide expansion in knowledge, an age of "wise men" emerged. However, many were unaware that it came with a downside:

> "Many of history's most celebrated creative GENIUSES WERE MENTALLY ILL, from renowned artists Vincent van Gogh... to literary giants Virginia Woolf and Edgar Allan Poe. Today, the fabled connection between GENIUS AND MADNESS is no longer merely anecdotal." [53]

Of course, we're not implying here that every single inventor of the recent past manifested mental instability. Nor are we saying that all forms of lunacy are the result of devils. What we're attempting to tap into here is the overarching picture showing how Satan is active in history, especially in these end times. Unclean spirits certainly can impart technical knowledge, and they certainly can cause madness. The fact that there's a link between madness and genius helps demonstrate this, and in turn, creates a potential that the "smarts" of many, both today and in the recent past, may be the result of INDWELLING DEMONS. Remember our study on devil-possession and how we demonstrated that some demoniacs manifest, not as lunatics, but as WISE MEN? (more on this later)

---

[53] Wolchover, Natalie. "Why Are Genius and Madness Connected." (Live Science, Future US Inc, June 2, 2012), https://www.livescience.com/20713-genius-madness-connected.html.

IS A SPIRIT DRIVING INNOVATION?

Much of the time, inventions are driven by need. A man needs to eat, so he plants a garden and learns to tend and keep it. A man needs to protect his family from the elements, so he provides clothing for his wife and children and builds them a house. A man needs to get around quickly, so he acquires horses and builds wagons to fill the demand. However, contrary to popular belief, "necessity" is not always the grounds for invention. The basic needs of man (food, water, clothing, shelter, transportation) don't always dictate why a thing is created. In his work, *The Evolution of Technology*, secularist and professor Emeritus at the University of Delaware, George Basalla, writes:

> "We are often told that automobiles are absolutely essential, yet the automobile is barely a century old. Men and women managed to live full and happy lives before Nikolaus A. Otto devised his four-stroke internal combustion engine in 1876. A search for the origins of the gasoline-engine-powered motorcar reveals that IT WAS NOT NECESSITY THAT INSPIRED ITS INVENTORS to complete their task. The automobile was not developed in response to some grave international horse crisis or shortage. National leaders, influential thinkers, and editorials WERE NOT CALLING FOR THE REPLACEMENT OF THE HORSE, nor were ordinary citizens anxiously hoping that some inventors would soon fill a serious societal and PERSONAL NEED for motor transportation. In fact, during the first decade of existence, 1895-1905, the automobile was a toy, a plaything for those who could afford to buy one." [54]

---

[54] Basalla, George. *The Evolution of Technology* (Cambridge University Press: New York, New York, 1988), p. 6-7

These remarks touch on a fact of modern technology of which most are uninformed. Much of the innovation of today comes without any sort of public demand or need:

> "Technocrats invent because they can, not because of a demonstrated need to do so." [55]

There are hundreds of experiments going on today in laboratories around the world that have nothing at all to do with the "needs" of man. And many times, society ends up reaping the fallout. Like loss of jobs, for example. So, where's the demand for all the junk they're making? Did you know that for many of the devices of the nineteenth and twentieth centuries, public demand was so low, that THE INVENTORS HAD TO CREATE A MARKET? Like the origins of the automobile mentioned above, the public didn't need the inventions, and in many cases, didn't want them. They saw no need for most of the things and viewed the novelties as unnecessary. Public need and demand WAS NOT THE DRIVING FORCE behind these new creations. This includes things like the telegraph, telephone, record player, television, light bulbs, bicycles, airplanes, personal computers, cell phones, etc. According to Linda Simon, author of *Dark Light: Electricity and Anxiety from the Telegraph to the X-Ray*:

> "...few saw a market for telephones in the home... Inventing a need for this new device proved to be a formidable challenge. ...a telephone in the home seemed frivolous and potentially invasive." [56]

In a synopsis for his book *American Lucifers: The Dark History of Artificial Light*, associate professor of history at Lafayette College, Jeremy Zallen, writes::

---

[55] Wood, Patrick. "New Navy Weapon Can Literally Stop You From Talking" (Technocracy News & Trends, Coherent Publishing, 8, September, 2021), https://www.technocracy.news/new-navy-weapon-can-stop-you-from-talking/

[56] Simon, Linda. *Dark Light*. (Harcourt Inc: San Diego, CA, 2004), p. 64

"The myth of light and progress has blinded us. In our electric world, we are everywhere surrounded by effortlessly glowing lights that simply exist, as they should, seemingly clear and comforting proof that human genius means the present will always be better than the past, and the future better still. At best, this is half the story. At worst, it is a lie." [57]

Many of today's new computerized gadgets and electronics are in the same predicament. Take driverless cars, for example. Where are the throngs of Americans lined up insisting that self-driving cars be made? Do you know of any red-blooded Americans, anywhere, who are begging science to take away their freedom to drive their vehicles? Are all the truckers and semi-drivers (the lifeblood of the economy) demanding it? No. There is no demand. It's being done simply because the ability exists. Average citizens are not calling for it. Another good example of this today is Amazon's "Echo Dot." The Echo Dot is a speaker that you hook up to the internet. If you place one of these things in every room of your house (and have compatible appliances), it allows you to talk to your refrigerator, talk to your oven, talk to your car, your television, your remote control, your thermostat, your vacuum cleaner, your lights, and the list grows daily (more on this later). Who's demanding such things? "Not I, said

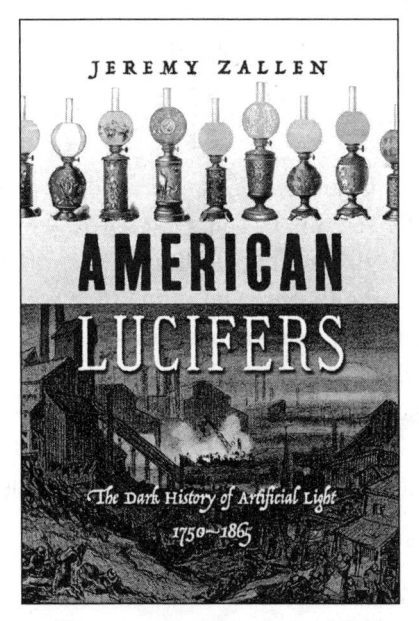

---

[57] Zallen, Jeremy. "American Lucifers: The Dark History of Artificial Light, 1750-1865 Paperback – August 1, 2022" (Amazon)

the duck." When the internet was released to the public in 1994, no one was calling for it. Although the technology had been around in a primitive form since the early 1980s, most people in '94 never knew such a thing existed, or even what it could do, or what it was for.

Due to the increasing automation and computerization of today's society, many see massive job loss on the horizon. How does job loss fill a "necessity"? The "necessities" of giant companies (Facebook, Amazon, Google, etc.) are beginning to drive the technological market and override the necessities of the average person. Automation cuts costs for these corporations by eliminating the need to hire employees (*"For the love of money is the root of all evil..."* 1 Tim. 6:10). Because of this, rumblings of a solution are now being heard calling for a "universal basic income" (UBI). This is a setup where future governments practically pay their citizens not to work.

From the outside, a kind of creative arrogance appears to be what's going on today. We can especially see this in fields like DNA, where science is doing unthinkable things like mixing humans with animals at the genetic level. Many corporations seem to be endlessly birthing new inventions simply because they can. But suppose man's inventive ambitions are really THE RESULT OF A DRIVING SPIRIT? Does the Bible say anything about such a concept? Yes. The Bible says that the lost man lives his life in accord with (in agreement with, corresponding with, concurring with) a spirit that works through him, and it's not the Holy Spirit:

> "...*in time past* [before salvation] *YE WALKED according to the course of this world, ACCORDING TO THE PRINCE OF THE POWER OF THE AIR, THE SPIRIT THAT NOW WORKETH in the children of disobedience:*" Eph. 2:2

Do you see that? Do you see there's a "*spirit*" working through fallen man? This spirit is driving him and pushing him and leading him in directing the "*course of this world*". And what is "*the course of this world*"? Is it a thing moving closer to God or away from Him?

What follows is an investigation into geniuses, demons, electricity, lightning, and other aerial mysteries. These will hopefully shed more light on the spirit propagating the current trajectory of today's worldly system. In the meantime, the Christian is not to get overly worried. Although these things can often seem overwhelming, God is in control:

> "REST IN THE LORD, and WAIT PATIENTLY FOR HIM: FRET NOT THYSELF because of him who prospereth in his way, BECAUSE OF THE MAN WHO BRINGETH WICKED DEVICES TO PASS." Psa 37:7

PART VII

THE GOD OF FORCES

Satanology - History - Prophecy - Technology

"...yea, also the heart of the sons of men is full of evil, and madness is in their heart while they live, and after that they go to the dead." Ecclesiastes 9:3

DAWN OF THE MAD SCIENTIST

EARLIER IN the book, we addressed supernatural events and how they can manifest as either overt or covert phenomena. The residing of unclean spirits within a human host was one of the topics which fell into this category. To summarize what was stated previously, while some individuals who are possessed may display outward symptoms of being demonically inhabited (like the maniacs of the Gadarenes), others show more subtle signs or none at all. We concluded the section by saying that demon possession doesn't always result in an individual becoming the town "crazy," sometimes the possessed may come across as the exact opposite – a man of high intelligence (and in some instances both of these symptoms can be manifest). Some of the Bible's examples of this included witches, sorcerers, magicians, and wizards.

According to Skeat, the word "witch" can mean "a wizard, to practice sorcery" (casting of lots, divination by the assistance of evil spirits, magic) or "to turn aside, conjure away, exercise." But it is also a variant of the Anglo Saxon word "witga" meaning "wise man, a prophet, a soothsayer." The title of "wizard" also infers one who is "wise-like." Wizard is simply the word "wise" with an "-ard" suffix, like the words "cow-ard" or "slugg-ard." The name "magician" also has ties to the same, being rooted in the word "magi," a Persian priest, a wise man, a mage. [58] In plainer words, all these titles are tied to A FORM OF WISDOM, yet, not the wisdom of God. Scripture ties them to THE WISDOM OF UNCLEAN SPIRITS.

How a person becomes a "genius"--an exceptionally gifted, talented, or learned person with creative power--is a great mystery to modern science. But the fact that the man of today labels certain endowed people as "geniuses" is ironic. Webster's 1828 Dictionary lists six definitions for the word. The meaning which tops the list is the oldest:

> "Among the ancients, a good or evil spirit or demon supposed to preside over a man's destiny in life..."

The word is from the identical Latin word, "genius," which indicates an "attendant spirit present from one's birth, innate ability or inclination." Also related to this is the word "genie" or "jinn," which is Arabic for "demon." Thus, the implications of being called a "genius" is twofold. One meaning can refer to one's inborn spirit (the spirit of man), the other an outside spirit (an unclean spirit, devil, or demon). Scottish folklorist and occult scholar, Lewis Spence, writes of the word:

> "Genius: Is generally used as THE NAME OF A SUPERIOR CLASS OF AERIAL BEINGS, holding an intermediate rank between mortals and immortals. That, at least, appears to be the signification of 'Daemon,' the corresponding term in Greek." [59]

The etymological link between geniuses, genies, jinn, and demons is interesting. It substantiates why the adage "genius borders insanity" is often found to be true. Demons can give people the brains to do things,

---

[58] Skeat, Walter W. *An Etymological Dictionary of the English Language.* (Dover Publications: Garden City, NY, 2005), p. 354, 719, 720

[59] Spence, Lewis. *An Encyclopedia of Occultism.* (Citadel Press & Carol Publishing Group: Secaucus, NJ, 1996) p. 177

but such possession may also produce other effects. Some highly intelligent people are free from any outward signs of devil activity, but others aren't. Many of the so-called "geniuses" of the world have also been certified as mentally unstable. Some "smart people" have "gone crazy," and many serial killers have genius-level intelligence. What this all serves to demonstrate is that SOME MEN OF HIGH INTELLIGENCE MAY BE THE RESULT OF DEMON POSSESSION. A fact that undergirds the proposition of the demonic impartation of knowledge. Some of history's most well-known figures, both famous and infamous, who were known to be afflicted with mental illness mark them as potential candidates for this. Abraham Lincoln, Isaac Newton, Nikola Tesla, Wolfgang Amadeus Mozart, Charles Darwin, Michelangelo, Ludwig van Beethoven, Alexander The Great, Adolf Hitler, Joseph Stalin, Winston Churchill, and Vladimir Putin are a few. In the world of killers, Ted Bundy, Ted Kaczynski, and Jeffrey Dahmer all had very high IQs or genius-level intelligence. Cain, the world's first murderer was probably a "genius." After he KILLED HIS BROTHER, he went and BUILT A CITY (Gen. 4:17). That's no feat for a dummy (we'll talk more about this later in the book).

Of course, as we've already addressed, true devil-possession doesn't need any outward markers to be a reality (see pages 55-57). Some people have them, some don't. The mystery of simultaneous invention and the proliferation of technical knowledge can both be tied to the operation of devil spirits. Of course, talking about devils and devil-possession in the twenty-first-century is frowned upon. But the tossing about of clinical words like "schizophrenia," "bipolar," "multiple personality disorder," and "dissociative identity disorder," does not negate scripture. In fact, it shouldn't be too shocking to discover that some modern psychiatric hospitals secretly harbor a belief in demons:

> "I had the nurses tell me, and I heard one doctor tell me, unofficially, off the record, okay, that there is a fine line between mental illness and [demon] possession. And that there are people in there that are probably possessed.

But they [the institution] will never, ever, ever, never tell anybody this officially. That shook me to my core." [60]

"You can think whatever you want to think about demon possession. But before you open your mouth and show your ignorance, you really need to get a job and work in a psychiatric hospital, because I have. When I was going to Bible college, I used to work at Escambia General Hospital. And every now and then, I'd have to work in the psych ward – Ward B. ... And the thing was divided into two parts. The first part had the people who were just mildly depressed... Then, they had the really back section which was, like, maximum security in the psychiatric ward. And that's where you really had some people which, I'm convinced, were demon-possessed. ... And I remember one time...I'll never forget, we were sitting back there in the maximum security part, and one young man...he said, 'the Lord said unto me, come unto me and I will make you KILLERS of men!' And by the way, this thing here about these people that would scoff at demon-possession have never really dealt with some of these people who have serious, serious psychological problems. And...a lot of those cases back there in the maximum security psychiatric ward, the psychiatrists, they didn't know *what* to do! ... One time...this one patient called me, and I said, 'yeah, how can I help you?' And he said, 'Hey,' he said, 'you can't see that little green man over there in the corner, can you?' Thank God, I didn't see nothing, amen? I don't want to see him or anything he's doing! I've never seen any demons. I don't want to see any." [61]

---

[60] Former security guard, Michael Nesbitt, from the show HAUNTED HOSPITALS.

[61] Carl Deems, "Insanity! By Dr Bill Haag." YouTube, March 1, 2018, 39:32, https://www.youtube.com/watch?v=Vy3ZwbfHWj0&list=FLiMPRqybPlZtEarPy pugE_w&index=6&t=16s

Dawn of the Mad Scientist | 143

Christian author and former psychiatric hospital staff member, David Heavener, once worked in an "M4" ward. Nurses and others who had a residency there were limited to shifts of three months at a time due to "the emotional stress of the working environment." Heavener readily admits that several of his encounters were with patients who were probably possessed, although his supervisors scoffed at the idea:

> "...the origin of the world of mental health and its original purpose...was never to cure, but to separate. But the question is: Separate society from what? The evil forces of the past [demons] exist in the present. ... Almost every patient was paranoid, schizophrenic, manic-depressive, or catatonic––well, that was according to their charts. But I knew something different was going on. ... Even though I hardly had a clue what I was doing, because I had no mentors and very little Bible knowledge, I would privately command those demons to leave patients until they would calm down. I kept my actions low-key in order to avoid getting into trouble with the hospital staff." [62]

---

[62] Heavener, David. *End-Times Investigations with David Heavener*. Crane, MI: Defender Publishing, 2022. p 26, 27, 29, 37

Science can only study the physical. It has no access to the spiritual. But the centuries-long association of GENIUSES with MADNESS, and the self-aggrandizement of worldly wisdom, knowledge, and science, is where we get the theme of the "mad scientist" (a demonized person who possesses advanced wisdom and knowledge). The last two centuries can rightly be labeled as the "Age of the Mad Scientist."

According to Harvard graduate, Eric Gastfriend, ninety percent of all the people who've ever earned PhDs are alive today. [63] Think about that. If you were to count all the scientists alive today, dating from today's oldest living scientist, up to the present, you'll find more scientists in this period than in ALL PREVIOUS ERAS COMBINED. In 1910, less than 2,500 PhDs were issued worldwide. In 2010, over 140,000 were given. Scientists are growing at an exponential rate.

So, what do our discussions on technology, and the dissemination of technical knowledge, have to do with the Prince of the Power of the Air? Understanding how information can be propagated to the masses through unclean spirits helps us to realize how the Devil could be manipulating mankind today. This goes hand-in-glove with the scriptures which describe the Prince of the Power of the Air as *"the spirit that now worketh in the children of disobedience"* (Eph. 2:2). The will and knowledge of Satan is funneled to man via these spirits. Like the four hundred lying prophets of Baal, many men then conceive ideas at the same general time. One of the fields of technology to balloon the fastest was KNOWLEDGE REGARDING THE AIR. This enabled man to quickly GO TO AND FRO in the earth, and move UP AND DOWN IN IT (compare with Job 1:7 & 2:2). This is why we've run this rabbit trail after having briefly addressed the birth of aviation. Men of prior ages could travel *"to and fro in the earth,"* but until the advent of the airplane, he could not move *"up and down in it."* Today he can.

---

[63] Gastfriend, Eric. "90% of all the Scientists who Ever Lived are Alive Today" (Eric Gastfriend, 5, November, 2015), https://ericgastfriend.com/index.php/2015/11/05/90-of-all-the-scientists-who-ever-lived-are-alive-today/

Before man could advance from balloons to motorized, flying vehicles, however, he had to be INTRODUCED TO A MYSTERIOUS FORCE. Without this strange force, much of the advanced technology of our age would simply not exist. Many ancient peoples reserved this enigma for the gods. However, we know it as "LIGHTNING" – energy produced regularly in Earth's atmosphere and later discovered to be analogous with ELECTRICITY (Benjamin Franklin, 1752). Now that we've talked about the Devil and air; the Devil's relationship to storms; and the Devil's knowledge of aircraft, we're now going to look at another facet of this matter. One of the primary ingredients that often accompanies a storm is LIGHTNING. Does Satan have a relationship with this? Could lightning be linked in any way to the Devil's *"power of the air"*?

A BAFFLING, UNEXPLAINED CONNECTION

Scripture states that at death a spirit vacates the body. An event often referred to as *"giving up the ghost"*:

> *"Then Abraham GAVE UP THE GHOST, AND DIED in a good old age, an old man, and full of years..."* Gen. 25:8

> *"And Isaac GAVE UP THE GHOST, AND DIED, and was gathered unto his people..."* Gen. 35:29

> *"But MAN DIETH, and wasteth away: yea, man GIVETH UP THE GHOST, and where is he?"* Job 14:10

> *"And Ananias hearing these words fell down, and GAVE UP THE GHOST..."* Act 5:5

Science, on the other hand, states that at death all ELECTRICAL ACTIVITY in the body ceases.

146 | A Baffling, Unexplained Connection

With these two statements, one clear conclusion about death is drawn from the Bible, another conclusion is drawn from science. Carefully read those things again and think about how they're related. Regardless of anyone's opinion about it, the fact cannot be escaped that death, when taken in light of both the Bible and science, exposes a mysterious link between GHOSTS AND ELECTRICAL PHENOMENA. Note what one website has said about the human brain and electricity:

> "Without electricity, you wouldn't be reading this [internet] article right now. And it's not because your computer wouldn't work. It's because your brain wouldn't work. EVERYTHING WE DO IS CONTROLLED AND ENABLED BY ELECTRICAL SIGNALS RUNNING THROUGH OUR BODIES." [64]

What's "running through our bodies"? Electricity. This is an established fact of science. Does this mean that "electricity" may actually be a "spirit"? No. The parallel does indicate, however, that the two are most certainly related somehow. The details involved in such an association are unknown. The connection could include any number of things. I don't profess to know the exact relationship between these matters, but that doesn't stop me from attempting to discern the phenomena from the word of God (1Th. 5:21, etc.).

Regardless, the correlation suggests that SOME ELECTRICAL INCIDENTS (not all) may be the residual of, or some kind of leftover from THE SPIRIT REALM. For example, "footprints" are not a literal part of living things. Footprints are impressions made by feet that have already passed through an area. A footprint is evidence that a foot exists, but it's not the very foot itself. The word can also be applied to THE LEFT-BEHIND EVIDENCE of a thing, or the area occupied or affected by something. ARE SOME FORMS OF ELECTRICITY THE "FOOTPRINTS" OF SPIRITS?

---

[64] Layton, Julia & Mark Mancini. "How Does the Body Make Electricity — and How Does It Use It?" (Howstuffworks, InfoSpace Holdings 1, August, 2022), https://health.howstuffworks.com/human-body/systems/nervous-system/human-body-make-electricity.htm

A Baffling, Unexplained Connection | 147

In an attempt to better understand this, consider that we know that nature (the ordinances of God) creates electricity through lightning. Man has also recently discovered how to transport or store electricity (power stations, hydropower plants, generators, batteries, etc.). Do spirits emit some form of this energy as well? Does Satan's control over vast hordes of evil spirits give him the means to manipulate, or to even summon such mysterious forces? Does the Devil sometimes manipulate the air, either separately or in conjunction with unclean spirits, to create his own lightning? If this sounds improbable, would it really be a shock to discover that the fallen being whom God has named *"the prince of the power of the air"* could do this? Does the Bible associate Satan with any kind of ELECTRICAL PHENOMENA?

Consider that in Arab legend stories often centered around an adventurous boy who encountered mystical artifacts. Upon acquiring these items (gold rings, bottles, lamps), the boy discovered that he could summon genies by rubbing them. A "genie" or "jinn" is a DEMON SPIRIT. Rubbing a metallic object (like a golden lamp) CREATES STATIC ELECTRICITY.[65] This concept infers that the demonic realm (or spirit realm) can somehow be accessed or activated through the generation of electricity. At the very least, it substantiates some sort of unknown connection between the two. Where did the authors of these stories get such an idea? Is it all a fairytale, a complete fabrication and work of man's imagination, or

---

[65] FOOTNOTE: Gold is one of the best conductors of electricity. Most modern electronics have portions of gold for this very reason. More about this later.

148 | A Baffling, Unexplained Connection

In 1901, one year after publishing *The Wonderful Wizard of Oz*, children's author L. Frank Baum, published *The Master Key*. The image above is a vintage advertisement for the children's novel. The story centered around a young boy who accidentally conjures "the deamon of electricity" with his electrical equipment. Baum's use of the title "Master Key" is interesting. In the Bible, the master key is the Lord Jesus Christ, not some electric devil (Lk. 11:52). Where did Baum get his ideas for such things? See page 101 for more about Baum.

is there more to this? Was this idea pulled from thin air or, perhaps, from the Prince of the Power of the Air? Does electricity open a door to demon activity, or perhaps in some cases, it's simply evidence of demon activity? Could the Devil exercise some form of "covert supernaturalism" through this mystifying force? If you don't believe he's doing this, what's preventing him from doing it? Is it because you don't believe he has the ability? What if you discovered he did? How deep does the rabbit hole between the spirit world and the electric world go?

BLINDED BY THE LIGHT

Some of what we've already said about air, storms, and the Devil, applies to this next subject. For the sake of brevity, however, we're not going to repeat where these things are alike. But, in dealing with the matter of LIGHTNING, the Prince of the Power of the Air is taken a step deeper. As this study unfolds, you will discover that this phenomenon leads into the fields of electricity, devil-possession, occultism, and even modern technology. If this sounds far-fetched, keep reading. There's a lot you've never been told.

> [17] *And the seventy returned again with joy, saying, Lord, even THE DEVILS ARE SUBJECT UNTO US through thy name.*
> [18] *And he said unto them, I beheld SATAN AS LIGHTNING fall from heaven.*
> [19] *Behold, I GIVE YOU POWER to tread on serpents and scorpions, and over all THE POWER OF THE ENEMY: and nothing shall by any means hurt you.*
> [20] *Notwithstanding in this rejoice not, that THE SPIRITS ARE SUBJECT UNTO YOU; but rather rejoice, because your names are written in heaven.*
> Lk. 10:18-20

The phrase *"Satan as lightning fall from heaven"* immediately follows the comments of the disciples who professed to God that devils were *"subject"* to them through the name of Jesus. Some believe this phrase implies that when Christ said *"I beheld Satan as lightning fall from heaven,"* he was referencing something the seventy did to cause the Devil to fall. However, I don't believe this to be the case. In looking closer at Christ's reply, the Bible-reader must note that, while it's true the born-again Christian, through the Lord Jesus Christ alone, has power over the enemy; be assured that NO SAINT CAN MAKE SATAN FALL FROM HEAVEN, regardless of any authority we may be given over him. Through Jesus, the Christian has the power to *"rebuke"* the Devil (Jude 1:9); *"resist the Devil"* (James 4:7); give not *"place to the devil"* (Eph. 4:27); *"stand against"* the Devil (Eph. 6:11), and recover ourselves from *"the snare of the devil"* (2Tim. 2:26), but we can't cause him to *"fall from heaven"* as is stated in these verses. It is the will of the Devil himself that precipitated his own fall (Isa. 14:12-14, Ezk. 28), and only God who will cast him out of heaven (see Rev. 12:7-10). Therefore, it appears that Christ's remark of beholding Satan *"fall from heaven"*, in the context of these verses, had nothing at all to do with something the seventy did to him. Rather, it's addressing THE ABILITY AND EXTENT OF SATAN'S POWER. Christ is contrasting one power against another. Note how the words of the Bible are clear that two things are being measured against each other:

> *"...I give YOU POWER...over...THE POWER OF THE ENEMY..."* Lk. 10:19

This, I believe, is why Christ alludes to *"lightning"* within this discussion. So, if Christ is referring to the Prince of the Power of the Air's authority over lightning, how are air and lightning related?

Lightning is an air-centric phenomenon and one of the world's most powerful forces. In fact, lightning contains the hottest temperatures mankind has ever directly encountered. The NOAA National Severe Storms Laboratory says that lightning is *"...50,000 degrees Fahrenheit, much hotter than the surface of the sun."* [66] Reporting on the formation of lightning, the UK-based Tornado and Storm Research Organization has stated:

---

[66] "Lightning Basics" (NSSL NOAA National Severe Storms Laboratory, U.S. Department of Commerce), https://www.nssl.noaa.gov/education/svrwx101/lightning/

"Lightning is the response to TURBULENT AIRFLOW... Lightning is a very long electric spark...greater than about 1 km [3280 feet]...generally associated with thunderstorms, but rarely lightning can strike from a clear blue sky." [67]

Note that "turbulent airflow" precedes the fall of a bolt of lightning. Without the invisible activity of AIR, lightning as we know it, is not possible. Since scripture identifies the Devil as *"the prince of the power of the air,"* then this, in turn, implies that he has immense control over both THE PRODUCTION OF LIGHTNING and THE MANIPULATION OF ELECTRICAL ACTIVITY. His ability to utilize these is impossible to distinguish from its natural production. The phrase *"I beheld Satan as lightning fall from heaven,"* I believe, is a reference to this power. And who could dare argue that lightning is not power? If it is anything, it is EXACTLY THAT. The average bolt of lightning is said to harbor 100 million to 1 billion volts of electricity.[68] This is why, earlier in the book, we covered the Devil's interactions with Job. Remember the *"fire"* that fell from heaven which burned up Job's servants and sheep, a power which scripture ascribes directly to the hand of Satan?

> "[12] *And the LORD said unto SATAN, Behold, all that he [Job] hath is IN THY POWER...* [16] *...FIRE...IS FALLEN from heaven, and hath burned up the sheep, and the servants, and consumed them..."* Job 1:12 & 16

The *"fire"* named here can be either literal FIRE FALLING FROM HEAVEN or BOLTS OF LIGHTNING. The correlation between the two is that the word "fireball" is a classic name given to the thunderbolt. In many cultures of antiquity, fire from the sky was

---

[67] Doe, Robert K., *Extreme Weather*, John Wiley & Sons Ltd., Chichester. 2016, p. 195, 209
[68] "Frequently Asked Questions About Lightning" (NSSL NOAA National Severe Storms Laboratory, U.S. Department of Commerce), https://www.nssl.noaa.gov/education/svrwx101/lightning/faq/

While scripture shows that lightning can signify the return of Christ (Mt. 24:27, Lk. 17:24), more often it is used by occultists to symbolize the Devil. Nineteen-sixties pop culture Satanist, Anton Zandor LaVey, often wore a medallion of an inverted pentagram superscribed by a thunderbolt. Note LaVey and the replica above. Why link an electrical symbol to the Devil?

synonymous with lightning. This is not to say that the fire in Job was necessarily a bolt of lightning. It may very well have simply been literal balls of fire. But forcing the reader to choose between fire or lightning is not the point. Regardless of which of the two occurrences explain the details of the calamity, scripture shows that the Devil can be tied to both kinds of sky-based phenomena. The tragedy in Job may have been satanically-created or manipulated lightning, but it may have been satanically-created or manipulated fire. Don't forget, we're dealing with *"the prince of the power of the air"* here, a being with substantial ability, not some clown in red tights running around with a pitchfork. Vincent Gaddis, a former United Press (UPI) and Religious News Service (RNS) correspondent, observes:

> "Each year throughout the world there are thousands of fires of undetermined origin. Many of them start on high roofs and steeples. Brush, trees, bridges and roadbeds have been mysteriously set afire. And each year there

are strange explosions, some of which cause extensive damage. ... There are hundreds of fireball cases in my files that could be classified as DESCENDING SPHEROIDS OF RADIANT ENERGY, UNREALTED TO ELECTRICAL STORMS OR METEORS." [69]

Gaddis explains that these strange fires "are not meteors, although as they fall they may be misinterpreted as meteors. In these occurrences, no meteoric material is found... They simply fall, fade away or expire with an explosion of radiant energy and heat... They are not balls of lightning. ... They appear in all kinds of weather and in regions where electrical storms are rare occurrences. Frequently they are actually observed to fall from the atmosphere. And what comes down from up there, obviously, must have been up there in the first place, even though INVISIBLE OR UNDETECTED." [70]

Having fire and lightning in visible forms is bad enough, but "invisible"? Could there really be such a thing?

"During its...lifetime, the Empire State Building has been struck by lightning over a thousand times and has been the object of NUMEROUS STUDIES. Over the period of about ten years, several hundred lightning strikes were recorded electrically and photographed, but only about half the strikes produced a visible photographic image. ... These results suggest that currents in the range of 100 amperes would likely be subvisible, defined simply as NOT BEING VISUALLY PERCEIVED IN DAYLIGHT by the casual observer. ... If this theory is correct, many more victims may succumb to subvisible or INVISIBLE LIGHTNING than to its more visible forms." [71]

---

[69] Gaddis, Vincent H. *Mysterious Fires and Lights*. (New Saucerian Press: 2017), p. 71 [Reprint of a 1967 edition]

[70] Ibid. p, 70-71

[71] Friedman, John S. *Out of the Blue*. (Delta Trade Paperbacks: New York, NY. 2008), p. 5

In his excellent work, *Thunder and Lightning* (1905), French astronomer, Camille Flammarion (1842-1925), attempts to collect into one volume the many astounding mysteries surrounding lightning. He writes:

> "It would be an interesting thing to make a careful study once a year...of the habits and customs of thunder and lightning. Perhaps in this way we should succeed one day in determining the still mysterious nature of these elusive forces. I, for my part, have been engaged upon the task for many years past. It has produced a big accumulation of records... I have hundreds of quaint records before me. Impossible to deduce any kind of law from them all. YOU ARE TEMPTED TO BELIEVE THAT THE ELECTRIC CURRENT HAS A BRAIN." [72]

Because of the ability of the Devil to control or mimic elements of nature (air, fire, etc.), many in old times RECOGNIZED LIGHTNING AS HAVING A CONNECTION TO THE SUPERNATURAL. This was due, no doubt, to the ancient, antediluvian knowledge of the Devil that earth's first father's possessed (Adam, Enoch, Noah, etc.). A knowledge that's reflected in the Bible's oldest book, the book of Job. However, over time, this knowledge became perverted and twisted by superstition and false religion. Many beliefs in myth and false religion contain perversions of Bible facts, and lightning is no exception:

> "By the ancients... [lightning] was not regarded as merely a blind force but a gigantic INTELLECTUAL ENTITY--A BEING rather than an elemental force." [73]

---

[72] Flammarion, Camille. Thunder and Lightning. (London, England: Chatto & Windus, 1905), p. 1 & 14

[73] Hall, Manly Palmer. The Mystery of Electricity. (Abelard-Schuman: London, 1930), p. 13

Of course, lightning, in and of itself, is not an entity, as some ancients supposed. But electrification certainly has some sort of unknown ties, as we've already noted, with SPIRIT ACTIVITY. This is not only true in the fact that God has direct power over it (Psa. 148:8, 2Sam. 22:15), but the Devil has direct power over it (Lk. 10:18).

Now realizing this, we must consider why in the world would God waste his time, and my time and your time, to warn us of the Devil's authority over wind, fire, and lightning, IF THE DEVIL NEVER PLANNED ON USING this tremendous *"power of the air"* AGAINST US? Can you answer me that? Because, if Satan ever did use this power he would certainly USE IT TO DECEIVE. His objective towards man has always been deceit. From the time he first appeared to man (Gen. 3), until his destruction (Rev. 20), THE DECEPTION OF MANKIND has always been his goal. So, in regards to this *"power of the air"* [lightning], would there be any reason for the knowledge of the air, or things of the air, to increase in the Bible's prophesied end-times? Or, perhaps, when the Lord tells us that Satan is *"the prince of the power of the air,"* maybe it doesn't mean anything significant at all? At least, that's what the Devil wants us to believe.

THE MYSTERY OF ELECTRICITY

I know that the title of this section may sound strange to some readers. Electricity is a "mystery"? Since when? Isn't this a subject that science hashed out and solved over two centuries ago? Doesn't twenty-first-century man have this thing figured out? Well, that's what they WANT you to think, and many of them DO think. That's the illusion. But bear with me, it's imperative that the Bible-believer not lose sight of what we're dealing with here. And WHAT WE'RE DEALING WITH IS A THING MUCH BIGGER THAN SCIENCE. This thing we call "electricity" somehow parlays over into the realm of spirits. The Bible knows that there's a real, active invisible world, but modern man does not (public schools, colleges, universities, academia, etc.). This is why we addressed Satan's connections with weather and natural phenomena in the first parts of this book. The DEVIL'S CONNECTION TO WEATHER AND NATURE SHOULD PROVIDE A GATEWAY into understanding what we're about to get into. Now we're going to start bringing these things down to modern reality. Or, at least, show the potential of how such potent satanic influence can affect man TODAY – in the twenty-first century. The Bible doesn't call Satan *"the god of this world"* for no reason. He's still the owner of that title (see 2 Cor. 4:4).

For starters, although the word "electricity" has been around since the early seventeenth century, today a multiplicity of things have been labeled with this single word. Consequently, THERE'S NO SINGLE DEFINITION for "electricity," even though many authorities pretend that there is. Because of this, there is no way of precisely defining it. The Devil has a long history of playing word games and CONFUSING MANKIND WITH WORDS (Gen. 3:1-5). When it comes to the word "electricity," this was his joke and a way of sowing more confusion around an issue that was already complex and mystifying (1Co 14:33). Would the Prince of the Power of the Air have a legitimate interest in bewildering man about phenomena of the air? Think about it. William J. Beaty, Research Engineer at the University of Washington, has been writing on the fallout of such semantics since the late 1990s:

> "... If we wish to agree on a single correct definition of 'electricity,' which definition should we choose? ...the few textbooks which do use the scientific definition are all seventy years old, or older [and by the 2020s, 90 years old]. ...approximately TEN SEPARATE THINGS have the name 'electricity.' THERE'S NO SINGLE STUFF CALLED 'ELECTRICITY.' ... Mrs. McCave was invented by Dr. Seuss. She had twenty-three sons. She named them all 'Dave.' Whenever we ask 'What Is Electricity,' that's just like asking Mrs. McCave 'who is Dave?' ... There can be no answer since the question itself is wrong. It's wrong to ask 'who is Dave?' because WE'RE SILENTLY ASSUMING THAT THERE'S ONLY ONE... For the same

reason, WE'LL NEVER FIND A SIMPLE ANSWER TO THE QUESTION 'WHAT IS ELECTRICITY?' ... We must accept the fact that, while SEVERAL DIFFERENT THINGS do exist inside wires, PEOPLE WRONGLY CALL ALL OF THEM BY A SINGLE NAME. ... if you ask 'What is electricity?', then all of the answers you'll find will just confuse you, and you'll never stop asking that question." [74]

As it currently stands, electric charge is called "electricity;" electric energy is called "electricity;" electric current is called "electricity;" and the list goes on. And this confusion created by mislabeling doesn't even begin to touch on the mysteries which continue to surround the various things named "electricity." While, certainly, we've come a long way since Ben Franklin's verification that lightning is an electric spark, there's still much that science doesn't understand. For as long as man has been investigating this thing, there have always been those who were willing to admit that we still do not know what, exactly, we're dealing with. And we're not talking about crackpots, here. We're talking about established authors, journalists, and scientists:

> **1889** – "What is electricity? NO ONE KNOWS. It seems to be one manifestation of the energy which fills the universe, and which appears in a variety of other forms, such as heat, light, magnetism, chemical affinity, mechanical motion, etc." [75]

> **1889** – "What is electricity? We do not know, and for practical purposes it is not necessary that we should know. We are only concerned in what its properties are –– how we can make it obedient to our will." [76]

---

[74] Beaty, William J. "What Is 'Electricity'?" (Science Hobbyist, Bill Beaty, 1996), http://amasci.com/miscon/whatis.html

[75] Benjamin, Park, The Age of Electricity. (Berwick & Smith: Boston, MA), 1886 p. 35

[76] Citing from an article in *Electricity in Homes*, 1889. Simon, Linda. *Dark Light* (Harcourt Inc: San Diego, California, 2004), p. 247

1905 – "Electricity is not a form of energy, any more than water is a form of energy. Water may be a vehicle of energy when at a high level or in motion; so may electricity. Electricity cannot be manufactured, as heat can; it can only be moved from place to place, like water; and its energy must be in the form of motion or of strain. Electricity under strain constitutes 'charge'; electricity in locomotion constitutes a current and magnetism; electricity in vibration constitutes light. WHAT ELECTRICITY ITSELF IS WE DO NOT KNOW, but it may, perhaps, be a form or aspect of matter." [77]

1930 – "...though the wonder of electricity grows with every passing day, the nature and source of its marvelous energy remain an impenetrable mystery. WE KNOW IT NOT FOR WHAT IT ACTUALLY IS but for that which it is able to accomplish." [78]

1967 – "Electricity is a universal physical energy MANIFESTING IN MANY FORMS...Its primary source, which would determine what electricity is, HAS NOT YET BEEN ASCERTAINED." [79]

21st CENTURY – "Electricity is all around us--powering technology like our cell phones, computers, lights, soldering irons, and air conditioners. It's tough to escape it in our modern world. Even when you try to escape electricity, it's still at work throughout nature, from the lightning in a thunderstorm to the synapses inside our body. BUT WHAT EXACTLY IS ELECTRICITY? This is A VERY COMPLICATED QUESTION, and as you dig deeper and ask more questions, THERE REALLY IS NOT A DEFINITIVE ANSWER, ONLY ABSTRACT REPRESENTATIONS of how electricity interacts with our surroundings." [80]

Understanding lightning and electricity has long been a mystery.

So, whether modern man thinks he knows what "electricity" is, or not, there is still plenty of mystery that surrounds it. Don't be fooled by those who would say otherwise. Lightning, for example, is one of the most outstanding and well-known displays of electrical phenomena. And yet, while science knows SOME things about this, there are a lot of things it doesn't know. In many ways, THE LIGHT EVENT IS A PARADOX. Its formation contradictory and baffling. Physicists recognize that lightning's most prominent place is found IN THE AIR (lightning flashes and lightning bolts), and yet the air is not a conductor of electricity. The National Oceanic & Atmospheric Administration's National Severe Storms Laboratory admits:

> "The creation of lightning is a complicated process. ... THERE IS STILL DEBATE about exactly how a cloud builds up electrical charges, and HOW LIGHTNING FORMS." [81]

---

[77] Beaty, William J. "Electricity is Not a Form of Energy" (Science Hobbyist, Bill Beaty, 1999), http://amasci.com/miscon/energ1.html

[78] Hall, Manly Palmer. *The Mystery of Electricity*. (Abelard-Schuman: London, 1930), p. 23

[79] Gaddis, Vincent H. *Mysterious Fires and Lights*. (New Saucerian Press: 2017), p. 178 [Reprint of a 1967 edition]

[80] Blom, Jim. "What Is Electricity?" (SparkFun, SparkFun Electronics), https://learn.sparkfun.com/tutorials/what-is-electricity/all#getting-started

[81] "Lightning Basics" (NSSL NOAA National Severe Storms Laboratory, U.S. Department of Commerce), https://www.nssl.noaa.gov/education/svrwx101/lightning/

To say that "there is still debate" about the formation of lightning (i.e. scientists disagreeing on what's true and what isn't), is just a roundabout way of professing that the phenomena largely remains an unexplained mystery. Here's an eye-opening remark made in 2012:

> "But for all we know, LIGHTNING MIGHT AS WELL COME FROM ZEUS. Counting Ben Franklin's kite-and-key experiment as the starting point, 250 years of scientific investigation HAVE YET TO GET TO GRIPS WITH HOW LIGHTNING WORKS. ...LIGHTNING CONFOUNDS MUCH OF SCIENTISTS' UNDERSTANDING OF BASIC PHYSICS." [82]

Imagine twenty-first-century man professing that our understanding of lightning is currently so shallow that such phenomena "confounds" us and "might as well" have supernatural origins like "Zeus." Lightning physicist, Joe Dwyer, of the Florida Institute of Technology iterates:

> "How do you get a spark going inside a thunderstorm? The electric fields never seem to be big enough inside the storm to generate a spark. So how does that spark get going? ... After you get it started, how does lightning propagate for tens of miles through clouds? THAT'S AN AMAZING THING—HOW DO YOU TURN AIR FROM BEING AN INSULATOR INTO A CONDUCTOR?" [83]

The idea of electrical conductors and insulators has been around since the mid-1700s. According to basic physics, a "conductor" is a thing that permits the free flow of "electrons." An "isolator" prohibits this flow. While air is considered a prohibitor of such a flow, it is also one of the most abundant producers of electrical activity – via

---

[82] Wolchover, Natalie. "Lightning Still Largely a Mystery" (LiveScience, Future US, Inc., 26, September, 2012), https://www.livescience.com/34245-lightning-mystery.html

[83] Ibid.

The Mystery of Electricity | 161

storms. This is the conundrum. The chief scientist for the Space-based Nuclear Detonation Detection program at Los Alamos reports:

> "Despite all this knowledge, lightning is still poorly understood." [84]

Nikola Tesla was one of the towering "geniuses" of his day. He ranks among those who reportedly have some of the highest IQs in the world. Labeled everything from a "wizard" to an "Electric Messiah," Tesla's lifelong work in this field, incredibly, still led him to ask in a letter to a friend (1939) at the end of his life:

> "Day after day I have asked myself 'what is electricity?' and HAVE FOUND NO ANSWER. Eighty years have gone by since that time and I still ask the same question, UNABLE TO ANSWER IT. Some pseudo-scientist, of whom there are only too many, may tell you that he can, but DO NOT BELIEVE HIM." [85]

Nikola Tesla worked with electricity for most of his life, but admitted he had yet to penetrate what it was.

If a man of Tesla's mind was admitting to the fact that he didn't know "what is electricity," then how can we be assured of its true nature? Some may say, "science tells us..." Yes, but what about the Bible? What does it have to say about such things? Can we not start

---

[84] Light, Tess Lavezzi. "Unraveling the mysteries of lightning" (Huffpost, The Huffington Post, 20, June, 2017), https://blog.nationalgeographic.org/2017/05/02/unraveling-the-mysteries-of-lightning/

[85] Carlson, W. Bernard. *Tesla: Inventor of the Electrical Age*. (Princeton University Press: Princeton, NJ, 2015), p. 18

there in getting some sort of definitive answer? Electrical events, certainly, have a connection with nature. There's no doubt about that. The phenomenon is also related to other things, however. We mentioned this earlier (see page 145). Science has known for years that the human body is a conductor of electricity. What many refer to as "brainwaves" are defined as "electrical impulses." Doctors measure these with a machine called an "electroencephalogram." Look at that word. "Electro," means electricity. "Encephalon" is a Greek word for what's inside the head. Science associates our mind with our brain. The Bible associates our mind with our spirit (Eph. 4:23, Ph. 1:27, etc.) At death, ALL ELECTRICAL ACTIVITY IN THE BODY CEASES. Scripture, on the other hand, tells us that when a person dies, THEIR SPIRIT DEPARTS.

While there's no proof that electricity itself is a spirit (and we're not saying that it is), the fact that electrical activity in the body ends at the same time our spirit departs is SURELY INDICATIVE OF SOMETHING SIGNIFICANT. Regardless of the reason, this helps illustrate that ELECTRIC PHENOMENA AND SPIRITS SHARE SOME SORT OF CLOSE, UNEXPLAINED CONNECTION. When this association is coupled with Satan's power over MANKIND, LIGHTNING, and EVIL SPIRITS, then a picture begins to form that some manifestations of electricity may be much different than what modern science thinks it is. If that sounds improbable, don't be too quick to spurn the idea of supernatural involvement. Note the words of King Solomon:

> *"Curse not the king, no not in thy thought; and curse not the rich in thy bedchamber: for A BIRD OF THE AIR SHALL CARRY THE VOICE, and that which hath wings shall TELL THE MATTER."* Ecc. 10:20

When addressing birds in the first sections of the book we talked about this (see page 25), but it's worth addressing again. In looking at this verse, the question that immediately jumps to mind is "how in the world does a bird carry the voice or tell of a matter that's in our thoughts?" Can "birds," as we know them, literally do this? No. But a "bird" can carry the voice when the bird is not a bird but is symbolized by a bird. Under the command of the Devil, foul spirits can TAKE TO THE AIR AND SPREAD MAN'S VOICE. You either believe that or you don't. But since this is a Bible fact, does it not point, perhaps, to some kind of spiritual insight into the true workings behind some electronic devices like the "telephone"? A device that twenty-first-century man now takes for granted with his "iPhones" and "smartphones" –– devices, powered by electricity, that can *"carry the voice"* from one location to another, and *"tell"* a matter.

THE PRINCE OF

THE POWER OF

THE AIRWAVES

What if there's more to radio waves, airwaves, and electromagnetic energy than what science can detect? Can or do certain spirits work in conjunction with these invisible forces? Is it possible that twenty-first-century man is (1) blinded to what these truly are, (2) ignorant of where such things originate, or (3) how such things are controlled? What if Satan has some sort of hold over this phenomenon? You may deny this, but your proof is what, exactly? My proof that science can be unaware of the workings of spirits is that the science of biology knows nothing about them. When we consider the ignorance of science regarding the presence of THE SPIRIT WITHIN THE HUMAN BODY, then THE INABILITY OF SCIENCE TO RECOGNIZE SPIRIT ACTIVITY IN ANY FIELD OF STUDY becomes apparent. Hundreds of years of physical scrutinizing and study have revealed nothing about this. In fact, current science will tell us, "conclusively," that the spirit isn't there. Thus, scripture defines this age as one of *"EVER LEARNING, AND NEVER ABLE to come to the knowledge of the truth"* (2Tim. 3:7). While "truth," specifically as mentioned here, concerns the truth of the saving work of the Lord Jesus Christ, it can certainly include a whole realm of truths to which fallen man is blinded. Is the field of physics any more knowledgeable about these things? Why should it be? Some may be dismissive of these ideas because they can't understand how spirit interaction would be carried out. But the Bible doesn't ask us to "understand" how that a spirit resides within each one of us, it simply reveals that it does. What about spirit operation in other areas? Must we know the technicalities of interaction to believe that it's possible? No. Then what of the Prince of the Power of the Air? Concider this:

> "Electricity was commonly symbolized by the serpent because of its motion. Electricity passing between the poles of a spark gap is serpentine in its motion. Force projected through atmosphere was called The Great Snake." [86]

The Bible shows that when the god of this world blinds the minds of men, they are unknowingly caught in *"the snare of the devil"* and *"are taken captive by him at his will"* (2Tim. 2:26). They do what Satan wants them to do and they only know what he wants them to know. Man thinks he's so smart, and yet all along he's being played by the Devil:

> *"...the god of this world hath blinded the minds of them which believe not..."* 2Cor. 4:4

WHAT YOU WERE NEVER TOLD ABOUT LIGHTNING

The evidence, supported by both severe electric shock victims and those who have been struck by lightning, demonstrates that such bodily trauma may result in the permanent acquiring of, or

---

[86] Hall, Manly Palmer. *The Mystery of Electricity.* (Abelard-Schuman: London, 1930), p. 32

temporary acquisition of, what many describe as metaphysical or psychic abilities, such as divination, necromancy, clairvoyance, healing, or manifestations of poltergeist activity, phenomena which Holy Scripture has long associated with witchcraft, demonism, and devil-possession:

> "Although the effects of being struck by lightning vary from one individual to another, no one is ever the same as before they were struck. Some survivors undergo a kind of 'SPIRITUAL AWAKENING,' or at the very least acquire a deeper interest in spiritual matters. ... The alleged development of psychic abilities IS NOT AN UNCOMMON FEATURE among cases where people have survived a LIGHTNING STRIKE." [87]

As we began to point out in the previous section, there exists a puzzling, intimate tie between electricity and spirit activity. And apparently, literal contact with electric phenomena can sometimes open a door to this event. The "spiritual awakening" mentioned above, is not due to the individual having a close brush with death where they are then put in mind of their mortality. No. This kind of "awakening" is speaking of "New Age" type thought, like matters of mysticism, out-of-body experiences, and so forth. Many Native Americans have been aware of this aspect of lightning for centuries. Often, the most powerful and respected among them have gone through such a process:

> "According to ethnologist and psychologist Holger Kalweit, in shamanic traditions the world over, BEING STRUCK BY LIGHTNING is one of the ways by which people are INITIATED INTO SHAMANISM." [88]

---

[87] Proud, Louis. *Strange Electro Magnetic Dimensions*. (New Page Books: Pompton Plains, NJ, 2015,) p. 165, 169

[88] Ibid. p. 172

"The initiation of a shaman takes on various forms ... The most dramatic INITIATION BY LIGHTNING BOLT; thus, many societies have the category of folks who BECOME SHAMANS AFTER BEING STRUCK BY LIGHTNING; these are referred to as 'lightning shamans.' They are OFTEN VENERATED AND FEARED AS THE MIGHTIEST SHAMANS..." [89]

Lightning-strike experiencer, Elizabeth Krohn, and author Jeffrey Kripal, who holds a chair in Philosophy and Religious Thought at Rice University state:

"...the shaman is sometimes identified or 'chosen' by a lightning strike. He or she has literally been touched or elected by the heavens. Sometimes, like some ancient superhero...a lightning bolt is displayed on the shaman's ritual garb. In one case reported among the Sudanese of Africa, the individual was 'dead' for two days, that is he became a shaman through what we would today call a 'near-death experience.' In one Canadian indigenous culture in British Columbia, the

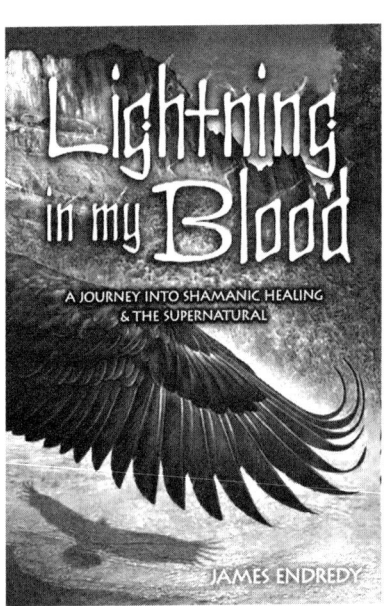

Lightning in My Blood: A Journey into Shamanic Healing & the Supernatural, a book on devil activity and lightning.

---

[89] Craffert, Pieter F. *The Life of a Galilean Shaman: Jesus of Nazareth in Anthropological-Historical Perspective.* (Cascade Books: Eugene, OR, 2008), p. 213

spirit itself is believed to come down 'in the shape of a stroke of lightning.' Another Eskimo shaman received his power when he was struck by a 'ball of fire,' perhaps ball lightning. ... The general religious notion here is that A PERSON HIT BY LIGHTNING HAS BEEN CHOSEN BY THE SPIRITS and initiated by the Thunder Being... The POWER SURGE is believed to give the individual special wakan, that is, sacred or mysterious powers. Such powers might include what we call clairvoyance and telepathy. It might also ENABLE THEM TO COMMUNICATE WITH THE SPIRIT WORLD." [90]

Interestingly, within the Native American culture, we often find a carved BIRD surmounting a wooden "totem pole." This bird, called a "thunderbird," represents THE SPIRIT OF LIGHTNING. We've already talked about how scripture uses the bird to picture unclean spirits. This is no different. Many tribal people believe that this "spirit bird", through the force of lightning, can instill special power or magic into certain individuals. In that the natives recognized that some sort of spirit was, evidently, working through an electrical event, they are correct. However, as a Bible-believing Christian, I shouldn't have to tell you that a "shaman" is simply another name for "witch." This is

---

[89] Craffert, Pieter F. *The Life of a Galilean Shaman: Jesus of Nazareth in Anthropological-Historical Perspective*. (Cascade Books: Eugene, OR, 2008), p. 213

[90] Krohn, Elizabeth G., Kripal, Jeffrey J. *Changed in a Flash: One Woman's Near-Death Experience and Why a Scholar Thinks It Empowers Us All*. (North Atlantic Books: Berkeley, CA. 2018), p. 218-219

why shamans are also known as "witch doctors." The Bible ties such pagan practices with those which have familiar spirits, consult with familiar spirits, and work with familiar spirits (Lev. 19:31, 20:27, Deut. 18:11, 1Sam. 28:7, 2Kgs. 23:24, etc.). Scripture warns us against things like "shamanism," not because they're fake, but because THE POWERS BEHIND THEM, whether acquired via lightning or otherwise, ARE REAL AND DEMONIC. Native Americans who have become Christians after receiving the Lord Jesus Christ as their Savior have admitted to this:

> "After many of the Indians of Martha's Vineyard were converted to Christ, they testified that before their conversion they really had intercourse with demons." [91]

It seems one way to sometimes acquire demons is to access them via ELECTRIC PHENOMENA like shock or lightning strikes. Since the Bible shows that the Devil has power over the air, and phenomena of the air, such possibilities shouldn't be all that surprising. In fact, this phenomenon within native shamanic cultures doesn't end with them. Some readers may be tempted to overlook these things, assuming that this strangeness is only related to primitive, superstitious tribalism. But this is not the case. Sometimes we find modern "psychics" connecting the genesis of their abilities to this same thing.

In 1975, Dannion Brinkley, author of *Saved by the Light, At Peace in the Light,* and *Secrets of the Light,*[92] acquired the ability to supposedly communicate with spirits after being struck by lightning:

> "Hi everybody. I'm Dannion ... I travel around the world speaking to sold-out audiences, doing workshops, and leading [New Age] spiritual journeys to sacred sites where

---

[91] Daniels, J.W. *Spiritualism Versus Christianity*. (Miller, Orton & Mulligan: New York, NY, 1856), p. 45

[92] FOOTNOTE: The world "light" in all of the titles of Dannion Brinkley's books is indicative of his initial lightning-strike experience, thus we can read them as *Saved by the Lightning, At Peace in the Lightning,* and *Secrets of the Lightning*.

I share this simple message: You are a great, mighty and powerful spiritual being with dignity, direction, and purpose. ...BEFORE THE LIGHTNING HIT ME I didn't believe anyone could READ MINDS or TRAVEL INTO OTHER DIMENSIONS. Now, I've become everything I didn't believe. ...Today...one of my deepest beliefs – there is no such thing as death!" [93]

In 2021, popular investigative journalist and talk radio host, George Knapp, interviewed Brinkley. In that interview, Brinkley reported:

"Lightning came down the phone line. ...into the house, it went into the side of my head above my ear, it went down my spine, it welded the nails of the heels of my shoes to the floor. It threw me up in the air, I see the ceiling, it slams me back down, A BALL OF FIRE COMES THROUGH THE ROOM... And in the course of that, I had what is now known in 1975 as a classic near-death experience. ...when you get to talking about being dead...I got it down pat. ...I've been with more than 2,000 people going from this world to the next world. And I can tell you this...that there might be people who know more about the death experience, or the life experience than me, but at the bedside, THERE'S NOBODY WHO KNOWS MORE. I've been dead four times. ...Let me tell you what happens based on my own experience...I go to this place where light is... And it was to educate me about the nature of the physical being as AN ELECTRIC ENTITY. ...I am a member of the No Vet Dies Alone advisory board, and I helped co-write the standard end-of-life care model for the Veterans Administration. ...and understand that nobody dies. Nobody. I have lived my entire life based on

---

[93] "Dannon Brinkley on how to become a psychic" (www.meditationadvice.com), https://medium.com/@meditationadvise/dannion-brinkley-on-how-to-become-psychic-f2d58c21cdef

171 | What You were Never Told about Lightning

SECRETS of the Light
LESSONS FROM HEAVEN
Dannion Brinkley and Kathryn Brinkley
Author of the *New York Times* bestselling SAVED BY THE LIGHT

In 1975, Dannion Brinkley was hit by a bolt of lightning. Not long afterwards, he acquired metaphysical, New Age, powers and began preaching that the words of the Holy Bible should not be trusted.

> the battle for the souls of humankind... So is there a life after death? Absolutely. Do you die? That is impossible. It cannot happen. There is no possible way. Are you going to hell? I just can't figure out how...I have never been there. ...people need to not be afraid of something that does not happen. ...you will not die. It will never happen. Never. ... If I didn't go to hell, in the last four journeys, NOBODY'S GOING TO HELL, okay...you're not going to go to hell." [94]

According to this 2021 interview, Mr. Brinkley seems to think he's in "a battle for the souls of humankind." But, I've got news for him. If there is "no Hell," as Mr. Brinkley's experiences have taught him, then Jesus Chirst is a liar. And not only that, if there is no Hell, then

---

[94] Knapp, George. "After 3 near-death experiences, this man's mission is to comfort dying veterans" (Fox 59, Nexstar Media, Inc, 5, May, 2021), https://fox59.com/news/after-3-near-death-experiences-this-mans-mission-is-to-comfort-dying-veterans/

THERE IS NO BATTLE. No man's soul is in jeopardy. Dannion's wasting his time, and everyone elses. Because, according to the "Gospel of Dannion," whether you're trusting the shed Blood of the Lord Jesus Christ, buttered toast, or SpongeBob Squarepants, we all go to heaven.

In any case, should we heed the words of Dannion Brinkley, a man who was struck down by lightning and began preaching that old, old sermon, *"ye shall not surely die"* (Gen. 3:4)? Can we take solace in Mr. Brinkley's so-called "near-death experiences" that Hell does not exist? What does the Lord Jesus Christ have to say about this? After all, Dannion's not the only one who's died and come back to tell about it. Did the Lord come back preaching "there is no Hell"?

> *"I AM HE THAT LIVETH, AND WAS DEAD; and, behold, I am alive for evermore, Amen; and have the keys of hell and of death."*   Rev. 1:18

> *"But I will forewarn you whom ye shall fear: Fear him* [Jehovah], *which after he hath killed hath power to* CAST INTO HELL; *yea, I say unto you, Fear him."*   Lk. 12:5

Dannion is a liar. He's simply another false teacher of *"good words and fair speeches,"* and today men like him are a dime a dozen (Rom. 16:18). When Dannion finally meets his Maker, his next book will be titled *In Hell with the Light*. Because, the supposed "light" he's received after his encounter with electricity is not the light of God:

> *"Take heed therefore that the light which is in thee be not darkness."*   Luk 11:35

But, if you think that certain Christians (Mk. 4:17, Lk. 8:13, 1Cor. 3:1, etc.), or people who think they're "Christian," can't be fooled by Brinkley's preaching, you're wrong:

> "My name is David March. In 2015, I was angry with the religious beliefs I'd grown up with all my life –– that some people go to Heaven, and most people go to Hell when

they die because they didn't accept Jesus... And I learned about a thing called 'near-death experience,' and that millions of people had died, had an experience with God, or universe, or spirit, or consciousness, or whatever you want to call it. And there was no judgment, and there was no division of Heaven or Hell, and they came back to talk about it. One of the most powerful stories that I read was from a man called Dannion Brinkley. His story changed my perception about God..." [95]

We've spent the last few pages talking about the life and beliefs of one "Dannion Brinkley." The reason I've parked here a little longer is because Mr. Brinkley is a very good example of a twenty-first-century individual who's had a scientifically-unexplainable incident with ELECTRIC FORCES. While I wouldn't say that I exactly trust Mr. Brinkley, I would say that I believe him when he says that he is a spiritually different man today, than before his lightning encounter. Brinkley's experiences serve to demonstrate that acquiring mystical, occult-like abilities, and doctrines of devils, VIA LIGHTNING, are not limited to the "shamans" of indigenous peoples. A man who's had no contact with early natives has inadvertently confirmed what shamans teach by having a comperable experience. Something strange is taking place within these people that's invisible to the naked eye and unexplainable in medical terms. But the talents they're learning are not unique with lightning-strike victims. Such things have a long history within WITCHCRAFT and DEMONISM.

Unfortunately, Brinkley's not alone in his lies and in making lost sinners *"twofold more"* the children of Hell (Mt. 23:15). Psychic necromancer George Anderson "is widely considered by those in the medical, scientific and religious fields to be the world's greatest living medium." [96] The famed psychic has admitted of his CONSULTING

---

[95] Exploring the Human Journey, "Dannion Brinkley NDE! Dead and back 4 times!." YouTube, May 26, 2019, 1:07:03, https://www.youtube.com/watch?v=7gYGl5QXeMQ

WITH SPIRITS that it's not like a literal face-to-face discussion, but more "LIKE GETTING AN ELECTRICAL CHARGE ALL THROUGH YOURSELF."[97] Spirit contact is like receiving an electrical charge? That's an interesting answer, but why am I not surprised? Anderson has also claimed that such communication can be interrupted during lightning storms.[98] His books deny the reality of "evil spirits," claiming "they don't exist." He also denies that spirits can "possess" people and that all supposed "demonic possession" is simply mental illness, even though the Lord Jesus Christ demonstrated otherwise (Matt. 8:16, 8:28, 12:28, Mk. 1:39, etc.). Although one of Mr. Anderson's books is titled *Lessons from the Light*, scripture reports:

> "To the law and to the testimony: IF THEY SPEAK NOT ACCORDING TO THIS WORD, it is because THERE IS NO LIGHT IN THEM." Isa 8:20

"Getting struck by lightning often means instant death, but Sonia Benson is one of the mysterious exceptions. She not only survived the strike, SONIA DEVELOPED A PSYCHIC SIXTH SENSE. Over the years, she's used her LIGHTNING POWERS, to help solve crimes that have stymied law enforcement. ... Somehow, Sonia was able to connect the [police] agents to a string of clues, people's names, initials, and details about a murder... a mysterious LEGACY OF THE LIGHTNING SHE ENCOUNTERED decades earlier."[99]

---

[96] "About" (George Anderson: The World's Most Scientifically Tested Medium), https://georgeanderson.com/about/

[97] "Psychics - George Anderson." Unsolved Mysteries, (Cosgrove Meurer Productions & First Look Media, 2004), disc. 2

[98] Ibid.

[99] "Sabine Thing - Lightening Psychics." Monsters & Mysteries in America, S3, E2, 2015. Amazon Prime, https://www.amazon.com/amazonprime.

Patrick McGuire, a former reporter for the Baltimore Sun, stated of Benson's abilities:

> "You can't really explain it, because some things are unexplainable. The logic says, 'this is crazy,' but then, how do these things happen?..." [100]

How, indeed!

In July 1997, Shane Smith began having spirit visitations following an encounter with a lightning bolt. After months of hospitalization and rehab, he reported:

> "I noticed something was different. I started to sense things more deeply. I STARTED TO SEE SPIRITS. I knew they were in the spirit world, but I was just shocked that I WAS ABLE TO SEE THEM SO CLEARLY." [101]

Greta Alexander was a well-known professional psychic from Illinois. In 1961, both she and her house were hit by a bolt of lightning. She also suffered an electric shock not long after the incident. Shortly after these encounters, "...Alexander's psychic abilities were 'awakened.' She found herself answering the telephone moments before it rang, and noticed she was able to 'read' the minds of others." In 1974, she began helping law enforcement with missing person cases. Police were astonished at some of the details she was able to uncover. [102]

In 2004, three members of the Ellickson family were struck by lightning. All three were knocked to the ground. Their 18-year-old

---

[100] "Sabine Thing - Lightening Psychics." Monsters & Mysteries in America, season 3, episode 2, 2015. Amazon Prime, https://www.amazon.com/amazonprime.

[101] Ibid.

[102] Proud, Louis. *Strange Electro Magnetic Dimensions*, (New Page Books: Pompton Plains, NJ, 2015), p. 171-172

Spirits began manifesting to Shane Smith after he was hit by a thunderbolt.

daughter, Erin, stopped breathing and her heart stopped. After rescue arrived and brought Erin back, she later reported of a "near-death experience":

> "I saw God. He was talking to me. He said I was struck by lightning. I was in awe. I said to Him, 'Get off your - - - [*profanity omitted*] and start doing something!' It was a nice experience." [103]

Miss Ellickson reportedly also spoke with her deceased "grandmother" during this event. "It isn't time for you to be up here. Get back down where you're supposed to be," the entity told her.[104] While I don't doubt that this girl had some sort of spiritual experience, to imply that the lightning strike supposedly allowed her to visit heaven and speak with God and her dead loved one, is not in accord with the Bible. What is in accord with scripture, is that these things were lying "familiar spirits" impersonating God and Miss Ellickson's grandmother. I also find it stunning that while supposedly in heaven, this teen curses "God" to his face, and then describes the event as "nice." Really? (see Lev. 24:15-16)

French astronomer Nicolas Camille Flammarion, writes:

> "Lightning has sometimes worked marvels on the blind, deaf, and dumb, to whom it restores sight, hearing, and speech. A man who had the whole of his left side paralyzed from infancy was struck on August 10, 1807. He lost consciousness for twenty minutes, but after some days he gradually and permanently recovered the use of his limbs. ... On the other hand, he became deaf. ...we owe no gratitude to lightning. There are too many miseries for a few happy results. The balance is really too unequal."[105]

According to the Bible, blindness, deafness, and dumbness are some of the very infirmities which unclean spirits can inflict (Mt. 12:22, Mk. 9:25). It would not be surprising to learn that demonic miracles could undo the same (Rev. 16:14).

Mr. Flammarion continues to describe from his records various baffling mysteries for which lightning has reportedly been responsible:

---

[103] Friedman, John S. *Out of the Blue*, (Delta Trade Paperbacks: New York, NY, 2008), p. 197

[104] Ibid.

[105] Flammarion, Camille. Thunder and Lightning, (Chatto & Windus: London, England, 1905), p. 118-119

1.) Hurdling prey through the air for 30, 40, and 50 yards.

2.) Shaving individuals of hair and beards to where it never grows back.

3.) Stripping victims from their clothes, shredding clothes, or carrying clothes great distances away.

4.) Human petrification where the victim remains sitting or standing in an immobile, statue-like state.

5.) Splitting people in half, vertically.

6.) Complete bodily disintegration into ash.

7.) Mass killings of people and partial or whole herds of animals and flocks of birds.

8.) Lightning has been known to leave behind a nauseous, sulfurous vapor or strong stench. [106]

In summarizing his vast collection on lightning phenomena, Flammarion writes:

> "The brilliancy of lightning hides itself from us in the darkness of impenetrable mystery. But we feel that there is an immeasurable power, and unimaginable force which rules us. ... It would seem as if lightning were a subtle being... It is like an elemental spirit, keen, capricious, malicious or stupid, far-seeing or blind, willful or indifferent, passing from one extreme to another, and of a unique and terrifying character. We see it twisting into space, moving with astonishing dexterity among men, appearing and disappearing with rapidity...it is impossible to define its nature. ... The phantasmagoria of lightning leaves us perplexed. All these observations are extraordinary and very disconcerting. The facts contradict

---

[105] Flammarion, Camille. Thunder and Lightning, (Chatto & Windus: London, England, 1905)

each other and lead us to no actual conclusion. ...Lightning may be the daughter of goblins. ... Though it may often strike innocent victims blindly and ferociously...at times it seems to show a certain amount of intelligence." [107]

Flammarion's not alone in this opinion:

"...I think it's fair to say there is an intelligent component to lightning. It almost seems to have a mind of its own." [108]

You've now been introduced to a rare phenomenon. One that's hardly ever talked about -- parallels between electricity, lightning, and the spirit world. This scientific age doesn't want you to believe what's been presented here. That's why they scorn it and mock it as "superstition" or "nonsense." But that's what the Devil wants. He wants YOU (the Bible-believing Christian) to be uncomfortable in your beliefs, and he wants THEM (the rest of the unsaved world) to be comfortable in their deception.

I believe that modern science and academia have put mankind in a box and will not let him look outside of it. This "box" builds up a wall, and creates the illusion, that everything of any consequence has been figured out or will eventually be figured out. They believe that all they have to do is just "learn a little bit more" and they'll have all the answers. This unrelenting trust in science goes beyond simple lessons which use solid, evidence-based science. THIS IS THE FAITH OF SCIENTISM (1Tm. 6:20). A religion where the power of scientific knowledge is stretched into philosophical speculations. This worldly arrogance is one of the hallmarks of this age (2 Tim. 3:1-7). Science writer Thomas Burnett remarks:

---

[107] Flammarion, Camille. Thunder and Lightning, (Chatto & Windus: London, England, 1905), p. 89, 91, 124-125, 128

[108] Proud, Louis. *Strange Electro Magnetic Dimensions*, (New Page Books: Pompton Plains, NJ, 2015), p. 174

"SCIENTISM...IS A SPECULATIVE WORLDVIEW about the ultimate reality of the universe and its meaning. ... Scientism restricts human inquiry. It is one thing to celebrate science for its achievements and remarkable ability to explain a wide variety of phenomena in the natural world. BUT TO CLAIM THERE IS NOTHING KNOWABLE OUTSIDE THE SCOPE OF SCIENCE would be similar to a successful fisherman saying that whatever he can't catch in his nets does not exist. Once you accept that science is the only source of human knowledge, you have adopted a philosophical position that cannot be verified, or falsified, by science itself. It is, in a word, UNSCIENTIFIC."[109]

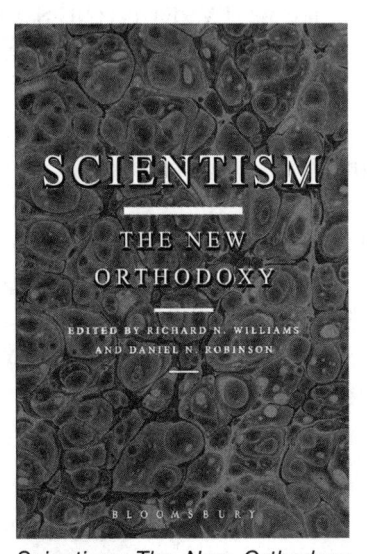

Scientism: The New Orthodoxy addresses how our modern technological age has created an over-reliance on technology, and how this leads to the false notion that technology can sovle all problems. The book touches on how this false science is growing into a quasi-religion.

"In science [of today] effectively all ideas are 'just' theories. Scientists often use concepts from the philosophy of science to make some semantic distinctions between laws, theories, hypotheses, and the like. So when a scientist talks about a 'law' of nature, he or she is referring only to a standard observation (given some strict parameters),

---

[109] Burnett, Thomas. "What is Scientism?" (Dialogue on Science, Ethics, & Religion, American Association for the Advancement of Science, 21, May, 2012), https://www.aaas.org/programs/dialogue-science-ethics-and-religion/what-scientism

NOT AN ABSOLUTE requirement. A basic principle in science [today] is that any law, theory, or otherwise can be disproven if new facts or evidence are presented. In science... EVERYTHING'S A THEORY. PROOF DOESN'T EXIST. NOTHING IS CERTAIN." [110]

Today, regardless of this attitude (which is a paradox when dealing with true "science"), mainstream academia are always the "experts." They're the high priests and the ones supposedly with all the knowledge. Yet, they never take into account the reality of spirits. And no amount of scientific equipment will provide them with the answers they need to realize this. This is God's joke on them. And now you know, as we've stated previously, why it's written:

"...the world BY WISDOM knew not God..." 1Cor. 1:21

Because science pushes an elitist image of itself onto the public, the perception is that they generally know everything there is to know about lightning, tornados, and other related phenomena. This is what the average person believes. THIS ILLUSION HAS BUILT UP A WALL THAT SUPERNATURALISM IS NONEXISTENT. This is part and partial to our day.

However, despite their haughty attitudes, thousands of things continue to happen that science has no answers for. Gravity, for example, is full of mysteries. When you dig deeper into the nuances and details of many supposed "established laws," you discover that mainstream science is in the dark on a lot of it, not just wind and electrical phenomena. What else are they not telling us?

Untold numbers of people are seeing things and experiencing things, daily, THAT SCIENCE CANNOT EXPLAIN. What does the modern

---

[110] Daley, Beth. Forget what you've read, science can't prove a thing. The Conversation. Published: April 20, 2011. http://theconversation.com/forget-what-youve-read-science-cant-prove-a-thing-578

egghead do about these reports? He ignores them. He pretends they don't exist. After all, he has "science" to lighten his path:

> "As much as we like to walk around with the confidence that we know this planet and we understand the planet we live on, there seems to be NOTHING BUT MYSTERY on this planet." 111

There's more to man, the world, and the universe than any scientist knows anything about. The Bible says to this attitude:

> "Wherefore let him that thinketh he standeth take heed lest he fall."   1Cor.10

SOMETHING UNKNOWN IS IN THE AIR

Yes, something unknown is in the air and it has been frightening and baffling mankind for centuries. In a letter to an 1856 French science journal we find:

> "...I hold a discovery which frightens me... There are two kinds of ELECTRICITY; one, brute and blind...the other is INTELLIGENT AND CLAIRVOYANT. The electrical ball or the globular electricity contains a thought which disobey Newton... we have in the annals of the academy THOUSANDS OF PROOFS OF THE INTELLIGENCE OF THE ELECTRIC BOLT..." 112

---

[111] David Whitehead, Investigative Journalist, Radio Host [quote taken from tv series THE UNEXPLAINED, 2019
[112] Excerpt from a letter by a "Jobard of Paris" publishing in the French paper *L'Ami des Sciences* (Friend to Sciences), March 2, 1856, p. 67. Also see Blavatsky, Helena. *Isis Unveiled*, (The Aryan Theosophical Press: Point Loma, CA, 1877), p. 188.

Although this sounds sensational, twenty-first-century man is not exempt from this astounding statement. Reports that fall along these same lines have been going on for a long time. Exactly what this unidentified "lightning" phenomenon is, science has no answer. There are several theories and guesses, of course, but the thing that's kept this riddle in obscurity is that facets of it contradict established laws of physics. Because of this, and despite the accounts of hundreds of witnesses, mainstream science has been reluctant to recognize it. Pertinent to the subject of this book, however, this enigma involves UNEXPLAINED PHENOMENA IN THE AIR:

– **THE UNINVITED KITCHEN GUEST:** In 1961, a "fireball" was seen floating inside the kitchen of Mrs. Doris Wills, a resident of Glouchestershire, England. Startled, the witness ran from the room and to the second floor only to have the ball follow and pass her on the stairway. Moving into a bedroom where two young boys were, the orb then zipped out an open window, whereupon it was followed by a thunderous crash. [113]

– **INVADING THE BEDROOM OF CHILDREN:** In the 1950s, two young sisters from Lewis Center, Ohio, witnessed a ping-pong-ball-sized, glowing orb enter through their open bedroom window. The small ball was reportedly as bright as a lightbulb, "...not at all like a lightning bug––much bigger and moving differently. ... It seemed as if the trajectory was intentional, rather than random. ...it seemed as if it were browsing around, rather than flying mechanically. It did not just fly in the center of the room, but around the periphery." The mysterious sphere circled the room three times without hitting anything and then suddenly disappeared. Terrified, the sisters went running and screaming out of the room. [114]

---

[113] Bord, Janet and Colin. Unexplained Mysteries of the 20th Century. (Contemporary Books : Chicago, IL, 1989), p. 131-132

– **THE KEYHOLE INTRUDER:** In 1953, the Blumenthals of Washington, D.C. observed a strange event. As a thunderstorm passed through the region, on their patio appeared a small, loud, sizzling point of light. To their fright and astonishment, the light moved up to their French doors, reshaped itself into a pencil-like rod, passed through the door's keyhole and into their house. Once in the room, the intruder changed back into its former spheroidal shape, but now it was about 10 inches in diameter. After floating stationary for a few seconds, the light suddenly shot towards the ceiling and exploded. No one was hurt, but they were certainly left stunned.[115]

– **AN EXPLODING ROD:** In 1907, three men standing outdoors in Burlington, Vermont suddenly became alarmed after a loud blast rudely interrupted their conversation. One of the witnesses, Mr. William H. Alexander, later reported: "I observed a torpedo-shaped body some 300 feet away, stationary in appearance and suspended in the air about 50 feet above the tops of the buildings. In size, it was about 6 feet long and 8 inches in diameter, the shell or cover having a dark appearance, with here and there tongues of fire issuing from spots on the surface... When first seen, it was surrounded by a halo of dim light, some 20 feet in diameter." [116]

– **THE FIERY JUGGERNAUT:** In November 1872, four persons in Banbury, England "...heard a whizzing, roaring sound like a passing train, which attracted their

---

[114] Scott, Irena McCammon. *Inside the Lightning Ball*, (Flying Disk Press: Yorkshire, England, 2018), p. 37, 39

[115] Gaddis, Vincent. *Mysterious Fires and Lights*. (New Saucerian Press, 2017), p. 54

[116] Corliss, William R. *Handbook of Unusual Natural Phenomena*. Avenel, NJ: Gramercy Books & Random House, 1977) p. 22

A mysterious, floating orb of light enters the window. (c. 1800s)

attention, and then saw a huge revolving ball of fire traveling from 6 ft. to 10 ft. off the ground. The smoke was whizzing around and rising high in the air, and a blast of wind accompanied it, carrying a cloud of branches along and destroying everything in its way. The havoc done is very considerable--large trees bodily uprooted, others broken off about 10 ft. from the ground. ... The 'ball' was attended by a sulfurous odor and ultimately seemed to vanish without a sound." [117]

– VIOLATING A YOUNG WOMAN: In August 1791 a young woman witnessed a small fireball "about the size of a billiard ball" travel along the ground and up to her feet. After caressing them, the spherical light then "made its way up under her clothes, and issued again from the middle of her bodice, and, still keeping its globular form

---

[117] Ibid., p. 22

darted off into the air and exploded noisily. When it got under her petticoats, they blew out like an umbrella, and she fell back. Two witnesses of the scene ran to her assistance, but she was unhurt. A medical examination revealed only a slight erosion of the skin, extending from the right knee to the middle of her breast; her chemise had been torn in two along the same line, and there was a hole through her bodice where the thunderbolt had got out." [118]

– OPENING DOORS: In another account (date unknown), "a fireball fell upon the door of a house, pushed it violently open, and made its way into the kitchen. ... After bursting [but not apart], the fireball made its way up the chimney, from which it removed a mass of soot, smelling somewhat of sulphur." [119]

– THE FOREST MENACE: In 1923, a globe of light was spotted in a wooded area in Chevy Chase, Maryland. The witness, a scientist, testified that the ball was about the size of a child's balloon and floating, roughly, about eight feet off the ground. Moving towards the viewer, the orb came in contact with a tree, when suddenly "a cloud of dust was formed by a dynamite-like explosion". Upon investigating the horrendous bang, the light had vanished leaving behind shattered bark which eventually killed the tree. [120]

– RISING OUT OF THE SEA: In November 1872, an "...enormous fireball was seen to rise slowly out of the sea

---

[118] Flammarion, Camille. *Thunder and Lightning.* (London, England: Chatto & Windus, 1905) p. 6-7

[119] Ibid, p. 70

[120] Bord, Janet and Colin. *Unexplained Mysteries of the 20th Century.* (Contemporary Books : Chicago, IL, 1989), p. 130-131

to the height of sixteen or seventeen meters. It traveled against the wind and came quite near the vessel from which it was being watched. Then it turned towards the southeast and disappeared. The apparition lasted about five minutes." [121]

− PASSING THROUGH GLASS: On July 27, 1952, a luminous, "purplish" bubble was seen in Hamburg, Germany, moving outside a house window. Reportedly, the thing had abruptly manifested following a lightning flash. Without warning, the orb entered the house through the pane of a closed window. The glass was unharmed, but upon entering the room, the fireball exploded. [122]

− HARMLESS TO METAL & MELTING METAL: In 1958, a pastor in Jim Thorpe, Pennsylvania reported seeing an illuminated spherical shape enter his bathroom. The yellow, grapefruit-sized light entered through a screened window without causing any type of damage. After rolling around on the floor at the man's feet, "...it then hopped up into the bowl of the wash basin and melted in two portions the steel chain holding the rubber stopper..." It then disappeared, presumably down the drain. [123]

− FIRE ORBS ENTERING CHURCHES: Not only does this phenomena have a history of entering houses and other structures, it's also found its way into churches.

---

[121] Flammarion, Camille. *Thunder and Lightning*. (London, England: Chatto & Windus, 1905) p. 68

[122] Bord, Janet and Colin. *Unexplained Mysteries of the 20th Century*. (Contemporary Books : Chicago, IL, 1989), p. 133

[123] Gaddis, Vincent. *Mysterious Fires and Lights*. (New Saucerian Press, 2017), p. 55

In the book *Extreme Weather: Forty Years of the Tornado and Storm Research Organization* (TORRO) it's recorded that accounts "...of fireballs falling upon churches, or infiltrating their interiors, are very numerous." On October 21, 1638, Widecombe church in Devon "saw a great fireball come in at the window and pass through the Church." Apparently, the ball-shaped spark was accompanied by a tornado. "Luminous phenomena associated with tornados may assume the aspect of FIERY GLOBES." On another occasion in 1751, a fiery globe "...passed between people standing by the south window." A rolling light was then seen damaging a large stone, it suddenly "entered the belfry...ascended the steeple and melted the iron wire of the chimes and clock", then it threw "a large bell off the brass it hung upon...the ball seemed to defy gravity and caused successive episodes of structural damage without dissipating its energy." [124]

The fireball and tornado at Widecombe church (c. 1638)

– THE GREMLINS OF WORLD WAR II: On November 23, 1944, the 415th Night Fighter Squadron, a United States Air Force unit, encountered "eight or ten" red-orange, ghostly "balls of light." Pilots reported that the lights were "moving through the air at a terrific

---

[124] Doe, Robert K. *Extreme Weather*. Chichester. (John Wiley & Sons: West Sussex, UK, 2016), p. 215-216

speed." The apparitions then vanished, only to reappear farther in the distance. Then, without warning, they disappeared completely. Nothing was seen on radar. However, soon afterward, reports of aerial encounters with the strange spheroids, or similar, began cropping up the world over. The aerial lamps were known to follow, play with, and tease fighter and bomber pilots. They would appear singularly or in groups. The unexplained objects generally became known as "Foo Fighters," a corruption of the French word "feu," meaning "fire." They were also often called "kraut balls," "kraut meteors" by the RAF, and "gremlins." (Concerning this mystery, the following two pages show newspaper clippings from the time.) [125]

– THE COCKPIT CREATURE: In 1958, an Irish airline commercial plane had a large, orange, fiery sphere materialize between two pilots. The crackling, hissing ball then floated out of the cockpit, down the aisle, and exited via the rear bulkhead by passing through it. According to one of the pilots who witnessed the event, "Apparently, this sort of thing is encountered by airlines around the world several times a year." [126]

– AS SILENT AS DEATH: As a result of this persistent mystery, long time researchers of the strange and unusual, Colin and Janet Bord, have asked the question: "Is there perhaps a life form unknown to us which can make itself visible as a ball of light?" In answering this, they then give the account of, William Bathlot. A resident and farmer of Beaver County, Oklahoma, Bathlot witnessed several spherical light manifestations on his ranch during the

---

[125] Story, Ronald. The Encyclopedia of Extraterrestrial Encounters. (New American Library : New York, NY. 2001) p. 202-203

[126] Bord, Janet and Colin. Unexplained Mysteries of the 20th Century. (Contemporary Books : Chicago, IL, 1989), p. 133

Eerie Fire Balls Pace German Planes in West

NIGHT FIGHTER BASE, FRANCE. — American fighter pilots engaged in flying night Intruder missions over Germany report the Nazis have come up with a new "secret weapon." They are mysterious "balls of fire" that race along beside their planes for miles like will-o'-the-wisps.

Yank pilots have dubbed them "foo fighters" and at first thought they might explode, but so far there is no indication that any planes have been damaged by them.

Some pilots have expressed belief that the "foo fighter" was designed strictly as a psychological weapon. Intelligence reports seem to indicate it is radio-controlled from the ground and can keep pace with planes flying 300 miles an hour.

Lieut. Donald Meiers of Chicago said there are three types of "foo fighters"—red balls of fire that fly along at wing tip, a vertical row of three balls of fire that fly in front of the planes and a group of about 15 lights that follow the plane at a distance, flickering on and off.

A newspaper clipping from the February 21, 1945 issue of the *Laurel Outlook*, p. 7

MYSTERY FLARES TAG ALONG WITH U.S. NIGHT PILOTS

Yanks Call Nazi Weapon a 'Foo Fighter.'

A U. S. NIGHT FIGHTER BASE, France, Jan. 1 (*P*).—The Nazis have thrown something new into the night skies over Germany—the weird, mysterious "Foo-Fighter," balls of fire which race alongside the wings of American fighter planes flying intruder missions over the reich.

American pilots have been encountering the eerie "Foo-Fighter" for more than a month in their night flights. No one apparently knows exactly what this sky weapon is.

The balls of fire appear suddenly and accompany the planes for miles. They appear to be radio controled from the ground and manage to keep up with planes flying 300 miles an hour, official intelligence reports reveal.

early 1900s. On one occasion, frightened horses alerted him to the presence of a floating light ball which quickly disappeared. Upon approaching the area, Mr. Bathlot stated, "I felt like some sinister thing was watching my every move and cold chills ran up my back." In another encounter, Bathlot reports that he and another witness saw a light "...about a dozen feet in front of us as silent as death. It was transparent. We could see a bunch of sage brush right through its body. It hovered in the air approximately eighteen inches above the ground. We could see no body resembling bird or animal, nor could we see anything resembling legs to hold it up. It was just a ball of light." [127]

– CHASING A POLICE HELICOPTER: In 1993, a mysterious, orange, orb-shaped, light appeared in the skies above Louisville, Kentucky. No doubt, the incident would've been quickly dismissed had it not been for the fact that the witnesses were two veteran members of local law enforcement. As officers Kenny Graham and Kenny Downs were on routine patrol in their police helicopter, their eyes were met with a baffling sight. In the air directly ahead of them appeared a small, round, glowing ball with an orange, basketball-sized, core. The gleaming orb seemed to recognize their presence as it began to play with their vehicle, moving in tandem with it. Suddenly, it shot up into the sky at lightning speed and disappeared. "It had no propulsion, whatsoever," reported officer Downs, "You didn't see any jet engine. You didn't see any kind of smoke coming off of it. It was, like, floating. But it was floating at speeds I'd never witnessed before."

---

[127] Bord, Janet and Colin. Unexplained Mysteries of the 20th Century. (Contemporary Books : Chicago, IL, 1989), p. 145

FACING PAGE: A newspaper clipping from the January 2, 1945 issue of the Chicago Daily Tribune

Just when the officers thought the encounter was over, the thing returned. This time, the light began chasing them reaching speeds of 100 miles per hour. Two more Jefferson County police then spotted the orb from the ground. They attempted to give chase in their cruiser, but the thing was too fast. The flying object then appeared to fire upon the helicopter as three small balls of fire shot out of it and directly at the police. As the pilots quickly maneuvered to avoid being hit, they soon realized that the strange encounter was gone. "I just wish somebody would come forward, say, 'Hey, this is what you saw that night. This is the reason it was flying that fast. This is the reason it was circling you. But nobody ever has.'" Despite years of ridicule and ribbing, the officers still stand by their story. And they still have no clue what was witnessed in the air that night. [128]

– WEATHERMAN WITNESS: Storm tracker, Jim Cantore, of *The Weather Channel* encountered this phenomenon as a boy. "I've actually experienced it, believe it or not when I was a kid in Vermont," Cantore said of the mystery, "just kind of seeing this fuzzy ball, electric ball, dancing around, and it was out there for a while, and all of a sudden, it came towards me. It came into the room, bounced around, and then went out. That actually happened!" [129]

– LIGHTNING, ORBS & WINGED THINGS: In 1935, Betty Galvano was born in Atlanta, Georgia. Because of low blood oxygen, she went into a coma when she was just three months old. The doctors gave her three hours to live. During the tragedy, as a thunderstorm raged,

---

[128] *Haunted Highway,* Kentucky UFO Chase, First aired: Sep 14, 2011.
[129] *Top Ten Weather Mysteries*, First aired: September 78, 2016.

The Weather Channel

Meteorologist and *The Weather Channel* personality, Jim Cantore, witnessed a floating light orb as a child. "That actually happened", Mr. Cantore affirms.

Betty's mother saw "a ball of lightning." The orb floated across the lawn, then entered the house through the baby's bedroom window, hovered over to the child, and remained motionless directly on top of her. A nurse who witnessed the ball-like shape saw the child suddenly wake from its comatose state. At the age of three, Betty once again went into a coma. And once again it was during a thunderstorm. According to Betty, when "the lightning stopped," she awoke to see a "lady with wings dancing" outside her bedroom window. Scripture associates sightings of winged women with "wickedness." [130]

– GLOWING BLUE LIGHT SMASHES THROUGH HOUSE: In 2017, Mr. Michael Dodd, of Devon (a county in southwest England) found himself both terrified and stunned after a luminous blue ball entered his house through a "window, crossed his lounge, and passed through his patio doors." "It frightened the life out of me,"

---

[130] Friedman, John S. *Out of the Blue*. (Delta Trade Paperbacks: New York, NY, 2008), p. 202. (See Zech. 5:5-11 regarding winged women)

the 71-year-old Dodd reported. "It had an orange tail to it. I thought I was going 'round the bend, but I know what I saw. It's difficult to take in what actually happened." [131]

– A SURGE OF HIGH STRANGENESS: The 1970s saw a huge flap of bizarre events take place in Pennsylvania. At the time, radio communications expert Stan Gordon, was the head of a citizen-based, investigative organization staffed with concerned professionals and locals (police officers, scientists, former military specialists, etc.) who wanted to know more about these strange happenings. The group often worked hand in hand with local law enforcement and the Pennsylvania State Police.

In their records of over a hundred reports during that time, some included sightings of small, unexplained AERIAL LIGHTS. The shimmering orbs were seen entering vehicles and floating around the windows of houses. One case had them spying on two young girls. Other anomalous air-based phenomena included days and nights of strange, orange, "ominous" LIGHTNING. Since there were no storms associated with the flashes, the lightning seemed like "something other than a normal weather-related event."

One standout case involved all of the following characteristics: (1) a giant, luminous, barn-sized, flying red ball; (2) two large, hair-covered, green-eyed creatures; (3) a strong, nauseating sulfurous odor; and (4) demon-like possession of the witness who began viciously and unexpectedly growling like an animal before passing out. In the days immediately following the incident, the witness began having visions of strange, hooded men

---

[131] Henderson, Guy. *Pensioner's horror as ultra-rare ball lightning passes through his home.* Devon Live. Sept. 111, 2017. https://www.devonlive.com/news/devon-news/pensioners-horror-ultra-rare-ball-457467

dressed in black and began talking about end-of-the-world events. This is despite the fact that "...he was not a religious man, so these comments were out of place for him."

On one night in September 1973, startled witnesses admitted to observing a giant, hairy, man-like thing carrying a small, GLOWING SPHERE. As the creature ran across the road and into a wooded area, another strange object was seen maneuvering in the sky above the woods, where it projected down a beam of light.

On a different night, fellow team member Barry Clark was accompanying onlookers of extremely unusual lights, almost like a swarm of gleaming fireballs in the sky. According to Stan Gordon, the events of that night "had a profound effect on Barry's life." Shaken, Mr. Clark decided that he had had his fill of paranormal investigating. He quit the group. Evidently, however, the "paranormal" was not finished with him. In the mid-1990s, his young grandson began seeing things. "He kept telling us about 'people' that were coming into his bedroom through a hole in his ceiling," Mr. Clark said, "...I don't know if what I was doing back then [in the 1970s] triggered something, and then it carried over to my grandson? I don't know how that works. ... I talked to another person that was involved back then that said they were afraid." [133]

In summing up the hundreds of weird investigated events in Pennsylvania during that time, Stan Gordon has stated:

"...we are dealing with a phenomenon that appears to be outside of current scientific verification. ...encounters

---

[132] Gordon, Stan. *Silent Invasion*. (Stan Gordon: Greensburg, PA, 2010), p. 138, 238, 179, 196-198

[133] Breedlove, Seth. *Invasion on Chestnut Ridge*. Small Town Monsters, 2017

suggested in some cases that we might be dealing with an entity that has a physical and non-physical component to its existence. And what about the UFO sightings that could not be explained? ...some of these objects appear to be solid, constructed craft, while others are just LIGHT SOURCES. Some of them seem to be INTELLIGENTLY GUIDED AND CONTROLLED... I still do not have the answers as to why these events occurred, and what it really meant, but I have no doubt that many of these cases and the witnesses involved, appeared to be legitimate." [134]

In 1965, Stan Gordon began investigating strange happenings in Pennsylvania. A pursuit which continues to this day. He is widely considered an authority on such events. In an April 6, 2021 interview with podcast host Martin Wills, Gordon stated:

"...the evidence, more and more, as reluctant as I am to say it, but for lack of a better term, we might be dealing with something which is inter-dimensional... we're dealing with a phenomenon that's SO BEYOND OUR...PRESENT SCIENTIFIC UNDERSTANDING. I don't think anybody understands, including the government." [135]

In another account, Gordon reported:

"I've found that many low-level, close range UFO sightings and many...strange entity reports, they very commonly occur in the vicinity of energy sources. There are many sightings, for example, around radio communication towers, power plants, and high-tension power lines...it

---

[134] Gordon, Stan. *Silent Invasion*. (Stan Gordon: Greensburg, PA, 2010), p. 315, 319

[135] Willis, Martin. 04-06-21 Stan Gordon, The 1973 UFO-Bigfoot Wave & The Mini-UFO Phenomena. YouTube. Martin Willis Live Shows. April 6, 2021, 1:54:36, https://www.youtube.com/watch?v=TQvyl-UqguQ

Something Unknown is in the Air | 197

According to author and researcher, Stan Gordon, who's been investigationg unusual phenomena since 1965, many of these events occur near or around power sources like electric lines and such.

goes on, and on, and on. I have no doubt, whatever we're dealing with, THERE'S AN ENERGY CONNECTION there." [136]

Many more accounts of this astounding mystery could be listed. What's being described here is not like the modern UFO phenomenon where metallic-looking discs ("flying saucers") or triangles are seen flying through the air. These unidentified aerial lights, instead of outwardly appearing technology-based, seem more nature-based, yet they do not follow the laws of nature. As we've discovered, they've been witnessed to fall from the air, ascend from the sea, or rise out of the ground (one brave scientist said "from hell"). They've been seen descending from the sky, only to make a U-turn and head directly back up. They can also appear in a variety of sizes, shapes, and colors, and manifest a range of behaviors. From tiny sparks to giant, football-field-sized masses. From spheroids, rods, dumbbells, and ribbon-

---

[136] Paranormal Bigfoot 44:41 - 45:20 min.mark
1 Stan Gordon, The 1973 UFO-Bigfoot Wave & The Mini-UFO Phenomena. YouTube. Martin Willis Live Shows. April 6, 2021, 1:54:36, https://www

like forms, to amorphous blobs in white, yellow, red, blue, green, or various multicolors. As we've disclosed, many have materialized or entered into enclosed constructs like houses, churches, buildings, planes, or jet airlines. Scores of reports have also ascribed to them seeming "intelligence." They've been seen (1) flying, (2) rolling across the ground, and (3) changing abrupt directions; (4) entering houses through chimneys and open windows; (5) entering bedrooms; (6) hovering in midair; (7) splitting into smaller balls; (8) bouncing up into sinks and bathtubs; (9) melting steel; (10) squeezing through keyholes and under doors; (11) pushing open doors to houses; (12) passing through sheer panes of glass, or (13) the metal walls of aircraft, without leaving any evidence behind; (14) following or chasing people in rooms and up flights of stairs; or (15) circling its victims as if in an inquisitive, probing manner; (16) exploding; (17) traveling with the wind or against it; and (18) killing both people and animals. Like spirits, there is no known scientific way to prevent these things from entering man-made structures.

In 1753, professor Georg Richmann had a close encounter with one of these aerial things. Flammarion writes: "A globe of blue fire, the size of a fist, struck him on the head and stretched him stone dead." [137]

---

[137] Flammarion, Camille. *Thunder and Lightning*. (London, England: Chatto & Windus, 1905) p. 91

Throughout history, this enigma has been known by several different names including fireballs, thunderbolts, lightning balls, globular lightning, kugelblitz (sphere lightning), orbs, foo-fighters, and more. [138] But the modern name for this unexplained phenomenon is "BALL LIGHTNING." However, the problem with this modern name is that it's kind of like the breakfast cereal *Grape Nuts*. It's neither "grapes" nor "nuts" (although it may make you feel kind of "nuts" if you happen to encounter it). Sometimes it's not a "ball," and many accounts have no connection with "lightning" or storm activity. Call this mystery what you want, but it seems to run the gamut as far as its behavior. The weather research group, TORRO, affirms that so-called "ball lightning" is not "deliberate hoaxes," "psychological phenomena," nor "hallucinations." [139] Author and electrical engineer, Paul Sagan, states in the introduction to his 2004 book:

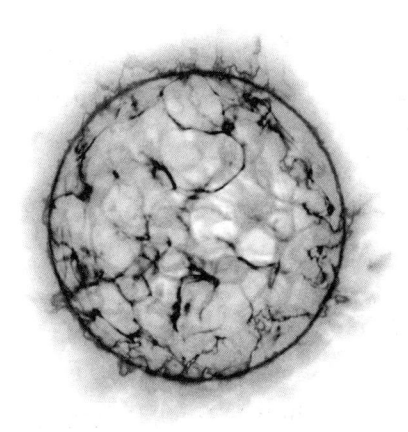

A Graphic represention of a light orb often called "ball lightning."

> "Ball lightning is a paradox of physics. By its mysterious propulsion, navigation, confinement and quasi (as if) intelligent behavior, ball lightning violates known physics and 'defies' gravity--and provides clues to a unified theory, the Theory of Everything--THE SACRED HOLY GRAIL OF PHYSICS.

---

[138] FOOTNOTE: Other perhaps related aerial phenomena include reports of so-called "corpse candles," "spook lights," "fairy lights," "will-o'-the-wisps," "jack-o'-lanterns" and the like.

[139] Doe, Robert K. *Extreme Weather*. Chichester. (John Wiley & Sons: West Sussex, UK, 2016), p. 210

Just a decade ago [mid 1990s], most scientists doubted that ball lightning even existed. But this is changing. Even the famous skeptics' association, the Committee for the Scientific Investigation of Claims of the Paranormal states on its Web site that ball lightning does indeed exist--but is unexplainable [scientifically].

All [scientific] theories have one thing in common--none work. Even Nobel Prize winners such as Oppenheimer knew of its existence and were puzzled. ... All existing [scientific] theories are fatally flawed. Many [scientific] theories begin by making restrictions and assumptions on boundary conditions that are untrue. But all theories ignore certain qualities, such as propulsion.

Ball lightning qualities defy conventional physical interpretation, which leaves physicists shaking their heads in amazement and frustration. As a result of these contradictions, physicists respond to ball lightning in one of several ways. Some avoid it; others deny it. Those who accept it attempt to explain it. This is impossible [scientifically]. ... So they ignore or deny unexplainable qualities and selectively accept only those properties that physics might explain. These theories are respectable. Some get published. None work." [140]

Peter van Doorn, a member of the UK-based Tornado & Storm Research Organization, has been the director of its Ball Lightning Research Division since 2002, and an ardent student of the phenomenon since 1986. Van Doorn writes:

"What in Heaven or Hell is 'Ball Lightning'? That indeed is a very good question, for not only are most of the

---

140] Sagan, Paul. Ball Lightning: Paradox of Physics (iUniverse Inc: Lincoln Nebraska, 2004), p. 1
FOOTNOTE: I've added the word "scientific" in brackets to this quote, because "scientific theories" are the only kinds of theories that Mr. Sagan is addressing. Like most scientists, Paul Sagan's not concerned with the supernatural.

inhabitants of this planet in ignorance of its existence, virtually the entire scientific community is also in the dark with regard to the circumstances of its formation, almost clueless to its structure, and, perhaps most disturbing of all, apparently unaware of its actual significance. ... Though undoubtedly real, the GLOs [Glowing Light Orbs] present an obvious barrier to any investigation by conventional science...how can something have an objective reality if it transgresses the demarcations of conceivable existence? ... Whatever the nature of this inexplicable phenomenon it is most definitely not a form of lightning. What lies behind this enigma is actually more alien to our understanding of the cosmos than most researchers could ever have imagined!" [141]

"The real mystery of ball lightning is not so much in its formation as in its abilities. If it is electrical in nature, why does it occasionally ignore conductors? Balls have skipped over steeples, bells, and transmission wires, yet continued on their merry, mysterious way. ...why does ball lightning sometimes exhibit animal-like curiosity in exploring houses and other structures?" [142]

---

[141] FOOTNOTE: The website titled "ball-lightning.info" no longer exists. For reasons beyond my control, the website orignially run by Peter van Doorn, from which this quotation is an excerpt, was taken down just a couple of months after I began researching this topic. According to the internet archive site *The Wayback Machine*, the web address "ball-lightning.info" which contained the references I've quoted, was live from about 2011 to 2019. Now, however, the address pulls up information completely irrelevant to the subject. The website "phenomena.org.uk," which is run by the meteorological artist Chris Chatfield, a colleague of Peter van Doorn, does have a link to the now-defunct page. This at least helps substantiate that the information contained in the quotation was taken from the original "ball-lightning.info" website and not the one that now exists. If you want to contact the creators of the missing website you can reach them at the following links:

1.) https://uk.linkedin.com/in/peter-van-doorn-15340455?original_referer=https%3A%2F%2Fwww.google.com%2F

2.) http://www.phenomena.org.uk/features/UFO%20Natural%20History/ufo.html

This photo of a small area of the aftermath of the Tunguska mystery was taken 19 years after the event (c. 1927) Due to political turmoil in Russia at the time, it was nearly 20 years before the Russian government undertook an official investigation.

In 1908, the largest known explosion in recorded human history occurred in a remote area of Siberia. Known as "The Tunguska Event," some unknown force detonated above the ground with the equivalent power of an apocalyptic discharge. To this day, no one (and I mean no one), knows what this thing was that blew up in the air over the desolate Russian landscape. A gigantic column of bluish light split the sky and was seen over a thousand miles away. People over 700 miles away heard the blast. From the shockwave's epicenter, hundreds of square miles of trees were flattened, displayed like the spoke of a giant wheel. A great cloud of smoke and debris stretched for miles up into the atmosphere. No crater was formed. No meteorite fragments have ever been found. Seismic stations all around the world registered the event. How could the cause of something so large continue to remain unknown? Could it happen again? If modern science is aware of this monstrous aerial event, do you think it slipped by God's attention? What about the Devil?

---

[142] Gaddis H., Vincent, *Mysterious Fires And Lights*. (New Saucerian Press: London. 2017), p. 50 [From the previoous page]

So, what are we to make of all these strange and weird happenings? One of the things I'm trying to do here is to GIVE THE READER A BALANCE. A balance that's in opposition to the continuously fed line that we get twenty-four hours a day that dictates "science has, or will have, all the answers." I'm here to tell you that modern science doesn't know half of what most people think it knows. We've disclosed some of these very subjects in this book. On occasion, secular researchers may mention unexplained mysteries. But they don't like to put across the image that they "don't know," so most of the time such things are simply kept hush-hush. Any time they do come out publicly and attempt to tackle an issue, their objective is always to try and explain a thing in "scientific terms." Well, what if there's no scientific answer? Are you going to try and force the matter into a "scientific theory"? Yes, and this is exactly what they do. However, whenever they do this, the assumption is that any form of supernaturalism was never the underlying cause. In other words, the first order of business is NATURE FIRST, GOD NEVER. The first order of business for the scientist of today is, NOT TO FIND THE TRUTH, but to kick out God or kick out the Devil and insist, "No, it isn't that." They pretend that the rightful position in approaching a situation is to never presume supernatural involvement, especially when first investigating a thing. But this is never the Bible's position.

The Bible's position is not, "in the beginning nature," but *"in the beginning God"* (Gen. 1:1). In fact, those same four words launch the entire Bible. Why? Because that is the underlying reality of all things. God is not the underlying *cause* of all things, but the Lord does have the answer to the cause. The Bible takes the position of SUPERNATURALISM, before considering NATURALISM. This is because we live in a SUPERNATURAL UNIVERSE, albeit fallen – a universe heavily influence and affected by the spirit realm (Psa. 8:4, Eph. 2:2, etc.). And such spirits have always been active in man's history. This is the exact opposite of the modern mindset. And it's despite the numerous accounts of so-called "ball lightning" reflecting some form of intelligence or behavior indicative of something greater than "nature" behind it. Are there things in reality that are outside the reaches of scientific measurement? Yes. There are plenty of witnesses to establish the reality of the light orb phenomenon, regardless if many in the mainstream choose to ignore it.

From a Bible-believer's perspective, I really couldn't care any less if "science" acknowledges a thing or not. Science doesn't recognize the resurrection of Christ, nor does it acknowledge any of the Lord's miracles. Nor the inspiration or preservation of scripture. It doesn't accept the reality of God or the Devil. And, according to the Bible, such beliefs are anti-Christ to the core. So, why should we listen to their biased opinions when the written words of God have already told us there's a *"prince of the power of the air"* at work? The modern Christian is already way-under-educated in this department (Demonology, Satanology), so why add to that ignorance with the opinions of men who never believed in God in the first place? [143] Do you know what were the first words the Devil ever spoke to man?

"Yea, hath God said..." Gen. 3:1

The first thing the Devil does is question God to sow doubt in the minds of men: "Did God really say that?"; "That's not what God said"; "You can't trust God's words"; "God didn't mean that, literally." How is mainstream science any different than this? Today, many scientists have the attitude that it's their duty to do this––to always challenge the idea that there's anything such as the "supernatural." Their

---

[143] FOOTNOTE: Please, don't get the idea that I'm somehow "against science." I know that it sure sounds that way by reading these things, and that's understandable. But, that's not what I'm trying to say. This book does not cover the instances where the Bible and science agree. If you want to read about that, you'll have to go somewhere else. But, please know that TRUE SCIENCE will support scripture. It also has limits, however, and will never be able to reveal to us the things that the words of God can reveal. Science can only provide a limited amount of light. The bottom line is that science should never dictate the Christian's reality. Much of the negativism that the reader will find in this book regarding modern science, is simply due to the fallout of a world run by sinners. It's not that I'm "anti-science," but that my allegiance is with the Bible first.

conclusion, especially beginning with the science of the Industrial Revolutions and Electric Age, is that NOTHING EVER IS:

> "It was in the nineteenth century, that period of hard-headed mechanistic science, that ball lightning was relegated to the category of myths. ... 'bigotry' is to be understood [as] the contemptuous dismissal by unbending orthodoxy of anything which is not clearly explainable by contemporary theories. It is this attitude which has delayed the acceptance and serious study of ball lightning by scientists for at least a century. The unwillingness to accept the unusual, does not apply to ball lightning alone." [144]

Like the fowls which snatch away the seed of God, modern science is quick to deny anything which scripture reveals about the world around is. However, not all scientists are narrow-minded or prejudiced. There are exceptions, but to say that they are "scarce" is an understatement. Peter van Doorn has at one time stated that he believes that "ball lightning" is an ancient preternatural invisible type of LIVING BEING. But they're not angels, and certainly not devils, according to his conclusions after 35-plus years of investigating this mystery. This is not exactly a biblical answer, but at least one scientist is being honest with the evidence and not afraid to step outside of conventional boundaries. And by the way, Mr. van Doorn is nowhere close to believing like a supernaturalist. He's just being avant-garde with the information he's collected. In any case, what he's studied has convinced him that SOMETHING INTELLIGENT is behind the so-called "ball lightning" phenomenon –– something in the air is alive!

If you're having a hard time in being convinced of any of this, think of it this way. Remember earlier how we talked about scripture using the BIRD to help teach us lessons about the SPIRIT WORLD? Well, guess what? One of the major things the bird typology discloses in

---

[144] Cade, C. Maxwell, and Davis, Delphanie. The Taming of the Thunderbolts: The Science and Superstition of Ball Lightning. (Abelard-Schuman: New York, 1969), p. 28 & 30

respect to demons is that SOMETHING IN THE AIR, OTHER THAN BIRDS OR BUGS, IS ALIVE. Did you get that? In fact, if fowl teach us nothing else about spirits, they do, at the most basic, fundamental level, reveal this one thing -- SOMETHING IN THE AIR IS ALIVE.

What we're dealing with here with this phenomenon is unlike anything associated with common meteors, comets, or meteorites that fall to the earth with no outward semblance of consciousness. Normal nature-based falling objects show no regard for things in their paths, be it trees, animals, people, or the ocean. Light orbs, on the other hand, behave strangely cognizant of their surroundings. This is not to say that the objects themselves are necessarily "alive," but perhaps are under the influence of that which is alive. A feat easily wrought by the Prince of the Power of the Air. This means that some aerial phenomena controlled by Satan may outwardly appear "supernatural," while other events controlled by Satan appear "natural." Scripture discloses to us both of these options regarding the Devil's power. The book of Job shows Satan working COVERT SUPERNATURALISM: When the fire falls with this event, no one's aware that the Devil's responsible (Job 1:16). Contrarily, Revelations shows Satan working OVERT SUPERNATURALISM: When the fire falls during this event, everyone's aware the Devil's responsible: [145]

> "And HE DOETH GREAT WONDERS, so that HE MAKETH FIRE COME DOWN FROM HEAVEN on the earth IN THE SIGHT OF MEN,"   Rev. 13:13

Do you know what the scientist will say when he's unable to explain strange happenings? He'll claim that, "Just because science can't explain it, doesn't mean it's supernatural!" But, do you know what?

---

[145] FOOTNOTE: Although the men in Revelations are not actually aware that the Devil himself is calling down the fire, the point is, that the witnesses recognize that the falling fire is not natural. The supernatural act is not hidden, but obvious, because it's being executed *"in the sight of men."* In fact the world will believe that this falling fire is a miracle of "God" (Just like Job's deceived servants Job 1:16).

Do you know what this dunderhead doesn't realize? He doesn't realize that JUST BECAUSE YOU CAN explain something "scientifically," does not mean in any way, that IT'S NOT SUPERNATURAL. Read that statement again and let it sink in. Modern Christians need to understand this fact, because IT IS THE CRUX OF THE ISSUE. And it is how the Lord *"...taketh the wise in their own craftiness."* (1 Cor. 3:19) In a way, this truth makes the mystery of light orbs (ball lightning, UFOs, etc) a red herring. The phenomena may make people think that the Devil's only involved with aerial anomalies that manifest in an apparent supernatural manner. But this has never been the case, according to the Bible. It's kind of like the difference between Satan using the Pharisees (Mt. 23, Jn. 8:44) and Satan using Judas Iscariot (Lk. 22:3). One pawn is obviously working for the Devil, while the other falsely seems not to be.

DEMON IN THE THUNDERBOLT

The 2005 science fiction film, *War of the Worlds*, begins with severe electromagnetic storms erupting all over the planet. Later, a news reporter discovers that lightning from these fronts is acting as conduits by which the invaders are descending to the earth and into the ground. Curiously, the spaceships of the visitors are never revealed, which is not usually the case with these types of films. Instead, the aliens' only means of arrival is shown via LIGHTNING. Once in the ground, the demons emerge, piloting (or possessing) giant, robot-like, three-legged, walking machines. All hell then breaks loose as the earth goes into great tribulation.

Since its beginning, science fiction (both literary and film), has had an extensive history of counterfeiting tidbits of scriptural truth. I've long said that science fiction is the Devil's prophecy. Satan often tells you through this medium what he's done, is doing, or is going to do. Why do you think this is the case? Because such stories represent FALLEN MAN'S IMAGINATION – these are the thoughts of those under the thumb of the god of this world. Remember earlier what the Bible revealed about man's "imagination"? Scripture generally always casts the word as something negative (see pages 99-101).

"I beheld Satan as lightning fall from heaven."
An image from the 2005, Steven Speilberg move, *War of the Worlds*. The dark blob in the upper left coner is the hand of a news reporter pointing to a television screen which shows lighting pulling an off-world creature through the air and down to the earth.

H.G. Wells' classic novel, *The War of the Worlds*, begins with the following 27 words:

"No one would have believed in the last years of the nineteenth century that this world was being watched keenly and closely by intelligences greater than man's..."

Yet, despite this being the opening sentence from one of the most famous science fiction novels of all-time, those who have always truly "believed" what this says have not been scientists or science fiction fans, but Bible-reading Christians. Such a scenario existed long before H.G. Wells knew how to read or write. The malevolent "intelligences greater than man's," watching us, have been with us since man's beginning (Gen. 3). We know them not as "Martians," however, but as Paul describes them *"spiritual wickedness in high places"* (Eph. 6:12). In this respect, Wells' words are true, abeit,

---

FOOTNOTE: See the book *What Dwells Beyond* for more on how Satan uses science fiction.

not as he intends them. His ideas present a counterfeit where the truth is taken and twisted into something it's not. With Wells, an invasion of beings from Mars is substituted for the dark spiritual forces currently in control of this world. As far as Speilberg's 2005 adaptation, there are aliens in this movie but, strangely enough, there are NO SPACECRAFT. This marked a very atypical slant for this genre of film. For the first twenty minutes of the film, the picture doesn't focus on extraterrestrials, ufos, or space ships, but on ELECTROMAGNETISM, STORMS, and LIGHTNING. Isn't that strange? Who ever heard of "aliens" having a connection with weather phenomena or lightning? Later in the film, the viewer gets a three-second glimpse of a sign that reads "The Devil has come." The subtle reality is that this film is not really about creatures from another planet, but SUPERNATURAL ENTITIES. Beings that, like Satan, can manipulate and mimic weather and natural events. I'm sure the producers, writers, and directors of the film had no idea that they were echoing the talents of a fallen being. But this ignorance is not unusual. Steven Speilberg's 1977 film, *Close Encounters of the Third Kind*, has similar undertones. The appearance of UFOs is met with CONTROL OVER ELECTRICITY with occurring blackouts, poltergeist activity, and many ufo witnesses become "possessed" and lead to a place known as "Devils Tower." Note what the Bible says about the Antichrist:

> *"But in his estate shall he honour THE GOD OF FORCES: and a god whom his fathers knew not shall he honour with gold, and silver, and with precious stones, and pleasant things."*   Dan. 11:38

Who is this *"God of Forces"*? The Prince of the power of the Air. "May *the Force* be with you," has long been a famous quip of science fiction fans.

The phrase *"God of forces,"* as found in the book of Daniel, helps demonstrate the superiority of the scriptures as preserved in the *King James Bible*. The ASV, NIV, NASB, NRSV, NKJV, etc. all replace the words with the ridiculous *"god of fortresses."* This transliteration completely loses all light to the cross references of the Devil as the prince of the *"power of the air"* (a force); a manipulator and controller of *lightning* (a force), *wind* (a force), and *other energies in nature* (Job 1:16, Job 1:19, Eph. 2:2, Lk. 10:18, etc.). The word *"forces"* as used, here has more in common with the word "power," than it does with any kind of physical building or structure (e.g. "...the prince of the POWER of the air..."). Where in scripture is the Devil ever referred to as a god of fortified places, fortresses? Nowhere. But he has clear and profound ties to THE FORCES OF NATURE. This truth is so pronounced that the Antichrist even personally demonstrates this during the Great Tribulation (Rev. 13:13).

Look up the word "force(s)" in any dictionary or thesaurus and you'll generally find one of these three words mentioned first: strength, power, energy. The forces in nature are analogous to all these words, and the Devil has control of them. This is what his title, the Prince of the Power of the Air, is all about. There's much more going on in this world behind the curtains than any public school teacher, college student, university professor, agnostic, or atheist knows anything about. The Bible has always known about it.

PART VII

UNCLEAN SPIRITS IN OUR DAY

Satanology - History - Prophecy - Technology

"And when they shall say unto you, Seek unto them that have familiar spirits, and unto wizards that peep, and that mutter: should not a people seek unto their God? for the living to the dead?" Isaiah 8:19

AGE OF ELECTRIC, AGE OF DEMONS

UNKNOWN TO most, the rise of the Electric Age (1800s) ran concurrently with a flurry of DEMON ACTIVITY, the ramifications of which are still being felt today. Modern scholars of both secular and occult persuasions admit to this. Of course, they don't necessarily claim "devils" were in operation, we have the Bible to tell us that, but they do recognize that the nineteenth century saw substantial growth in anti-biblical, anti-Christ beliefs:

> "Throughout Western history, from late antiquity to the present, there have been a number of related theological and philosophical currents that have been rejected as profane within some religious cultures and as regressive or irrational within certain secular discourses. However, following the discovery of ancient texts during the Renaissance, which led to the scholarly REVIVAL OF OCCULT SUBJECTS IN THE WEST, not only did aspects of these intellectual and spiritual currents become WIDELY ACCEPTED, but they have been DECEPTIVELY INFLUENTIAL within the history of ideas. Moreover, as a result of the erosion of Christianity's hegemonic position in Western societies, the modern turn to self, and

the questioning of deference to traditional authorities, many of the fields of discourse generated by the occult sciences have survived into late-modernity. Not only that, but, HAVING EXPERIENCED A SIGNIFICANT REVIVAL IN THE NINETEENTH CENTURY, they have been subsequently ADOPTED AND DEVELOPED in ways that can hardly be ignored by contemporary scholarship. 'The occult', broadly defined, haunts the TWENTY-FIRST CENTURY IMAGINATION, PERMEATES POPULAR CULTURE, and contributes to new spiritual trajectories. ...TODAY THERE IS A THRIVING OCCULTURE THAT SHAPES THE CONTOURS OF EVERYDAY LIFE. PARTICULARLY IN THE NINETEENTH CENTURY, THERE EMERGED a common trade in stock occultural elements, which...BEGAN TO SHAPE THE WESTERN IMAGINATION..." [146]

Thus, not only did this era witness the rise of several cults which would later plague America and the world like Mormonism (1830s), Seventh-day Adventism (1863), Jehovah's Witnesses (1870s), and Christian Science (1879), but it also birthed Marxism (1848), Darwinism (1860), Theosophy (1875), and the Ku Klux Klan (1871). But one of the major nineteenth-century outbreaks of devilment came with a movement that openly professed COMMUNICATION WITH THE DEAD. Called "Spiritualism," it began in Newark, New York in the small community of Hydesville, and in the very same county which gave us Joseph Smith's cult.[147] Also known as "Spiritism," it was nothing less than NECROMANCY. And like the new phenomena of electricity, and the technologies that came with it, its deceptive tentacles quickly began to embrace the world.

[146] Partridge, Christopher. *The Occult World* (Routledge: London, England, 2015), p. 1 & 11

[147] FOOTNOTE: Spiritualism was birthed in 1848, the same year as Carl Marx's Communist Manifesto, and about 10 miles from Palmyra, New York where Mormonism began a few years earlier. Both Hydesville (Spiritism) and Palmyra (Mormonism) are located in Wayne County, New York. Amazing isn't it?

A seance — Late 1800s

Spiritualism exploded on the scene in 1848 in the very midst of the burgeoning Electric Age. Also known as Spiritism, necromancy, or divination, the movement advocated communication with the spirit world, which it believed to be ghosts of friends and loved ones. From this came the "seance," and many other practices associated with the supposed communication with the dead. The Bible has always been against such things. It reveals that dead people are not the spirits with which these practitioners are in contact with. Their intercourse, rather, is with the unclean spirits of devils, often called "familiar spirits" (Lev. 19:31, etc.)

What the internet is to the twenty-first century, the telegraph was to the nineteenth century. Samuel Morse had been perfecting his machine since the late 1830s, and by 1844, he was ready to demonstrate it publicly. The telegraph was a mind-boggling new invention. Its ability of INSTANTANEOUS COMMUNICATION, in effect, eliminated time and space. No horse or train of the day could outrun, or even approach, the speed of its transmissions. Nothing like it had existed in the known history of the world. In his attempt to sell the telegraph to the US government, Morse himself had even warned that it had the potential to:

"...become an instrument of immense power, to be wielded for good or for evil...even in the hands of Government alone it might become the means of working vast mischief..." [148]

The public was not interested in such a device. To many, communicating thoughts through wires "had the aura of the occult." [149] To try to dispel this negative perception, when Morse finally did go public on May 24, 1844, he coded the words: "What hath God wrought!" The message was taken from the Bible (Num. 23:23). Many newspapers of the time attempted to reinforce Morse's description by calling the telegraph a "miracle" whose invention was supposedly linked to the divine. In any case, the new gadget quickly became popular in trade circles. By 1858 a transatlantic telegraphy cable had been laid. By the 1870s it was a staple in business. Although the average person outside of commercial life had little interaction with the device, this didn't stop publications from expounding on the wonders of its potential. The media proclaimed that, due to better communication among nations, the telegraph may ERADICATE WAR, or even GIVE BIRTH TO A COMMON WORLD LANGUAGE where citizens could take part in a GLOBAL COMMUNITY. [150] The era of man-made globalism had begun.

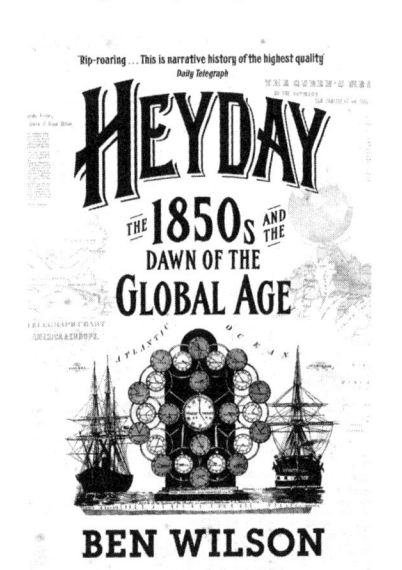

Only four short years after the advent of the telegraph, Spiritualism erupted in America (1848). Within five years of Morse's machine, a

---

[148] Simon, Linda. *Dark Light* (Harcourt Inc: San Diego, CA, 2004), p. 31

[149] Ibid., p. 32

[150] Ibid., p. 39

necromantic wave stretched across the Atlantic birthing a global phenomenon. According to Kathy Gutierrez, a professor of religion and an authority on nineteenth-century Spiritualism and esotericism:

> "Scholars have estimated that half of Americans experienced Spiritualism in some manner and certainly hundreds of thousands adhered to it rigorously enough to belong to organizations or to subscribe to Spiritualists newspapers." [151]

A former Research Fellow in Religious Studies at the University of Stirling, UK, has stated:

> "In the late 1920s and early 1930s there were around ONE QUARTER OF A MILLION PRACTICING SPIRITUALISTS and some TWO THOUSAND SPIRITUALIST SOCIETIES in the UK in addition to flourishing microcultures of platform mediumship and 'home circles'." [152]

Eight years into this hell-spawn (1856), Paster J.W. Daniels wrote in his book, *Spiritualism Versus Christianity* (1856):

---

[151] Partridge, Christopher. *The Occult World* (Routledge: London, England, 2015), p. 197

[152] Sutcliffe, Steven J. *Children of the New Age.* (Routledge: New York, NY, 2002), p. 35

FOOTNOTE: The image above is of a popular period book written and published in 1874 by physicist, William Crookes (1832-1919), in support of Spiritualism.

"Spiritualism proves itself to be THE ANTI-CHRIST MOVEMENT OF THE PRESENT AGE, and ONE OF THE WORST DELUSIONS which has ever afflicted the world. But it is not all to be met by sneers and cries of 'humbug,' 'ventriloquism,' 'collusion,' and 'cheat.' Intelligent men, learned men, and strong men, are wedded to the system. ...to whatever source this movement may be imputed, it is not the work of God, of holy angels, nor departed saints. We deem the intercourse sinful, fascinating, deceptive, and very dangerous. ... It is the avowed purpose of the Spiritualists to subvert Christianity and establish their own religion on its ruins. ... Spiritualism is filling our land with demoniacs." [153]

Secular historians agree that the "enemy" of the Spiritualist movement was, and still is, "run-of-the-mill Christians." [154]

From the height of the American Civil War to its end (1861-1865), the desire to have spiritual intercourse with the dead increased, and Spiritualism with it. Over the next 50 years, the movement gradually began to wane but saw a strong upsurge on the heels of World War I (1914 - 1918). One preacher, upon returning from England at the time, stated that "...spiritualistic meetings are being held all over the country, and there are seances on every street. So alarmed have the churches become that preachers are delivering sermons regarding it, and the religious press is printing weekly editorials." [155]

James Martin Gray (1851-1935), a contemporary of the time and former Dean of the Moody Bible Institute of Chicago reported:

---

[153] Daniels, J. W. *Spiritualism Versus Christianity*. (Miller, Orton & Mulligan: NY, 1856), p. vii, viii, 170 & 211

[154] Partridge, Christopher. *The Occult World*. (Routledge: London, England, 2015), p. 203

[155] Gray, James Martin, *Spiritism and the Fallen Angels in Light of the Old and New Testaments*. (Fleming H. Revell Company: Chicago, IL, 1920), p. 14

SPIRITUALIST   SATAN REPRESENTING DEPARTED FRIEND   MEDIUM
From a one-page broadsheet exposing Spiritualism   (c. 1865)

> "*The Sunday School Times* recently called it 'the devil's world-wide revival.' ... The scientists bear witness that while there is a large element of fraud in Spiritism there is still a residuum of facts demanding explanation." [156]

Secular journalist and author, Lewis Spence (1874 - 1955), who wrote the classic work, *An Encyclopedia of Occultism* (1920), stated about Spiritualism:

> "Although the movement in its present form [1920] dates to no further back than 1848, it is possible to trace its ancestry to witchcraft, demoniac possession, poltergeist disturbances, and animal magnetism. In these all the phenomena of spiritualism may be found, though the disturbing influences were not in the earlier instances identified with the spirits of the deceased. ...clear indications of demonic possession, had in their symptoms considerable analogy with modern spiritualism." [157]

---

[156] Gray, James Martin, *Spiritism and the Fallen Angels in Light of the Old and New Testaments.* (Fleming H. Revell Company: Chicago, IL, 1920), p. 33, 36

[157] Spence, Lewis. *An Encyclopedia of Occultism.* (Citadel Press & Carol Publishing Group: Secaucus, NJ, 1996) p. 380

Surprisingly, many of those who were attempting communications with the dead saw definite PARALLELS BETWEEN THEIR MOVEMENT AND THE NEW TECHNOLOGIES of the day. When the movement first began, the telegraph "became the primary metaphor for Spiritualist communication". [158] Messages sent and received, via the telegraph, SUGGESTED THE OPERATION OF INVISIBLE FORCES. Spiritualists viewed the human body in like manner, where it acted in place of the telegraph as a sender and receiver of the unseen. However, I'm not just picking on the telegraph. THE SPIRITUALIST MOVEMENT WELCOMED ALL ELECTRIC-AGE TECHNOLOGIES. For "Spiritualist and left-leaning Protestant groups...science was embraced... Ready to experiment with new machines, medical theories, and avant-garde forms of knowledge, Spiritualism remained convinced that science would further rather than erode religion." [159] In other words, electricity and technology were viewed as a means to helping heaven manifest on earth.

Although Spiritualism lacked any central or official governing body, there were beliefs common to all those who seriously adhered to it:

> "SPIRITUALISM'S GREATEST LEGACY WAS THE DISMANTLING OF HELL. By opening heaven to all and repeatedly finding an inclusive and superior culture in the afterlife, Spiritualists carried a new moral code across a century and several continents to inaugurate WHAT WOULD BECOME MULTICULTURALISM in the current world." [160]

Other common beliefs along with religious pluralism consisted of (1) the belief in communication between the living and the dead; (2) the continuation of the spirit after death; (3) the belief in the existence of

---

[158] Partridge, Christopher. *The Occult World*. (Routledge: London, England, 2015), p. 201

[159] Ibid. p. 204

[160] Ibid. p. 205-206

a "heaven" consisting of various tiers (usually seven) which one could progress through in the afterlife; and (4) the use of heaven "as a model for what an ideal earth might become." [161] Many later "Spiritualists became Theosophists or other more hardline occultists. ... Theosophy had its roots in Spiritualism: both Helena Petrovna Blavatsky and her life-long follower and patron Colonel Henry Olcott, were Spiritualists prior to the founding of the Theosophical Society in 1875." [162]

It's important for the Christian reader to understand what's going on here, spiritually speaking. When one steps back at looks at the history of the nineteenth-century, ELECTRIFICATION and the ADVANCED TECHNOLOGIES DERIVED FROM IT represent the defining characteristics of the age. Parallel to this, however, and in regards to spiritual matters, INTERCOURSE WITH DEVILS was the hallmark of the age. In light of what's been discussed up to this point, the fact that INCIDENCES OF ELECTRICITY AND DEVIL ACTIVITY SUDDENLY APPEAR TOGETHER ON A MASS SCALE should cause us to stop and think. Is it a coincidence that this worldwide eruption in demonism parallels the arrival of the electric age? Is it a coincidence that this demonism parallels an explosion of knowledge in its century and those that follow? Is it a coincidence that this demonism helped birth the modern ideologies of "liberalism" and "feminism"? The phrase "progressive" concerning certain political ideas is nothing new. The very words were often used to describe political offshoots of Spiritualism:

> "Early Spiritualism...perceived itself as a voice of the 'PROGRESSIVE' MOVEMENTS of the time." [163]

> "By the 1860s and 1870s, one could sit for spirit photographs, attend spirit lectures on A RANGE OF

---

[161] Partridge, Christopher. *The Occult World*. (Routledge: London, England, 2015), p. 197

[162] Ibid. p. 205

[163] Lewis, James R., Melton, J. Gordon, Ellwood, Robert. *Perspectives on the New Age* (State University of New York Press: Albany, New York, 1992), p. 61

PROGRESSIVE SOCIAL AND RELIGIOUS ISSUES, and take part in carefully orchestrated seances at which ghosts materialized, voices spoke through levitating trumpets, messages wrote themselves on sealed slates, and mediums' bodies emitted disconcerting quantities of a strange, filmy substance known as ectoplasm." [164]

"...[the nineteenth-century] is the turning point at which people could self-identify as Spiritualists, which carried, at least in the United States, ASSOCIATIONS WITH PROGRESSIVE POLITICS as well as religious pluralism." [165]

"...Most spirit mediums were women, with many voting-rights activists among them. MARY TODD LINCOLN BROUGHT A PROGRESSIVE INFLUENCE INTO THE CIVIL WAR-ERA WHITE HOUSE from those who claimed to speak to voices from beyond. Until her death, she never recanted her beliefs..." [166]

The primary leaders within the Spiritualist movement were women. Women made up the vast majority of those who engaged in its mediumship, trance channelings, spirit readings, automatic writings, automatic drawings, seances, talking in tongues, telekinesis, clairvoyance, table tipping, and more. In fact, three young girls helped open the floodgates for the phenomenon (Leah, Margaret, and Kate Fox – one of which was a 15-year-old, the other 12). Imagine, if you can, a religious movement started by a 12-year-old:

---

[164] Sword, Helen. Ghostwriting Modernism. (Cornell University Press: Ithaca, NY, 2002), p. 2

[165] Partridge, Christopher. *The Occult World*. (Routledge: London, England, 2015), p. 197

[166] Horowitz, Mitch. "Mary Todd Lincoln, Spiritualist" (Medium, 16, July, 2018), https://medium.com/s/radical-spirits/mary-todd-lincoln-spiritualist-9140788023711

"As for my people, children are their oppressors, and women rule over them. O my people, they which lead thee cause thee to err, and destroy the way of thy paths."
Isa 3:12

In 1856, Dr. William Ramsey wrote of a family in Philadelphia which had begun to partake in Spiritualist phenomena. The father of that family stated to the doctor:

> "'We can turn the tables in our house [levitate, move]—our little [14-years-old] daughter can do it easily; but we can't do it without her.' Upon having his daughter give a demonstration of these things, the father then asked her if she could attempt to write something through 'automatic writing,' which allows a spirit to guide one's hand. She did so and '...the question was put, 'who moves her hand?' Immediately, in large distinct letters, she wrote the word 'DEVIL.' When she lifted up her pencil and saw the word she had written, she dropped the pencil, and a shudder passed over her that shook her whole frame. She evidently felt afraid, and her parents were silent. They looked amazed. At length the father said, 'I guess we had better stop now.' ...the conclusion that our friend drew from what he saw was, that THERE MUST HAVE BEEN A MIND DIFFERENT FROM ANYONE THEN PRESENT, CONTROLLING HER HAND, for no one had suggested that name, and surely the little girl herself had not intended to write the word. What led her to do it? That is the question." [167]

In any case, this MASS COMMUNICATION with the dead, lead with the help of many *"captive silly women"* (2 Tim. 3:6), "...created a social code in which women became the perfect vehicles for a host

---

[167] Ramsey, William. *Spiritualism, a Satanic Delusion and a Sign of the Times.* (H. L. Hastings: Peace Dale, RI, 1856), p. 54

Early communication technologies: Telegraph, telephone, tell-a-woman.

of NEW COMMUNICATION TECHNOLOGIES... Mesmeric trance states and Spiritualist messages SET THE STAGE for a new sphere of female white-collar workers... Court stenographers, touch typists, short-hand takers, and telephone and telegraph operators..."[168] In plainer words, since it was primarily women who had experience in communication with demon spirits, this fostered an environment favorable to women in communications technologies.

One Christian doctor of the time, Sir Henry Lunn, stated of the predominance of women in the Spiritualist movement:

> "There can be nothing more pernicious [subtly harmful] for our nation than that sorrowing women, instead of seeking in quiet waiting upon God for the comfort which He gave to the sorrowing sisters of Bethany, instead of resting upon the profound truth which He proclaimed to them, *'I am the Resurrection and the Life, he that believeth on Me, though he were dead, yet shall he live,'* should seek by the wretched mechanism of planchettes [early Ouija boards] and by automatic writing to penetrate

---

[168] Partridge, Christopher. *The Occult World* (Routledge: London, England, 2015), p. 202

the mysteries which God in His wisdom has veiled from humanity. This way lies madness." [169]

SPIRITS OF THE TWENTY-FIRST-CENTURY

In the last several sections, we've covered some pretty interesting stuff. Earlier in the book, we mentioned that there exists some kind of perplexing relationship between ELECTRICAL PHENOMENA and the SPIRIT WORLD. The example we gave was that at death science says all such electric activity in the body stops, while the Bible says that at death the body surrenders up a ghost. This parallel between the two end-of-life events set the stage for other possible connections. Later, we cited cases of people being struck by lightning who then acquired various abilities often associated with mysticism and demonism including mind reading, astral projection, divination, healing, clairvoyance, necromancy, and such. Next, we looked at several instances of witnesses who had encounters with unexplained aerial lights, and how these mystifying orbs contradicted the laws of established physics, many times displaying seeming intelligence.

All of these things have helped illustrate that some electromagnetic events can manifest connections with spirit activity, not just the ceasing of electric current within the body at death. Many questions remain unknown regarding this. For example, in the cases of lightning strike victims who then obtain occult abilities, are these instances of the Devil manipulating natural lightning, or is something more spiritually intricate taking place? Why and how does demon possession take place with some people involved with what seems to be ordinary lightning bolt encounters? Can unclean spirits be transferred into people via lightning, or maybe, in certain cases, what

---

[169] Kernahan, Coulson. *Spiritualism: A Personal Experience and a Warning.* (Fleming H. Revell Company: Chicago, New York, London, 1920), p. 9-10

appears to be "lightning" is not lightning at all? Maybe the things these witnesses are seeing are actually evil spirits under the guise of electric phenomena? Regardless of what the specifics may involve, there's no doubt that some people have experienced demonism simply by coming in contact with electricity, or what outwardly appears to be "electricity." This leads to the question that if devils can have such an intimate relationship with electromagnetic events, WHAT ELSE ARE THESE SPIRITS CAPABLE OF WITHIN THE ELECTRIC SPECTRUM? This helps us realize the sweeping extent of the Prince of the Power of the Air and may give us more insight into why the scriptures speak of *"Satan as lightning"* (Lk 10:18).

In considering these things, it makes one wonder if there may be a kernel of truth to "Aladdin's Lamp" where a devil is manifest when some form of electricity is produced. Rubbing metal vigorously creates a static charge. For Aladdin, this act summoned a "genie" or "jinn." What if one of the reasons for the worldwide DEMONIC ERUPTION of the 1800s was, in part, THE RESULT OF MAN'S INVOLVEMENT WITH THE NEW POWER OF ELECTRICITY? Do the two events parallel each other because of this connection?

What if, like in the field of biology where science is ignorant of the spirit, that OTHER BRANCHES OF SCIENCE ARE EQUALLY IGNORANT OF SPIRIT ACTIVITY within those respective fields? We briefly mentioned this earlier, but does this indicate that CERTAIN FORMS OF MODERN SCIENCE ARE UNKNOWINGLY ACTING IN CONCERT WITH DEMONS? What if some of the things traveling through the air today are not actually what science says they are – electromagnetic waves, radio waves, cell phone waves, wired and wireless internet, etc? Could modern electrical technologies involve more than we realize? Could they have some sort of link to the spiritual? Is such a thing even possible? According to scripture, it is.

In trying to get you to think outside the box, this book has attempted to demonstrate this. I want you to put on your biblical thinking caps (1Th. 5:21, 2Ptr. 1:19); your supernatural thinking caps

When Aladdin rubbed his golden lamp a demon appeared. Metal rubbed vigorously creates a static charge, a form of electricity. Gold, by the way, is not only what Aladdin's lamp was made from, but is one of the most proficient conductors of electricity. Today, gold is one of the primary metals contained in electronic devices.

(1Jn. 4:1, Lk. 10:18); your spiritual discernment thinking caps (Eph. 6:2, 2Tm. 3:1). Don't be intimidated by the science-only crowd (1Tm. 6:20). Remember, the religious men in the bible who did not believe in spirits were the SADDUCEES (Acts 23:8). Many of these people had "*a form of godliness*," but DENIED THE POWER THEREOF (2 Tim. 3:5). Anyone who denies the power of God will certainly deny the power of the Devil (like the kind of "power" he wielded against Job – see Job 1:1 & 2). This describes modern academia perfectly, the ones who supposedly know all about electricity.

A huge percentage of the major technologies of the twenty-first-century is made possible by a force with ties to the phantom world. Could this be an indicator that Satan is more involved with society today than ever before in history? With all the technological things that have gone on WITH THE AIR and IN THE AIR in the past two centuries, what grounds do we have to stand on to say that the Prince of the Power of the Air is irrelevant? In the sections that follow we will briefly cover a few issues of modern technology which suggest demonic involvement.

PART IX

THE CITY WITH NO NIGHT

Satanology - History - Prophecy - Technology

"And the great city was divided into three parts, and the cities of the nations fell..."
Revelation 16:19

CITIES OF LIGHT IN A FALLEN REALM

AS COVERED earlier in the book, the nineteenth century witnessed a technological and spiritual revival. Both movements were complicit in helping to usher in modern "progressive" politics, feminism, multiculturalism, strong occult influences, and the dream of a united world. Even though the Commissioner of the US patent office had stated in 1899, "Everything that can be invented has been invented," new technologies were on the horizon which would continue to radically change everyday life. The bedrock that would make most all of these new devices possible was the strange, baffling force we call "ELECTRICITY."

Although the arrival of electrification helped birth the modern era, it also marked an acceleration in the biblically prophesied last days – a mind-boggling age of knowledge (Dan. 12:4) through which the rulers of the darkness of this world were attempting to build A COUNTERFEIT HEAVEN ON EARTH.

The first thing the Holy God spoke into existence during the six days of Genesis was "light" (Gen. 1:3). From the beginning of the 1800s and beyond, one of the most outstanding applications for the discovery of electricity, was in THE CREATION OF ARTIFICIAL LIGHT. This mirrored the spiritual condition of the age -- an era of both knowledge and light, neither of which had roots in God (Lk. 11:35, 1Tm. 4:1):

> "...advances in LIGHTING seem almost to have foreshadowed advances in THOUGHT: Professor John Carey has noted that the dawn of the age of enlightenment is usually put at the beginning of the 18th century WHEN STREET OIL LAMPS FIRST APPEARED in Paris, and that Nietzsche's announcement of 'THE DEATH OF GOD' COINCIDED WITH THE APPEARANCE OF THE ELECTRIC LIGHT BULB..." [170]

Get that last quotation.

The appearance of electric lighting coincided with Nietzsche's "The Death of God" proclamation. In other words, the age of artificial light birthed an age of spiritual darkness. That is profound. When mankind thought it was "evolving" and getting smarter, it was actually becoming more foolish (Rom. 1:22). Arc lamps preceded incandescent lamps, but both were experimented with throughout the nineteenth century. Gaslighting came before both (1790s), but much of the public had misgivings about the technologies. In 1816, one newspaper derided the installation of gaslights stating that it was "...an attempt to interfere with the divine plan of the world, which had preordained darkness during the night-time." [171] The article predicted that artificial light at night would embolden criminals, not deter them. The argument was that without the "...fear of darkness... drunkenness and depravity [will] increase." [172] Arc lightning fared no

---

[170] Henley, Jon. "Life before artificial light" (The Guardian, Guardian News & Media Limited, 31, October, 2009), https://www.theguardian.com/lifeandstyle/2009/oct/31/life-before-artificial-light

[171] Simon, Linda. *Dark Light* (Harcourt Inc.: San Diego, California, 2004), p. 72

[172] Ibid., p, 72

better. Robert Louis Stevenson, the author of *Treasure Island*, and *Dr. Jekyll and Mr. Hyde*, echoed this sentiment after accusing arc light of being "...horrible, unearthly, obnoxious to the human eye, a lamp for a nightmare!" [173]

In the 1870s, Thomas Edison, "The Wizard of Menlo Park," introduced a new incandescent lightbulb. Although Edison was not the only developer of the invention, he is the one credited with it. What resulted from Edison's technology, however, was not so much the perfect lightbulb, but the catalyst for A NATIONWIDE ELECTRIC POWER GRID. Edison's new bulb, in conjunction with the growth and spread of ELECTRIC POWER, played a major role in transforming everyday life.[174] Because of such a grid, society quickly began to morph from a more rural type setting into an urban setting.

Over the next fifty-or-so years, electricity became the standard in homes and businesses around the world. For the people of the time, the burgeoning ever-presence of electric lighting changed life as we know it. People could stay up late and didn't have to regulate their lives by the limited light of the sun. Sleeping patterns were altered as factories and employers began introducing "night shifts." In short, electric lighting birthed an earthly CITY WITH NO NIGHT ––a city that never sleeps. A kind of city which, up to this time, HAD ONLY EXISTED IN HEAVEN (Rev. 22:5).

If you're not quite getting this, you will. What we're dealing with here in the coalescing of these innovations (electric power and light)

---

[173] Simon, Linda. *Dark Light* (Harcourt Inc.: San Diego, California, 2004), p. 72

[174] FOOTNOTE: Thomas Edison was a Bible-rejecting pantheist who professed that nature was "God", and there was no such thing as spirits or a soul. Believe it or not, his delusion of reality was not much different than the mythology behind the *Star Wars* films. He believed that countless microscopic intelligences called "immortal units" or "life units" were the life-giving force behind all things. [see *Modern Mechanix and Inventions*. (October, 1933), p. 34-36] Although Edison was one of the key players in bringing artificial light to the world, he died on October 18, 1931, in complete and total spiritual darkness rejecting the Lord Jesus Chirst.

is not just the ability to build a city. But the ability for making GIANT, LIGHTED, GLOWING CITIES. When steel is added to the mix (an architectural technology that was growing parallel to all this) you not only get the capability for wide, horizontal cities, but vertical constructs which HAD NEVER EXISTED BEFORE. The year 1890 marked the birth of the "skyscraper" (see Gen. 11:4). When the Devil's influence is factored into these things, it's realized that today's world of great, spreading, electric-powered cities are MAN-MADE COUNTERFEITS OF THE CITY OF GOD. These places are not enlightened by the glory of God, but by some strange force with mysterious ties to the spirit world (see image on opposite page). Most people view the modern city as simply a part of urban technological evolution, being unaware of its spiritual significance. People don't think about the fact that such radical places have not existed for the majority of man's time on earth. Most people don't consider these electrically-illuminated places as a recent development, but that's what they are. But whether earthly cities are thousands of years old, or the new electrified versions, scripture does not have anything good to say about them.

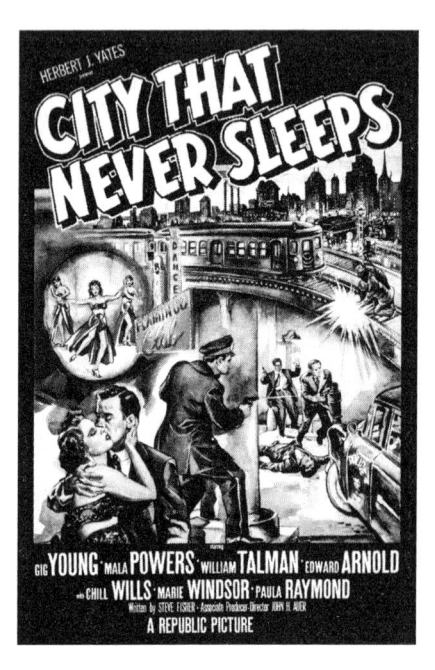

CITIES OF MEN, CITIES OF DEATH

Before the so-called "Age of Enlightenment" and the Industrial Revolution (see Part IV), cities were nothing like they are today.

Technology and industry have completely revolutionized this. There were no factories before this and no centralized means of employment for the average worker. Not only did the modern city bring these things with it, but along with this, other things were birthed. The Bible's history of the city shines a light on this matter.

Many are unaware of the fact that THE WORLD'S FIRST CITY-BUILDER in scripture was also THE WORLD'S FIRST MURDERER -- Cain, a man identified as being "*of that wicked one*" (1 Jn. 3:12). The Bible shows that the first city was built after Cain went "*out from the presence of the LORD*" (Gen. 4:16). Meaning that God was not involved with the building of earth's first city. The world's first city was named in honor of the seed of the world's first killer. Cain's first son was "*Enoch*," the name of the first city: [175]

> "*And Cain knew his wife; and she conceived, and bare Enoch: and he [Cain] builded a city, and called the name of the city, after the name of his son, Enoch.*" Gen. 4:17

The Bible is clear that the building of the earthly city was not inspired by the Lord. Of course, God could've just as easily built a city for the first man, Adam, but he didn't. God's city is not scheduled

A city of light in a fallen world

---

[175] FOOTNOTE: We know that Cain is the city-builder here, and not Enoch, for Enoch did not name his firstborn after himself, but called him "Irad." Thus, the one who names the city of Enoch "after the name of his son," is clearly Cain. Gen. 4:17-18

to arrive until sometime in the future (see Rev. 21). Man-made cities arrive at the beginning of the Bible. God's city arrives at the end.

Another early mention of "city" in scripture, is tied to the first major insurrection against God after Noah's Flood –– the building of the city and tower of Babel. Babel represents the first consolidated effort of man to build an anti-God world order (Gen. 11:1-9). The next mention of the word "city" is one that the Lord himself burned to the ground (Gen. 18 & 19). In fact, this was a group of cities – "*Sodom and Gomorrha, and the cities about them*" (Jude 1:7).

While cities in and of themselves are not evil, per se, these Bible verses do not cast their earthly origins in a good light. As we've mentioned, God himself is the builder of a City (Heb. 11:16). But the difference is that one type of city is BUILT BY FALLEN MAN, with the technology of man, the other, BY THE HOLY GOD, with the technology of God. In stark contrast, the city of God brings with it no more sorrow, no more tears, no more pain, and NO MORE DEATH (Rev. 21:2-4), but the cities of man are MARKED BY DEATH. This is why we've pointed out that the first earthly city was built by a murderer (1 Jn. 3:12).

> "*Woe to him that buildeth a town with blood, and stablisheth a city by iniquity!*" Hab 2:12

> "*Woe unto them that join house to house, that lay field to field, till there be no place, that they may be placed alone in the midst of the earth!*" Isa. 5:8

It's a statistical fact that crime increases with population density thus, as a general rule, the larger the city the higher the crime rate. This is why one of the things that industrialization and the modern city brought with it was MORE CRIME. With the advent of electric lighting and the introduction of "the city that never sleeps," cities could operate 24 hours a day. This also helped inflate the crime rate. It also brought to the forefront a type of criminal element not widely seen before – THE SERIAL KILLER. Dr. Frederic Reamer of Rode Island College, an authority on criminal justice, has stated:

> "I think the evolution of LARGE, URBAN, COMPLEX SOCIETIES can sometimes provide the INCUBATOR FOR MURDER." [176]

In 1888, London was rocked by a series of murders, the brutality of which was monstrous. From these incidents arose the legend of "Jack the Ripper," a man now labeled as the first modern "serial killer." This is in spite of the fact that, to this day, no one knows whether these crimes were perpetrated by a male or female, or whether it was the work of a lone killer or several. There are many theories, but not enough evidence to draw any hard conclusions. "Jack" got away with murder!

"Cities are murky places-- hatching grounds for monsters."
– John Geddes, MD

Five years later across the Atlantic, the 1893 Chicago World's Fair was putting America's most advanced technology on display and celebrating the dawn of the Electric Age. One centerpiece of the event was the climax of the electrical "Battle of the Currents." It featured the technologies of Thomas Edison, George Westinghouse, and Nikola Tesla. Little did they know, however, that literally right next door, in the very same city, at 701 West 63rd Street, was the makeshift "hotel" of America's first known and most prolific urban killer – Herman Mudgett (a.k.a. H.H. Holmes). During the 179 days that the Chicago Fair was open to the public, over 27 million people were in attendance. By the close of the exhibition, reportedly

---

[176] "America's Most Notorious Serial Killers: The First Wave". *Becoming Evil: Serial Killers*, S1 E3. Amazon Prime, https://www.amazon.com/amazonprime.

America's first mass killer was Herman Mudgett, alias "H.H. Holmes." Mudgett renovaded a floor in his building into a killing chamber aimed at targeting victims during the 1893 Chicago World's Fair. While the world celebrated the Electic Age, a new breed of wickedness was emerging.

hundreds of visitors had inexplicably disappeared. It was later discovered that Mudgett had refurbished part of an old pharmacy building to accommodate guests. But his drugstore makeover was obviously something more sinister. Allegedly it contained trap doors, chutes, maze-like hallways, an asphyxiation chamber, stairways to nowhere, fake walls and doors, and a dungeon with an operating table and a crematory oven. No one knows for sure how many fell victim to the maniac, but scores of human bones were later found in his "faux-tel" (fake hotel). The Encyclopedia Britannica reports that Holmes "confessed to 27 murders" but later upped it to 130. [177]

Although the crimes of the Ripper and Mudgett were an ocean apart, they were harbingers of things to come. Both were a product of the new, burgeoning industrial era and the MODERN CITY. Even the police of the time admitted this evil was something new:

---

[177] John Philip, Jenkins. "H.H. Holmes, Herman Mudgett" (Britannica, Encyclopædia Britannica, Inc.), https://www.britannica.com/biography/H-H-Holmes

"A modern, urban monster for a modernizing and increasingly URBAN AGE, Holmes was, according to Chicago police, a 'new class of criminal,' a man so monomaniacal about manslaughter that he turned his own hotel into a 'Murder Castle.'" [178]

Today, due to the ever-increasing urbanization of society, serial killers are becoming more and more frequent. Former FBI criminal profiler, Clint Van Zandt, estimates that "there's maybe 50 serial killers operating in the United States at any one time." [179] That's nearly one killer per state and it's all come about with the increased urbanization and electrification of the world. According to the Global Change Data Lab:

"By 1800...over 90% of the global population lived in rural areas. Urbanization in the United States began to increase rapidly through the 19th century, reaching 40% by 1900. By 1950 this reached 64% and nearly 80% by 2000." [180]

In 2007, world urbanization surpassed rural areas. By 2020, the world's urban population had swelled to over four billion where 55% of the global population now lived in urban areas. As the world continues to be more and more technologically entwined, rural populations will continue to dwindle. It is estimated that by the year 2050, two-thirds of the world will be city dwellers, and by the turn of the next century (or sooner), as the world inches ever closer to complete urbanization, the Earth itself will be one, giant, interconnected, megalopolis spread around the globe.

---

[178] Lenoir, Andrew. "H. H. Holmes: The Devil You Don't Know" (All Things Interesting, Oct. 31, 2019). https://allthatsinteresting.com/hh-holmes

[179] *The Unexplained*, S2 E15, Serial Killers, First aired: Saturday, March 12, 2021.

[180] Ritchie, Hannah & Roser, Max. "Urbanization" (Our World in Data, Global Change Data Lab, 2018), https://ourworldindata.org/urbanization

What Percent of the World's Population Lives in a City?
THE RATE OF GROWTH FROM 1700 TO 2016

United States Urbanization Growth ‑ ‑ ‑ ‑ ‑ ‑
World Urbanization Growth ───────

OurWorldInData.org/urbanization
Chart based on UN World Urbanization Prospects 2018 and historic sources.

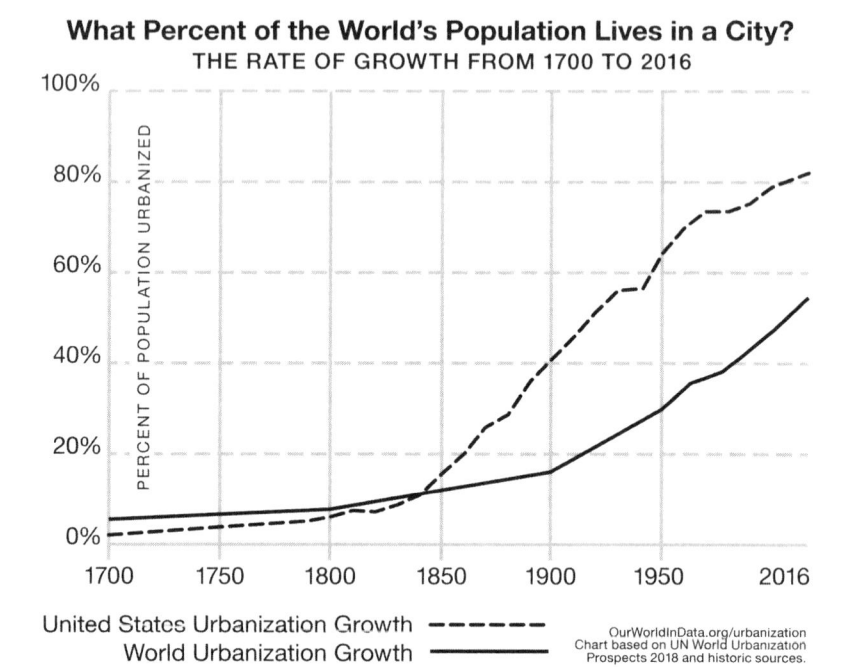

The chart above shows the explosion in urbanization after the advent of the nineteenth-century Electric Age. The growth of urban living has been phenomenal and it is on track to consume much of the rural world in the coming years.

"Megalopolis" is a compound word denoting a very large, heavily populated urban complex. This word originates from the Greek words "mégas" and "pólis," and means "great city." Without modern technology (and especially electricity) these modern, networked superstructures would not be possible. In fact, the global shift in urbanization began in the same century as electricity and its accompanying inventions. And it just so happens that "great city" is a Bible phrase used to primarily describe the last world government of Satan – BABYLON. In this context, the word combo is used nine times, the most of any city found in the word of God:

> "And a mighty angel took up a stone like a great millstone, and cast it into the sea, saying, Thus with violence shall that GREAT CITY Babylon be thrown down, and shall be found no more at all." Rev. 18:21, etc.

Cities of Men, Cities of Death | 241

The final city in the Bible is the Holy City, New Jerusalem (Rev. 3:12. 21:2. etc.). It's a massive, earth-shattering, megalopolis that's 1500 miles wide by 1500 miles tall (a true "skyscraper"). God's "city" appears to be one, large, single construct consisting of billions of individual "manisions" (Jn. 14:2), similar to what we would think of as a huge motel or apartment complex. Today, the largest residential building in the world is located in Kudrovo, Russia. The structure contains over 3,708 separate apartments, with around 20,000 residents and employees. Plus, it has seven groceries, three salons, a florist, a construction material store, a kindergarten, three cafes, a post office, a pharmacy, an outpatient hospital, a pet store, and more. It is a city within a city and another attempt by this fallen world to immitate what God ofers to the born-again sinner.

However, the final "great city" in scripture is God's City––the city which Satan is currently attempting to immitate on earth:

> "And he carried me away in the spirit to a great and high mountain, and shewed me that GREAT CITY, the HOLY JERUSALEM, descending out of heaven from God,"
>
> Rev 21:10

God's City is a PLACE OF LIFE (the last city named in the Bible). Man-made cities are PLACES OF DEATH (the first city named in the Bible). This is why there are no godly cities anywhere in this world (including "Vatican City"). There are a few God-fearing individuals and, perhaps, some godly communities, but there are no godly cities or nations. The first God-fearing man on this earth was a FARMER who lived in a GARDEN and tilled the ground, but IT TOOK A MURDERER TO BUILD A CITY (Gen. 2:5-8 & 4:17). Of course, if you live in a city this doesn't mean you're damned because of it or anything like that. These are simply the facts of a fallen world. There will be no godly city anywhere on this earth until God Himself places one upon it (Rev. 21). Until that time, man is going to try his best to build a utopia himself. A feat that is doomed to failure:

> "Except the LORD build the house, they labour in vain that build it: except the LORD keep the city, the watchman walketh but in vain." Psa. 127:1

Today, the modern city is taken for granted. But even so, society is not done molding them. In the twenty-first-century, new types of cities are beginning to take shape which will absorb the older, outdated ones. These modern metropolises represent a merger of technologies, including electricity, advanced electronics, and computer networks. Such places will be even greater imitations of God's City than those of the past. And to attempt to blindly lead mankind into it, these new constructs have been dubbed "SMART CITIES."

PART X

WHAT HATH THE DEVIL WROUGHT

Satanology - History - Prophecy - Technology

*"[10] ...that great city, the holy
Jerusalem, descending out of heaven
from God, [11] Having the glory of God:
and her light was like unto a stone most
precious, even like a jasper stone,
clear as crystal;"*   *Revelation 21:10-11*

THE SECRET OF CRYSTALS

IN OUR GEEKY age, we're constantly hearing new tech-related words and phrases. One of the labels we often hear today in conjunction with electronics is the word "smart." Although the term is evolving with newer and newer technology, "smart" is generally indicative of objects that have been computerized and integrated into a network. [181] According to one online dictionary:

> "The term 'smart' originally comes from the acronym 'Self-Monitoring, Analysis, and Reporting Technology' but [has] become widely known as 'smart' because of the notion of allowing previously INANIMATE OBJECTS—from cars to basketballs to clothes—to TALK BACK TO US and even GUIDE OUR BEHAVIOR." [182]

This new behavior-steering technology is a burgeoning field that is expected to rapidly increase in the coming years. However, the

---

[181] FOOTNOTE: The word "smart" is found only once in the Bible (Prov. 11:15), and it's not a reference to a person who makes wise choices, but to physical pain received from punishment. Webster says of "smart": "To be punished; to bear penalties or the evil consequences of anything."

[182] "smart tech" (Netlingo), https://www.netlingo.com/word/smart-tech.php

technology for it is already in wide use today. The more "smart" devices a person obtains, the more your home will become a "smart" home – intricately tied to the world's electronic web. Technocrats want us to have smart homes, in addition to smart cars, smart cities, smart nations, and eventually a smart world. But the thing that makes this kind of integrated computer technology possible is a thing called "smart materials" :

> "SMART MATERIALS: This catch-all term refers to a wide range of materials that are able to respond to their surroundings and change their properties. THE MOST FAMILIAR SMART MATERIAL IS QUARTZ. QUARTZ CRYSTALS PRODUCE ELECTRIC CURRENT when squeezed, and vibrate when ELECTRIFIED." [183]

> "QUARTZ CRYSTAL is the most widely used crystal when it comes to CONDUCTING ELECTRICITY. Its resistance to wear and heat, added to its ABILITY TO REGULATE ELECTRICITY, makes it a highly valuable substance for technology engineers." [184]

According to Webster, "QUARTZ" is a "species of SILICIOUS MINERALS, of various colors...frequently crystallized."

What we're attempting to get at here, and what the reader may not be informed about, is that the primary use of gemstones today (like quartz), is not in jewelry-making or ornamental work, but in COMPUTER TECHNOLOGY. *The New York Daily News* reports:

> "Natural crystals are so powerful that metaphysicians and healers throughout history have used them to alter

---

[183] Jackson, Tom. Engineering: *An Illustrated History from Ancient Craft to Modern Technology*. (Shelter Harbor Press: New York. 2016), p. 127

[184] Erickson, Michaelyn. "What Crystal Can Hold Electricity or Energy" (Sciencing, Leaf Group Ltd. / Leaf Group Media, 13, March, 2018), https://sciencing.com/crystal-can-hold-electricity-energy-6886479.html

the FLOW OF ENERGY in the physical world. ... These cultures utilized crystals in their work because they knew A SECRET THAT MODERN SCIENCE HAS ONLY RECENTLY DISCOVERED: CRYSTALS HAVE THE POWER TO TRANSMIT ENERGY. Scientists understand that applying pressure to certain crystals, such as quartz, GENERATES A SPECIFIC FORM OF ELECTRICITY. THE COMPUTER AND ELECTRONICS INDUSTRY DEPENDS UPON CRYSTAL TECHNOLOGY and COULD NOT EXIST IN ITS PRESENT FORM WITHOUT IT." [185]

"Quartz crystals are piezoelectric, a natural phenomena that has had A SIGNIFICANT EFFECT ON THE ELECTRONICS INDUSTRY. ...the piezoelectric properties of Quartz basically mean that it will create a very small electrical charge if it is squeezed. It will also CARRY AN ELECTRICAL CHARGE across the crystal, from one side to another. ... While it is charged, Quartz will oscillate (meaning it vibrates) exactly 32,768 times a second. By counting these oscillations, we can use Quartz crystals as a very accurate way of timekeeping." [186]

There are many different varieties of quartz including, but not limited to the AGATE, JASPER, ONYX, CHALCEDONY, AMETHYST, BERYL, and EMERALD. If you're a Bible reader these gems should be familiar to you. All of these stones (what man is now calling "smart materials") are named numerous times in the Bible IN CONJUNCTION WITH THE MOST ADVANCED TECHNOLOGIES ESTABLISHED BY GOD. Hello? Are you listening?

---

[185] Angel, Jennifer. "The power of crystal energy" (New York Daily News, 03, May, 2016), https://www.nydailynews.com/horoscopes/power-crystal-energy-article-1.2623109

[186] "Gemstone Family Tree: Quartz" (Gemporia, 23, October, 2019), https://www.gemporia.com/en-us/gemology-hub/article/1484/gemstone-family-tree-quartz/

In conjunction with precious stones, however, DIAMONDS AND GOLD are also important components of all these technical things. Like gemstones, they play an integral role in modern technology. Some even believe that "Silicon Valley" has the potential to one day become "Diamond Valley":

"...DIAMOND COULD POWER THE FUTURE OF ELECTRONICS: One company believes the diamond age is about to dawn. That makes diamond an attractive alternative for use in commercial electronics as silicon devices slowly reach their upper limits for speed and lower limits for size. But diamond is also uniquely equipped to improve applications in power electronics—the electronics used in sectors such as aerospace, transportation, communications, and power grid development that are designed to operate at high voltages." [187]

"...many consider that the industry is entering THE DAWN OF A DIAMOND AGE of Electronics. They believe the world's hardest-known natural material with exceptional electronic properties will take a variety of industries to the next level of performance." [188]

"...GOLD is the world's most reliable and durable ELECTRICAL CONDUCTOR, essential for computer electronics..." [189]

---

[187] Davenport, Matt. "Why diamond could power the future of electronics" (C&EN Chemical Engineering News, American Chemical Society, ACS Publications, 16, May, 2016), https://cen.acs.org/articles/94/i20/diamond-power-future-electronics.html

[188] Kahn, Adam. "Moore's Law and Moving Beyond Silicon: The Rise of Diamond Technology" (WIRED, Condé Nast), https://www.wired.com/insights/2015/01/the-rise-of-diamond-technology/

[189] "GOLD – NOT JUST FOR JEWELRY" (Straterra, October, 2018), https://www.wired.com/insights/2015/01/the-rise-of-diamond-technology/

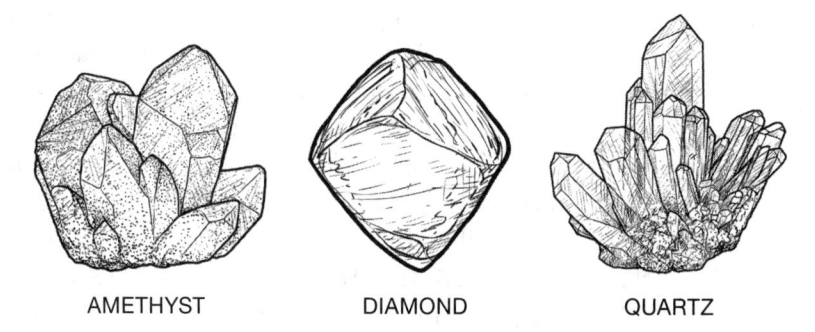

| AMETHYST | DIAMOND | QUARTZ |

Quartz is a prime material used in modern electronics. It is a "silicious mineral" and is the cause for the name behind "Silicon Valley," a region of high technology and innovation. Quartz comes in many forms, including the agate, jasper, onyx, chalcedony, amethyst, beryl and emerald. All of these can be found in the Bible being utilized by the Lord in holy, heavenly devices. Regarding the use of gemstones and electricity with twenty-first-century technologies, man has tapped into something, but he knowns not what.

Geology.com, one of the world's leading websites for Earth science articles, news, and geographic information, states:

> "THE MOST IMPORTANT INDUSTRIAL USE OF GOLD IS IN THE MANUFACTURE OF ELECTRONICS. ... A small amount of gold is used in ALMOST EVERY SOPHISTICATED ELECTRONIC DEVICE. This includes cell phones, calculators, personal digital assistants, global positioning system (GPS) units, and other small electronic devices. Most large electronic appliances such as television sets also contain gold. ... GOLD IS USED IN MANY PLACES IN THE STANDARD DESKTOP OR LAPTOP COMPUTER. The rapid and accurate transmission of digital information through the computer and from one component to another requires an efficient and reliable conductor. GOLD MEETS THESE REQUIREMENTS BETTER THAN ANY OTHER METAL." [190]

---

[190] King, Hobart M. "The Many Uses of Gold " (Geology.com), https://www.wired.com/insights/2015/01/the-rise-of-diamond-technology/

Hopefully, this information has helped you to understand that the uses and purposes of jewels reach far beyond their outward aesthetic. Such stones can alter the flow of light and can facilitate the movement of electric current. One of the most important things for the reader to get from all this is that the same materials that make up modern "smart technologies," are also a part of the most advanced technologies found in the Bible. Due to these similarities, I believe that MANKIND IS BEING LED BY THE DEVIL TO COUNTERFEIT GOD'S TECHNOLOGY WITHIN THE LIMITED RANGE OF HIS FALLEN MIND (Gen. 11:6). This means that God's and man's technologies, while not identical, they do share significant features. The fact that God's technology is infinitely more advanced doesn't prevent the Devil from attempting to duplicate it. If you're having a hard time accepting this, are we to believe that God is unaware of the technological capabilities of gems and precious stones? Was man the first intelligent being to conceive of such things? Is modern man's technology so advanced that it's outstretched the range of the Bible or God's knowledge? No. In fact, the truth is the opposite. The linking of quartz, gold, diamonds, and other gemstones, not with fashion, but with the ability to CARRY AND CONDUCT POWER did not originate in the minds of men.

LIKE LIVING STONES

I've dropped a couple of hints that modern technology, with its quartz and gold, is imitating certain heavenly technologies on a very primitive level. So, how does this work? The primary Biblical technologies we're concerned with here are (1.) the high priest's garments, (2.) the Lord's Chariot, and (3.) the city of New Jerusalem. All three of these things have an association with GEMSTONES and an ENERGY-LIKE POWER. Let's park here for a moment.

THE HIGH PRIEST'S BREASTPLATE – In looking at the high priest's breastplate, we find that it's construction was *"...for glory and for beauty"* (Ex. 28:2 & 40). While this sounds unimpressive on the surface (the Bible regularly understates things), the New Testament shows that these garments represented much more than what their appearance suggests. Instead of being regalia made solely for ritual and outward looks, the book of Hebrews reveals that they served as an *"...example and shadow of heavenly things..."* which were designed per a *"pattern"* (Heb. 8:5). The word "glory" in describing this apparel is especially telling. We can know this because "glory" can sometimes be descriptive of A THING THAT RADIATES LIGHT. Note the following examples:

1.) The glory of the angel of the Lord shines on the shepherds: *"And, lo, the angel of the Lord came upon them, and THE GLORY OF THE LORD SHONE round about them: and they were sore afraid."* Lk. 2:9

2.) God's glory lightens the earth: *"And, behold, THE GLORY OF THE GOD OF ISRAEL came from the way of the east: and his voice was like a noise of many waters: AND THE EARTH SHINED WITH HIS GLORY."*
Ezk. 43:2

3.) When Christ's glory is seen he is glowing: "[28] *And... he* [the Lord Jesus Christ] *took Peter and John and James, and went up into a mountain to pray.* [29] *And as he prayed, the fashion of his countenance was altered, and his raiment was WHITE AND GLISTERING...* [32] *But Peter and they that were with him were heavy with sleep: and when they were awake, THEY SAW HIS GLORY..."*
Lk. 9:28-32

4.) Saul is struck down and blinded by the glory of God: "...I could not see for THE GLORY OF THAT LIGHT...A LIGHT FROM HEAVEN, ABOVE THE BRIGHTNESS OF THE SUN" Acts 22:6-11 & 26:13

The Bible shows that the ephod, breastplate, Urim and Thummim sometimes functioned in tandem as a communication device between the Lord and certain individuals (see Sam. 23:9-12 & 30:7-8). The breastplate was made of gold and held twelve precious stones ordered in four rows of three (sardius, topaz, carbuncle, emerald, sapphire, diamond, ligure, agate, amethyst, beryl, onyx, jasper). The result was a GOLD and CRYSTALLINE DEVICE connected by GOLD WIRES (Yes, the *King James Bible* says "*wires*" see Ex. 39:1-4). Whenever this device was used to enquire of the Lord, God imparted power to it causing it to react and appear to COME TO LIFE (lighted, flashing gemstones, laser-like effects, or something similar). If this sounds questionable, keep in mind that the "*heavenly things*" (Heb. 8:5) which this device represented helps teach us this. In the New Testament, born-again saints are likened to a holy, royal "*priesthood*" of "*lively stones*" (1Ptr. 2:5 & 9). Did you get that? The Lord Jesus Christ is our Precious Stone (1Ptr. 2:6-7) from whom WE RECEIVE POWER. This is especially the case at the resurrection when we will be both "*raised in glory*," and "*raised in power*" (1Cor. 15:43). Thus, some type of Godly "power" is associated with the stones on the breastplate according to this typology. The gems are not simply there for ornamental purposes. At times, they appear "lively." If I were to guess what the power was that caused the stones to illuminate, I would have to say that it's the same power that raises the saint's body from the dead – the Holy Spirit of God.

Like Living Stones | 253

THE CHARIOT OF THE CHERUBIM – One of the most important features of the Lord's flying throne, is the cherubim which help both drive and power it. The Bible shows that when this thing is in flight (see Ezk. 1 & 10), the spirits of the cherubim are present in its "wheels." In conjunction with this, however, scripture shows that the glory of the Lord also has a profound connection with the device. Whenever this thing is in motion, it glows with a fire-like appearance. Note the words of Ezekiel:

"[4] *And I looked, and, behold, a whirlwind came out of the north, a great cloud, and a fire infolding itself, and A BRIGHTNESS WAS ABOUT IT...as the colour of AMBER... [13] ...like burning coals of fire, and like the APPEARANCE OF LAMPS...THE FIRE WAS BRIGHT, and out of the fire went forth LIGHTNING. ...[14] And the living creatures ran and returned AS THE APPEARANCE OF A FLASH OF LIGHTNING. ... [15] The appearance of the wheels and their work was like unto the colour of a beryl ... [20] ...and the wheels were lifted up over against them: for THE SPIRIT OF THE LIVING CREATURES WAS IN THE WHEELS. ... [21] ...and when those were lifted up from the earth, the wheels were lifted up over against them: for THE SPIRIT OF THE LIVING CREATURES WAS IN THE WHEELS. ... [26] And above the firmament that was over their heads was the likeness of A THRONE, as the appearance of a SAPPHIRE STONE: and upon the likeness of the throne was the likeness as the appearance of a man above upon it. [27] And I saw as the colour of AMBER, AS THE APPEARANCE OF FIRE round about within it, from the appearance of his loins even upward, and from the appearance of his loins even downward, I saw as it were THE APPEARANCE OF FIRE, and IT HAD BRIGHTNESS round about. [28] As the appearance of the bow that is in the cloud in the day of rain, so was THE*

APPEARANCE OF THE BRIGHTNESS round about. This was the appearance of THE LIKENESS OF THE GLORY OF THE LORD. And when I saw it, I fell upon my face..."
Ezk. 1:4, 13-15, 21, 26-28

The prophet Ezekiel also speaks of a cherub who once had *"every precious stone"* as his covering (the sardius, topaz, diamond, beryl, onyx, jasper, sapphire, emerald, carbuncle, gold – see Ezk. 28:13). Whether or not the four cherubim on the Lord's throne are adorned with gems, the scripture doesn't say. But whether they were, or weren't, the point is that God's flying throne shows us a link between energy-like power, light, and spirits. However, I would not be surprised at all to learn that all cherubim had a covering of gemstones.[191] And incidentally, the word *"amber"* (Ezk. 1:4) is where we get our word "electricity" even though the two words are nothing alike. The words "electric," electricity," and "electron," are also derivatives of this. Amber, in scripture, can be found in only three verses (Eze 1:4, 27 & 8:2). In these three references, it has a direct connection with only two types of living beings: GOD AND CHERUBIM.

THE CITY OF NEW JERUSALEM – As man gets closer and closer to the appearance of the Antichrist, it's becoming more apparent that the evolution of the city, through electricity and computer technology, is forming into a thing similar to the holy city of New Jerusalem. As is nearly everything the Devil does, however, it is a COUNTERFEIT. The special thing about New Jerusalem is that it is a place that God has prepared for the redeemed (Heb. 11:16, Rev. 21:2). Those who'll reside here are said to *"...have the mind of Christ"* (2Cor. 2:9, 10 & 16). Is the world today seeking global unity? There it is. Only the Lord can provide it in truth. Is the man of the twenty-

---

[191] FOOTNOTE: Some gemstones are called "eyes," including some forms of quartz, emeralds, and chrysolite. Compare these "eyes" with the cherubim in Rev. 4:8. Are these "eyes" precious stones?

first-century seeking peace? There it is. Only the Lord can provide it in truth. Is man pushing towards everyone getting along, thinking the same things, without conflict? There it is. Only the Lord can provide it in truth. In plainer words, everything that man wants today, God is going to provide. But man doesn't want these things GOD'S WAY. Mankind loves his sin too much, so he wants these things and his sin along with it – that's the whole problem:

"And this is the condemnation, that light is come into the world, and men loved darkness rather than light, because their deeds were evil."   Jn. 3:19

New Jerusalem is the real "smart city." It's not networked together by electricity, wires, and electronics, but by the Holy Spirit of God. It is the true city that never sleeps—the true City of Eternal Day:

[10] And he carried me away in the spirit to a great and high mountain, and shewed me that GREAT CITY, the HOLY JERUSALEM, DESCENDING OUT OF HEAVEN FROM GOD, [11] HAVING THE GLORY OF GOD: and HER LIGHT WAS LIKE UNTO A STONE MOST PRECIOUS... [23] And THE CITY HAD NO NEED OF THE SUN, neither of the moon, TO SHINE IN IT: for THE GLORY OF GOD DID LIGHTEN IT, and THE LAMB IS THE LIGHT THEREOF. ...[5] And there shall be NO NIGHT THERE; and they need no candle, neither light of the sun; for THE LORD GOD GIVETH THEM LIGHT: and they shall reign for ever and ever."   Rev 21:10-11 & 23, 22:5

Thus, it appears that what ELECTRICITY does for many man-made devices, by working through them; THE GLORY OF GOD does for some of Heaven's technologies, working through them. Once again, another parallel between spirits and electric phenomena is revealed. Sometimes, man's technology incorporates minerals and precious metals in its constructions. Some of Heaven's things involve the same. One kind of technology is primitive and unholy, the other advanced and holy. The technology of the Lord can truly be considered "hi-tech" -- THE TECHNOLOGY OF THE MOST HIGH. Amen!

THE FUTURE IS COUNTERFEIT

In Satan's desire to be *"like the most high"* (Isa. 14:12-14), the Bible teaches us that many of the things in scripture that are associated with God are also associated with the Devil. But the Devil's purpose for being involved in these is not the same as the Lord's. Satan's primary goal, especially as his objectives for mankind are concerned, is DECEPTION.

Much of what the world today identifies as "Satanism," while it is satanic, is simply the Devil's decoy designed to point away from HIS MOST SUBTLE, DECEPTIVE, AND DAMNABLE WORKS. I mean, people like "Anton Zandor LaVey," the founder of the Church of Satan (1966), are clowns for the most part (LaVey, in fact, was a former circus animal trainer). The real heavy-duty, satanic stuff is in things like the Roman Catholic Church, its papacy, cardinals, and "Marian" apparitions; as well as men like Joseph Smith who built the demonic empire deceptively known as "The Church of Jesus Christ of Latter-Day Saints." These are the kinds of things the Devil loves – RELIGIONS which outwardly claim "Christianity," while being thoroughly saturated with *"doctrines of devils"* (1Tim. 4:1). They are demon-run spiritual factories that crank out, by the hundreds, those made *"twofold more the child of hell"* (Mt. 23:15). I mean, not only do the members of these organizations need to see past the lie of their own self-righteousness to be saved (Rom. 3:10), but now they must discern the false "Christianity" that's been set before them. Most never make it, and that's the Devil's intent (Jn. 10:10).

When Satan wants to deceive, he appears as an angel of light, not a fallen angel. When Satan wants to deceive, he sends out his *"ministers of righteousness,"* who often can make the right decisions, even though none of these men were ever called of God (see 2 Cor. 11:13-15). This is how Satan can present a "Jesus" (a man who does right) and still not be presenting the Truth. Satan's "Jesus" can be the spiritual brother of Lucifer (the Jesus of Mormonism); or a wafer of unleavened bread that you can literally eat and who can be bossed around by a demon called "Mary" (the Jesus of Roman Catholicism); or not a part of the triune Godhead (the Jesus of the Jehovah's Witnesses), or a high-ranking shaman, wizard, or witch (the Jesus of Witchcraft or occultism).

Satanism, in its most dangerous form, will hold up before the world A JESUS, but it will not be THE LORD JESUS CHRIST of the scriptures. The Devil promotes *"another Jesus,"* presented through *"another gospel,"* which transmits *"another spirit."* The apostle Paul was concerned that many would be deceived by these very things (see 2 Cor. 11:4), and they are!

What this all demonstrates is that, contrary to popular perception, Satan is not trying to distance himself from God. The Devil wants to get as close to God as he possibly can without being detected. He wants to get right up next to God and be worshipped as God. He wants to deceive you into believing that when you think you're looking at "God," you're actually looking at him. To achieve this, the Enemy has created a vast system of COUNTERFEITS. We've already mentioned four counterfeits of "Jesus." There are many more (1Jn. 2:18). The Bible makes mention of this satanic set-up, the existence of which proves the goals of the Devil:

> "[13] *For such are false apostles, deceitful workers, TRANSFORMING THEMSELVES INTO THE APOSTLES OF CHRIST. [14] And no marvel; for SATAN HIMSELF IS TRANSFORMED INTO AN ANGLE OF LIGHT. [15] Therefore it is no great thing if HIS MINISTERS*

ALSO BE TRANSFORMED AS THE MINISTERS OF RIGHTEOUSNESS; whose end shall be according to their works." 2Cor 11:13-15

Here we see the scriptures making direct mention of this counterfeiting system, but it is further elaborated upon throughout the Bible. As a result of this, we find the Bible speaking of another spiritual *"father"* (Jn. 8:44); another *"son"* (2Th. 2:3); another *"Christ"* (Mt. 24:24); another *"spirit"* (2 Cor. 11:4, 1 Jn 4:3); another *"church"* (Rev. 2:9, 3:9); another *"gospel"* (2 Cor. 11:4); other *"apostles"* (2 Cor. 11:13); other *"prophets"* (Mt. 24:11, 1Jn. 4:1); other *"miracles"* (Ex. 7:22, Rev. 13:13-15); other *"wisdom"* (Ex. 28:17, Jm. 3:15). I could list twenty more, but I trust you're beginning to understand the extent the Devil's willing to go to in order to mimic God, or the thing's of God, with his own corrupt versions. This characteristic of Satan is so much the case, and so pronounced in scripture, that I wouldn't hesitate to call it a doctrine -- the doctrine of Demonic Counterfeits.

So, how does this truth relate to our subjects of the Prince of the Power of the Air and modern technology? These examples demonstrate to us that if the Devil is *"the god of this world"* as the Bible declares (2Cor. 4:4), then we should not be surprised to find him using mankind in an attempt to counterfeit what God has *"...prepared for them that love him."* (2Cor. 2:9) And this is exactly what he's doing. Some of these satanic imitations are delusions the Devil has fed to man to convince man that he can provide the promises of God to himself, without God's help. In these cases, the counterfeit is blatant and obvious. Other instances, however, exhibit knowledge of scripture, without the creators of the imitation having any real knowledge themselves. These kinds of cases show the hidden hand of Satan. While man may be blind to the spiritual significance of some of the things he's inventing, the Devil is not. This is just one of the reasons why the Bible says of the lost man that his eyes need opening to turn him from *"...THE POWER OF SATAN unto God..."* (Act 26:18) In the next section we'll address some of these counterfeits, both the obvious and the not-so-obvious.

PART XI

LAST DAYS WEB OF SATAN

Satanology - History - Prophecy - Technology

"[13]...I will ascend into heaven, I will exalt my throne above the stars of God: I will sit also upon the mount of the congregation, in the sides of the north: [14] I will ascend above the heights of the clouds; I will be like the most High."
Isaiah 14:13-14

THE NUMBERING OF PEOPLE

AS THE ELECTRIC revolution of the nineteenth-century continued to advance, America was growing and becoming more and more urbanized. The U.S. was also experiencing an immigration boom. Because of this, records of population growth and other statistics were needed to help in planning for the future. Although keeping track of all the burgeoning data was wrought with increasing difficulty due to outdated methods, new technologies were beginning to emerge which helped alleviate the problem. In 1890, the first electric tabulators were introduced with the U.S. Census. The brainchild of one Herman Hollerith, his tabulating machine became the cornerstone of the company which, in 1924, rebranded itself as International Business Machines, better known as IBM:

> "Herman Hollerith is widely regarded as the father of modern automatic computation. ...and he founded the company that was to become IBM. Hollerith's designs dominated the computing landscape for almost 100 years. ... He did not stop at his original 1890 tabulating machine and sorter, but produced many other innovative new

models. ... These inventions were THE FOUNDATION OF THE MODERN INFORMATION PROCESSING INDUSTRY." [192]

Hollerith's tabulator was a staple of the U.S. Census Bureau until 1951 when THE FIRST COMMERCIAL COMPUTER was introduced. So, why are we talking about these things? Two reasons. Firstly, THE NEED TO COUNT THE POPULACE created the need for THE WORLD'S FIRST COMPUTERS. Remember, earlier we stated that not all new inventions were being invented out of necessity. Well, the electric tabulator was an exception. Its calculating power was needed to help keep up with America's mushrooming population. This people-counter was the forerunner of the modern computer. In other words, had there been no need to NUMBER PEOPLE, the computer would not have been invented when it was. Secondly, and shockingly, the first time the name "*Satan*" is mentioned in the Bible we find:

"*And SATAN stood up against Israel, and provoked David to NUMBER ISRAEL.*" 1Chron. 21:1

The first appearance of the name "*Satan*" is tied to NUMBERING PEOPLE. Today, man has grown accustomed to being tracked and identified by numbers. This is especially the case since the later half of the twentieth century with the appearance of personal tracking and identification numbers like social security numbers, phone numbers, bank accounts, billing accounts, barcodes, passwords, credit cards, PINs, and so forth. The technology behind the Antichrist's "Mark of the Beast" system has been growing and attempting to materialize within the last several decades.

In 1973, the UPC barcode came out. Used to track products and inventory, the "Universal Product Code" consisted of a series of vertical, black bars and spaces of various widths. When two of the adjacent lines are paired together, they represent a coded number.

---

[192] "Herman Hollerith" (Columbia University Computing History, 11, August, 2022), http://www.columbia.edu/cu/computinghistory/hollerith.html

A laser scanner reads the bar and interprets it into numbers. Every barcode has three pairs of longer bars positioned on the left and right sides and in the center. These longer "guard bars" are used to divide the UPC into two numerical halves which separate the product's manufacturer number from the product number. And not only that, each guard bar represents the number SIX. So, there it is – 666. The UPC is a forerunner of the Antichrist's final numbering system which, likewise, will be "universal." Today, nearly everything is tagged and tracked. None of these things are an accident. Satan has a long history of numbering people. Some form of "mark" now seems to be awaiting, or in-the-making, at all times (UPCs, GPS, RFID chips, etc.). They're preparing us for the last straw. When the prophesied mark finally does arrive, no one will be able to function without it (Rev. 13:16-18). Those who refuse it will be killed (Rev. 20:4). You can credit the first electric, human-tabulating machines for paving the way. Thank you, Mr. Hollerith.

An earlier electronic, 666, numbering system

A BYTE FROM A FRUIT

In 1976, a new company known as "Apple Computer" privately debuted and introduced the first hobbyist computer (a single motherboard with no accompanying monitor or keyboard). Within the next several years, and the advent of the multi-million-dollar-selling "Macintosh" (1984), the company would balloon into the monster establishment we all know today – Apple Inc.

In connection with this landmark technology, the launching of a computer company named after a fruit was peculiar. Even the "Macintosh" personal computer was named for the McIntosh apple. Although no real significance was placed on this symbol by its founders, the company's first public logo and print advertisements cast this denial into question. Some have claimed that the first modern logo for Apple (1977) was designed as a tribute to "the father of computer science," Alan Turing. Turing was a computer scientist and homosexual who was arrested in 1952 by the British government and charged with multiple counts of "acts of gross indecency." He died in 1954 after purposefully eating an APPLE contaminated with cyanide. Thus, it's not too much of a stretch to see how people could associate a logo that used an apple, plus a bite, plus six rainbow colors (same as the sodomite flag), as a tribute to Alan Turing. And if that were not enough, the name "fruit," according to the dictionary, is sometimes used as modern slang for the homosexual, and the first widely published advertisement for Apple used the world's most famous naked man (see facing page). How many coincidences are needed to add up to a conclusion? Although Apple denies all of these things, as the old adage goes, where there's smoke, there's fire. [193]

Apple Computers logo (c. 1977)

But honoring a suicided sexual deviant is not the only theory behind the Apple logo. A bite taken from a fruit is emblematic of ACQUIRING HIGHER KNOWLEDGE, albeit forbidden knowledge:

"[16] *And the LORD God commanded the man, saying, Of every tree of the garden thou mayest freely eat:* [17] *But of the tree of the knowledge of good and evil, thou shalt*

---

[193] Hodges, Andrew. "Alan Turing — a short biography" (Alan Turing: The Enigma, University of Oxford, 1995), https://www.turing.org.uk/publications/dnb.html. Also see: "Alan Turing the father of artificial intelligence" (The Translation Gate), https://thetranslationgate.com/artificial-intelligence/

We're looking for the most original use of an Apple since Adam.

Note the words in the ad above: "...use of an Apple." What did Adam "use" the fruit for? He partook of it and was separated from the Holy God. Why would anyone want to associate their product with such an act? (c. 1976)

> not eat of it: for in the day that thou eatest thereof thou shalt surely die... [6] And when the woman saw that the tree was good for food, and that it was pleasant to the eyes, and a tree to be DESIRED TO MAKE ONE WISE, SHE TOOK OF THE FRUIT THEREOF, AND DID EAT, and gave also unto her husband with her; and he did eat."
> Gen. 2:16-17 & 3:6

The first advertisement for Apple Computers capitalized on its logo as having A CONNECTION TO THE FRUIT WITH WHICH SATAN TEMPTED ADAM AND EVE. Why would a product want to associate itself with Adam's "use" of this fruit (see the ad above)--the event which caused mankind's separation from God? Is this the underlying truth about all computers? Is the Devil USING THE COMPUTER

The first product offered by Apple Computers sold for $666 dollars. (c. 1976)

INDUSTRY to bring about his endgame to deceive everyone on the face of this earth? A plan to separate everyone, permanently, from their Holy Maker? Although the suggestion is profound, this is not the end of Apple Computer's curious behavior. The first Apple motherboards were advertised for $666.66. Explanations for this price tag give excuses as to why it had nothing to do with the Bible or the Devil. The claim is that it wasn't planned. Maybe it wasn't, but it sure seems the Devil's using them. As we mentioned earlier, any unsaved man is fair game to be used by Satan. No one has to worship the Devil, believe in the Devil, or even acknowledge the Devil to be his tool. The lost person, whether he realizes it or not, is *"...taken captive by him at his will."* (1Jn. 3:10, 2Tim. 2:26).

WHAT YOU NEVER KNEW ABOUT THE INTERNET

Everything you see on the internet, behind the window of your computer's monitor or smart phone, is not as it appears. The backbone of the world wide web is what is known as "source code." WordPress, the most popular content management system in the world, says of webpage creation:

"HTML, or Hypertext Markup Language, is the main language used to create web pages. ...In the HTML editor, EVERYTHING IS TEXT — A LINK IS TEXT, A QUOTE IS TEXT, even AN IMAGE IS TEXT." [194]

According to Skeat (1910), the English roots of the word "hyper" indicate "above, beyond, or super." The word "text" means "the words of an author; a passage of scripture" or "that which is woven" (like fabric or the connected words of a book).[195] Therefore, the word "HYPERTEXT" means THAT WHICH IS ABOVE OR BEYOND THE WRITTEN WORD. The internet's hypertext language WEAVES TOGETHER WORDS TO FORM A VIRTUAL REALITY. The interconnected elements of this source code are called a "web," and every "webpage" is a part of it. Thus, as WordPress has rightly stated, the internet is built upon words and "language used to create." Now, get that. By the use of words the internet creates images.

Surprisingly, THE CONCEPT OF CREATING A REALITY WITH WORDS did not start with the originators of the internet or world wide web:

> "[1] *In the beginning was the Word, and the Word was with God, and THE WORD WAS GOD. [2] The same was in the beginning with God. [3] ALL THINGS WERE MADE BY HIM; and without him was not any thing made that was made.*"   John 1:1-3

When God made reality, he created the world with WORDS. Just as hypertext words are the source of VIRTUAL REALITY, God's word is the root of ACTUALITY. It represents his absolute power, and is the ability to create simply by speaking words and causing a thing to exist (or not exist) by those words:

---

[194] "Beginning HTML" (Wordpress.com), https://wordpress.com/support/beginning-html/.

[195] Skeat, Walter W. *An Etymological Dictionary of the English Language.* (Dover Publications: Garden City, NY, 2005), p. 284, 638

EXAMPLE 1 - A REALITY CREATED BY WORDS

THE REALITY YOU SEE...

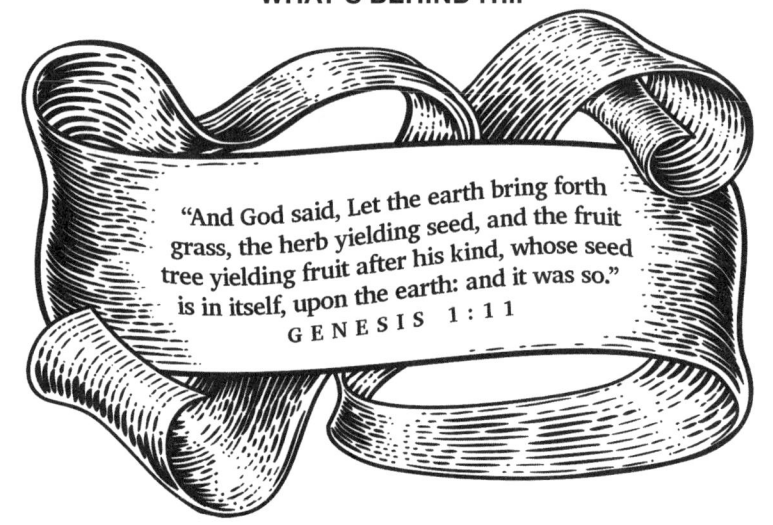

WHAT'S BEHIND IT...

"And God said, Let the earth bring forth grass, the herb yielding seed, and the fruit tree yielding fruit after his kind, whose seed is in itself, upon the earth: and it was so."
GENESIS 1:11

THE WORDS OF GOD.

EXAMPLE 2 - A REALITY CREATED BY WORDS

THE REALITY YOU SEE...

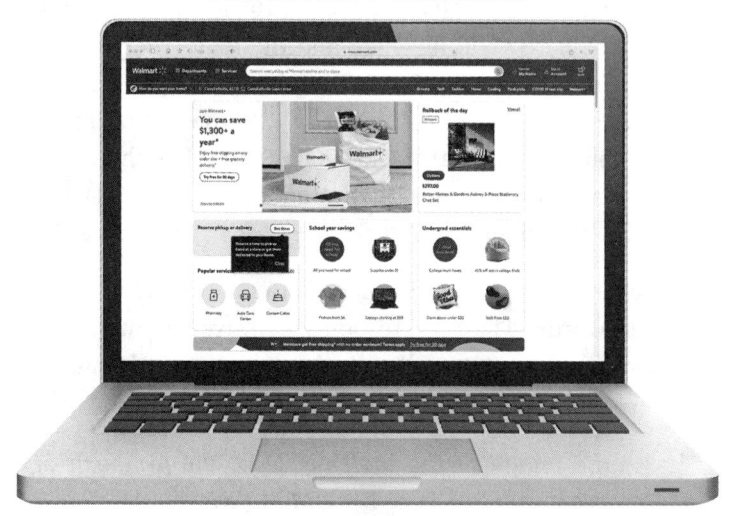

WHAT'S BEHIND IT...

HYPERTEXT SOURCE CODE.

[3] And GOD SAID, Let there be light... [6] And GOD SAID, Let there be a firmament... [9] And GOD SAID, Let the waters under the heaven be gathered together unto one place... [11] And GOD SAID, Let the earth bring forth grass, the herb yielding seed, and the fruit tree yielding fruit... [14] And GOD SAID, Let there be lights in the firmament... [20] And GOD SAID, Let the waters bring forth abundantly... [24] And GOD SAID, Let the earth bring forth the living creature... [26] And GOD SAID, Let us make man in our image..."
Gen. 1:3-26

These verses demonstrate the Lord's raw power to create reality with spoken words. The only reason the universe, and everything in it, doesn't immediately fall completely apart, is because God's Incarnate Word holds it together:

"[15] ...the image of the invisible God, the firstborn of every creature: [[16] For BY HIM WERE ALL THINGS CREATED, that are in heaven, and that are in earth, visible and invisible, whether they be thrones, or dominions, or principalities, or powers: ALL THINGS WERE CREATED BY HIM, and for him: [17] And he is before all things, and BY HIM ALL THINGS CONSIST."
Col 1:15-17

These things help illustrate that God's WORDS FORM AN IMAGE. What's being said here is that VIRTUAL REALITY IS A WORLD CREATED BY WORDS (hypertext), and ACTUALITY IS A WORLD CREATED BY WORDS (the Word of God). Two realities, each dependent upon words for its existence. One mirrors the other. Or, more precisely, one COUNTERFEITS the other. It's almost as if someone looked at the deep truths of God, reality, and the Bible, and asked themselves, "How can I create some form of technology based on this concept?" Did that literally happen? Is that how the founders of the internet brought forth their invention? Probably not. But the fact that the technology docs mirror this in a very primitive way, despite anyone's intentions, is just too much of a coincidence.

What You Never Knew About the Internet | 271

THE INCARNATE WORD OF GOD

THE WRITTEN WORD OF GOD

Scripture says Chirst is the Word of God *"made flesh"* (Jn. 1:14). As the Word Incarnate, he is *"the express image"* of God (Heb. 1:3)--he is an Image made of Words. The technology behind the internet uses this concept in a very basic way--every web page is an IMAGE made by WORDS.

1a.) Satan and the numbering of people.
2a.) Computers and the numbering of people.

1b.) Satan, a fruit, and Adam.
2b.) Computers, a fruit, and Adam.

3a.) Satan and 666.
3b.) Computers and 666.

4a.) A reality made by Words.
4b.) A virtual reality made by words.

We keep running into these strange "coincidences" where a tangential is created by technology crossing the words of God. What's going on? The Devil's fingerprints keep showing up in his handiwork. And the demonically-lead elites who run this world are not about to stop. The internet is not the end of it, but is helping to usher in the final downhill slide. The powers that be are not satisfied with only you being entwined in this web, they're gunning for everything you own –– and the coincidences continue.

BEHOLD, A VOICE OUT OF THE CLOUD

Today, a technocratic concept known as the "Internet of Things" (IoT) is emerging. This process seeks to embed internet connectivity into everyday objects so that every facet of our lives will soon be integrated into, and inextricable from, the world's electric web. This is the idea that you, your car, your home, your appliances, your stuff (cellphone, watch, refrigerator, doorbell, cat litter box, dog collar, vacuum cleaner, toaster, shoes, clothing, toys, coffee maker, television, smoke alarm, thermostat, lighting system, security system, etc.) will eventually all be a part of the internet (all of the things listed here are already offered as IoT devices with certain brands).

Behold, a Voice Out of the Cloud | 273

As is usually the case, modern society is singing the praises of this burgeoning tech, proclaiming that it will make the future much more "efficient." This may be true, but in 2017 the FBI issued a warning against the Internet of Things, citing a massive increase in hacker-induced cyber attacks and data breaches as being inevitable. Many today are already lamenting the severe weaknesses of security systems in IoT devices. In spite of the higher risks, no one is calling for the IoT to be shut down. They're plowing full steam ahead, regardless of the dangers, as if THIS IS SOMETHING THAT MUST BE DONE REGARDLESS OF THE CONSEQUENCES (a spirit is driving them forward. See pages 131-134). There are already BILLIONS of devices merged with the web.

In anticipation of the growing Internet of Things, the world's largest online retailer, Amazon, has created an artificial voice called "Alexa." [196] Inspired by the science fiction series, *Star Trek: The Next Generation* (1987-1994), Alexa is a cloud-based, artificial intelligence (AI) service that you can speak to from your home or cellphone which allows interaction between you and all of your internet-connected stuff. Generally, it allows you to turn these things on and off, simply by speaking (as if we're too lazy to do it ourselves). [197] When you speak to "Alexa," accessible through various electronic devices (Amazon's Echo Dot, etc.), A VOICE COMES TO YOU FROM THE CLOUD. But, the very idea that technology has formed this virtual scenario is mind-boggling. The "voice" being heard is not a real voice, and the "cloud" is not a real cloud, but it exists technologically, nevertheless. Why is this so profound? Again, because the concept of a voice emanating from a cloud did not begin with Amazon:

---

[196] FOOTNOTE: The name "Alexa" is meant to reflect the Library of Alexandria, Egypt, which attempted to collect all of the world's knowledge. "Amazon is attempting to do the same thing," according to their own Senior Vice President of Devices and Services, David Limp. Alexandria, Egypt is also the home of the family of corrupt manuscrpts which underlie all Bible versions outside the KJV.

[197] FOOTNOTE: The technical word "cloud" is always in reference to servers or programs, not connected locally within the same computer, but linked to via the internet.

The Lord Jesus Christ on the Mount of Transfiguration, the event of the real *"voice out of the cloud."* God was telling man to listen to the voice of Christ.

> *"While he yet spake, behold, a bright cloud overshadowed them: and behold A VOICE OUT OF THE CLOUD, which said, This is my beloved Son, in whom I am well pleased; HEAR YE HIM."* Mat 17:5

> *"And there was a cloud that overshadowed them: and A VOICE CAME OUT OF THE CLOUD, saying, This is my beloved Son: HEAR HIM."* Mar 9:7

> *"And THERE CAME A VOICE OUT OF THE CLOUD, saying, This is my beloved Son: HEAR HIM."* Lk. 9:35

This company hopes that whenever we think of A VOICE FROM THE CLOUD, we do not think of the Lord Jesus Christ first, but an AI, named "Alexa." If this is not the subtle replacement of God with a

TALKING IMAGE, then what is? At the very least, it's a step in that direction, regardless of people's indifference about it. Can you not see that this is helping pave the way for the last-days image of the beast? The more science can steal the words of the Bible and apply those words to their devices, the closer we inch to calling technology "God."

David Limp, the executive in charge of Amazon's cloud-based Alexa service has stated:

> "Alexa has a whisper mode, where she'll whisper to you and understand your whispers. ... Beginning in 2020, Amazon is rolling [has rolled] out frustration detection features, so Alexa will be able to understand and acknowledge when you're getting frustrated with her." [198]

Amazon's 4th-Gen Echo Dot speaker secretly doubles as a CIA-NSA bug.

"She" hears us. "She" understands us. "She" knows when we're frustrated with "her." (She sees us when we're sleeping. She knows when we're awake) They're personifying this talking tennis ball as if it were alive. They want us to love it, speak to it, and welcome it into our homes as if it were one of our own family members. This is a subtle ploy, because supposedly helping you navigate everyday life is not all Amazon's smart speakers can do:

> "Through Amazon, which is now valued at nearly a trillion dollars and includes a cloud computing division that has A MASSIVE CONTRACT WITH THE CIA, [Jeff] Bezos is in a unique position to PLAY A ROLE IN

---

[198] Bizzaco, Michael, Rawes, Erika, Wetzel, Kim. "What is Amazon's Alexa, and what can it do?" (Digital Trends Media Group, 30, March, 2021), https://www.digitaltrends.com/home/what-is-amazons-alexa-and-what-can-it-do/3711

SHAPING not just THE FUTURE OF COMMERCE, but also THE FUTURE OF WORK, TECHNOLOGY, AND NATIONAL SECURITY. ... The increasingly ubiquitous voice known as Alexa took Amazon's DATA GATHERING to a new level. Since it first launched its Echo Dot smart speaker in 2014, Amazon has marketed the voice known as Alexa as a virtual assistant who makes NAVIGATING DAILY LIFE more efficient and entertaining. But Alexa is also a way for the company to EXTEND ITS DATA GATHERING... AMAZON EMPLOYS THOUSANDS OF PEOPLE AROUND THE WORLD TO LISTEN TO AND TRANSCRIBE SOME VOICE RECORDINGS [in our homes] in an attempt to improve the Alexa algorithm." [200]

Amazon is lying when it tells you that "improving the Alexa algorithm," is its sole purpose for eavesdropping on us. Their contract with the CIA betrays this excuse. In fact, in 2021 Amazon Web Services was awarded a secret contract with the National Security Agency worth over 9 billion dollars. [199] What does a simple online shopping website have to do with "national security"? Exactly.

The Internet of Things is the basis for all emerging "smart cities." Amazon's Alexa AI service is on the ground floor in helping build this – an electronic "Tower of Babel" with its own "voice from the cloud." No doubt it's all a forerunner to the ultimate and final speaking image. But, unlike "Alexa," no one will dare become frustrated when speaking to it:

---

[199] Bizzaco, Michael, Rawes, Erika, Wetzel, Kim. "What is Amazon's Alexa, and what can it do?" (Digital Trends Media Group, 30, March, 2021), https://www.digitaltrends.com/home/what-is-amazons-alexa-and-what-can-it-do/3711

[200] Konkel, Frank. "NSA Awards Secret $10 Billion Contract to Amazon" (Nextgov, Government Media Executive Group, 10, August, 2021), https://www.nextgov.com/it-modernization/2021/08/nsa-awards-secret-10-billion-contract-amazon/184390/

> "And he had power to GIVE LIFE UNTO THE IMAGE of the beast, that THE IMAGE OF THE BEAST SHOULD BOTH SPEAK, and cause that AS MANY AS WOULD NOT WORSHIP THE IMAGE of the beast SHOULD BE KILLED."   Rev 13:15

The sole purpose of Amazon's talking image is to make money for its master. If in doing this it helps the Antichrist rise to power, then we should be able to see more clearly why scripture declares *"the love of money"* as *"the root of all evil"* (1Tim. 6:10). Money is Amazon's reason for doing these things, it's not the Devil's reason. Satan often uses man's covetousness to reach his own goals.

LIFE IN A WEB

In sucking mankind deeper and deeper into technological world integration, a "metaverse" is now under development by several large corporations including, but not limited to, Meta (formerly known as Facebook), Google, Apple, Amazon, Microsoft, Snapchat, Sony's Epic Games division (publishers of the popular online game "Fortnite"), and LEGO (the makers of the children's plastic construction block toys). All of these businesses are considered "metaverse companies." Essentially, the metaverse is the next step in the evolution of the internet, and connection to it will require some form of real-world oversight and governance. It will also mark a time when integration for many will mean the elimination of screens and physical hardware that will give way to neurosurgical implants allowing for perpetual, lifetime connectivity.

In May 2022, the World Economic Forum (WEF) gave the following general outline for what the metaverse, in part, will be:

> "...a future persistent and INTERCONNECTED VIRTUAL ENVIRONMENT where social and economic elements MIRROR REALITY. Users can interact with it and each

other simultaneously across devices and immersive technologies while engaging with digital assets and property. ... This will have significant impacts on society. Just as the internet and smartphones transformed our social and commercial interactions, the metaverse could change the way people and businesses communicate, and operate, in innovative yet unpredictable ways. ...the metaverse will be shaped by three potential technological innovations, including VIRTUAL REALITY (VR), AUGMENTED REALITY (AR), and BRAIN-COMPUTER INTERFACES (BCI)." [201]

In speaking of machine-mind interfaces, technology which allows man to communicate directly with computers, neurosurgeon and science fiction author, Eric C. Leuthardt has stated:

"A true fluid neural integration is going to happen. It's just a matter of when. ... With current technology, I could make an implant—but HOW MANY PEOPLE ARE GOING TO WANT THAT NOW? I think it's very important to take practical, short interval steps TO GET PEOPLE MOVED ALONG THE PATHWAY TOWARD THIS ROAD of the long-term vision." [202]

Note that brain surgeon, Eric Leuthardt, recognizes that this type of thing is currently not in demand. Like many of the technologies of the nineteenth century (the telegraph, the telephone, etc.), the invention precedes the need and the market must be created. Dr. Leuthardt

---

[201] "Defining and Building the Metaverse" (The World Economic Forum, initiatives.weforum.org) https://initiatives.weforum.org/defining-and-building-the-metaverse

[202] Piore, Adam. "The Surgeon Who Wants to Connect You to the Internet with a Brain Implant" (MIT Technology Review, 30, November, 2017), https://www.technologyreview.com/2017/11/30/146863/the-surgeon-who-wants-to-connect-you-to-the-internet-with-a-brain-implant/

admits that getting people to want this stuff is a "long-term vision." First, a desire for the tech must be fostered to get people to want to go down this path.

Although the metaverse already exists in infancy, its designers intend it to be an even more immersive experience than the web of today. It is "Web 3.0," the third stage in the evolution of the World Wide Web (Web 1.0 began in 1989, and Web 2.0 emerged around 2004). Some have defined the coming metaverse as a time when "... our digital lives – our online identities, experiences, relationships, and assets – BECOME MORE MEANINGFUL TO US THAN OUR PHYSICAL LIVES." [203]

In October 2022, it was reported that the pioneering virtual reality platforms, The Sandbox and Decentraland, were both tanking as metaverse experiments. After eleven months and eight months respectively of live online activity, the projects reflected little public interest.[204] But, since when has low consumer appeal stopped these people? The billion-dollar programs will no doubt trudge ahead, despite the massive shortfalls. As was noted earlier, a spirit is driving innovation (see pages 131-135).

As if there are not already enough things in the world to occupy man's attention, the coming "Web 3.0" will cast a massive stumbling block in his path. Part of the Devil's intent, no doubt, is to distract man from his need for salvation in the Lord Jesus Christ:

> "[13] *So are the paths of all that FORGET GOD; and the hypocrite's HOPE SHALL PERISH:* [14] *WHOSE HOPE*

---

[203] Nevradakis, Michael. "WEF Launches 'Metaverse' Initiative, Predicts Digital Lives Will Become 'More Meaningful to Us Than Our Physical Lives'" (The Defender, Children's Health Defense, 02, June, 2022), https://childrenshealthdefense.org/defender/wef-metaverse-digital-physical-body/

[204] Tangermann, Victor. "$1.2 Billion Metaverse Horrified by Report It Only had 38 Active Users" (Camden Media Inc, 11, Oct, 2022), https://futurism.com/the-byte/metaverse-decentraland-report-active-users

SHALL BE CUT OFF, and WHOSE TRUST SHALL BE IN A SPIDER'S WEB." Job 8:13-14

BUILDING AN ELECTRIC ETERNITY

Part eleven of this book has addressed several things that show the Devil's fingerprints in the technologies of our day. But if you think this is where technology stops, as far as its attempts to counterfeit certain truths and promises of God, you're wrong. Modern science is not satisfied with simply providing us with an electric web to entangle ourselves. The same powers pushing this technological false hope, have plans to provide to us ETERNAL LIFE.

Any being willing to stand up and challenge the holy, Almighty God, must certainly have a few loose screws somewhere. This is the core of sin. An illogical brain too stupid to recognize that the sinless Creator wants what's best for us. But to reap these benefits, we must first deny ourselves and listen to God. This is where most people rebel, however. They want to have their cake (God's promises) and eat it too. Man's "eat it too" is his love of sin. And this is exactly what many scientists today are targeting. Patrick Wood of the excellent *Technocracy News & Trends* writes:

> "Silicon Valley is steeped in Transhuman ideology and focussed on ITS QUEST FOR HUMAN ENHANCEMENT AND ETERNAL LIFE. The problem is, their science of Transhumanism is cracked, in other words, it is bordering on 'pseudo-science'. Nevertheless, THESE ARE THE PEOPLE WHO ARE BUILDING THE TECHNOLOGY TO RUN THE WORLD. ... Technocrats believe humans are little more than a randomized bag of atoms and molecules, and hence, humans are on a par with any

Building an Electric Eternity | 281

Consider the fact that God has a plan to make men immortals, and now modern technology is working on a plan to make men immortals. Since God and modern science both have the same goal, wouldn't God be pleased with modern technology because of it? Wouldn't such man-made technology be a good thing? No. Why not? What's the difference? The difference is holy and unholy, sinless and sinful, pure and corrupt. *"Who can bring a clean thing out of an unclean? not one."* (Job 14:4) The problem with man today is that he has no concept of the "holy." He has no standards for it. The reason for this is simple. Man's wisdom is corrupt. He has no fear of God: *"The fear of the Lord is the beginning of wisdom: and the knowledge of the holy is understanding."* (Pro 9:10) Man's technology can't purge his conscience of sin, only the Blood of Christ can do that. Man-made immortality is "Hell on wheels."

other biological or non-biological thing. Their extremely low view of humanity leads them to think that we can and should be 'engineered'... Transhumans can't get THE DREAM OF ETERNAL LIFE out of their head. Since the

Transhuman community heated up in the last 30 years, thanks to advancing technology, there has not been one single scientific breakthrough that has moved them one inch closer to achieving immortality. Undeterred, they continue to look for the big 'breakthrough' that will save them from death." [205]

The important thing to understand from this is that many of the same people and companies who are building the technology of today (iPhones, computers, the internet, etc.) are the same ones pushing artificial eternal life. If this madness were not enough, there are professing "Christians" today who are jumping on this hell-bound train. In 2014, the Christian Transhumanist Association was founded. The CTA is committed to holding up transhumanist ideology as supposedly a way of "participating with God in the redemption, reconciliation, and renewal of the world." This is the same line of thinking that early, nineteenth-century spiritists held regarding the technologies of their day. As one authority has rightly stated:

> "Ready to experiment with new machines, medical theories, and avant-garde forms of knowledge, Spiritualism remained convinced that SCIENCE WOULD FURTHER RATHER THAN ERODE RELIGION." [206]

The very idea that eternal life can be manufactured like a machine is rank heresy. Such a belief ignores the sin nature of man (Heb. 9:14, 22). Scripture says that if this is your mindset, you're cursed:

> *"Thus saith the LORD; CURSED be the man that TRUSTETH IN MAN, and maketh flesh his arm, and whose heart departeth from the LORD."* Jer. 17:5

---

[205] Levin, Susan. "Silicon Valley's Transhuman Obsession Is Fundamentally Flawed" (Technocracy News & Trends, Coherent Publishing, 30, March, 2022), https://www.technocracy.news/?s=eternal+life

[206] Partridge, Christopher. The Occult World (Routledge: London, 2015), p. 204

Transhumanists are attempting to CREATE IMMORTAL SINNERS. They have no concept of an eternity *"wherein dwelleth righteousness."* (2Ptr. 3:13) God will not tolerate a sinner who has immortal life. This is the very reason Adam was driven from the garden after he ate the forbidden fruit. You either take salvation God's way (Rom. 5:16), or you don't get it at all:

> "[22] *...lest he [Adam] put forth his hand, and take also of the tree of life, and eat, and LIVE FOR EVER:* [23] *THEREFORE THE LORD GOD SENT HIM FORTH FROM THE GARDEN of Eden...* [24] *So HE DROVE OUT THE MAN; and he placed at the east of the garden of Eden Cherubims, and a flaming sword which turned every way, to keep the way of the tree of life."* Gen. 3:22-24

Eternal life is one of the most important issues addressed by the Bible. Acquiring such is fundamental to man's need for a Saviour–the Lord Jesus Christ. Christians need to recognize, now that the secular world is beginning to discuss things like ETERNAL LIFE, that the addressing of such vital scriptural issues signals that man is nearing something momentous. Not in the fact that something marvelous is about to happen, but that attempts to artificially duplicate immortality demonstrate THE MOVING OF SATAN'S HAND AT DEEP LEVELS IN SOCIETY (the Devil's original lie was *"Ye shall not surely die..."* Gen. 3:4). The only remaining matter to hash out is the reality of God. Since the world is now injecting TECHNOLOGY into its concept of an endless life, does this indicate it will eventually inject a technological perspective on God? Consider that the book of Daniel tells us that when Satan takes the world throne, he will be worshiped as *"the God of forces"* and one that will be honored with *"gold, and silver, and with precious stones"* – the very ingredients of SMART TECHNOLOGY (Dan. 11:38). The profound thing about Daniel uniting the word *"forces"* with gold, silver, and gems is that the primary force in the world today that's associated with these things is ELECTRICITY, formerly known as LIGHTNING:

> *"...I beheld Satan as lightning fall from heaven."* Lk. 10:18

What if, in speaking these words, Christ wasn't only teaching us important details regarding *"the prince of the power of the air,"* but was literally PROPHESYING OF FUTURE EVENTS? A future where the Devil would be manipulating and imitating such forces to where he leads the whole world into worshiping him. Electricity is the backbone of modern technology. Lighting is the backbone of electricity. Without it there is no world wide web, no interconnected future, and no technological world order.

THE PROBLEM WITH TECHNOLOGY IS SIN

It's often been said that "technology is neither good nor evil." I would generally agree with this, but the concept can't be taken all the way in light of scripture. Ask yourself if such an accusation can be leveled at God regarding the Lord's technologies? Are heavenly technologies "neither good nor evil"? Take the holy city of New Jerusalem, for example. Is it neither good nor evil? What about the Ark of the Covenant which the Lord forbad anyone from touching lest they die? Was it a neutral thing? (Num. 4:15, 2Sa. 6:6) When the Philistines stole the Ark of the Covenant from the Israelites did the Ark then become evil because an evil people then had it? No (1Sa. 6). What about the Chariot of the Cherubim? Is such a thing separate from being good or evil, or is it like any man-made device? Can the technologies of God be neutral? I don't think so.

While the literal materials used in the construction of an invention are not innately "good" or "evil" (metal, wood, concrete, stone, silver, gold, plastic, etc.), the issue with a device is not simply with THE PHYSICAL CONTRIVANCE ITSELF, but with THE INVENTOR OF IT. But comparing God's technology to man's technology may not be exactly fair. After all, man can't create anything that's "holy," unless God has a direct hand in it (Psa. 127:1). What the Christian mustn't ignore is that THE DEVIL CAN ALSO PLAY A ROLE IN

TECHNOLOGY. When this happens, does the technology remain neutral? Take the city and tower of Babel, for example. Was it good, evil, holy, or unholy? Someone may say, "Yeah, but had good, godly men built..." -- but good, godly men didn't. The Bible has an advantage in these things because IT KNOWS MAN'S HEART AND CAN SEE THINGS IN HINDSIGHT, whereas we cannot. The Bible knows the future, and looking at man's technology from God's perspective, it can look back and see the whole of these things. Do you believe that the Holy God of history is going to look at any technology of fallen man as a good thing? I don't believe that the Lord's looking down on earth today and thinking, "Look at all that neutral technology going to waste!" And I don't think any Bible-believer would dare classify the Tower of Babel as being a "neutral" development. Its intent was certainly unholy (Gen. 11:1-9). The ironic thing about this is that "Babel" is being built all over again today with modern technology. The only difference is that God's not stopping it. Is God allowing this to move forward in our twenty-first-century because it's a good thing? No, he's letting it move forward because it's the fulfillment of prophecy (see Zep. 3:8).

When we take into account the increase in knowledge in the last days (Dan. 12:4); and take into account the rampant wickedness, unholiness, deception, and demon activity; and take into account that this is a time when the world is preparing itself to crown the Devil; then I would not hesitate to call the technology of our age "evil". And I don't believe that the Lord would be disappointed in us for making such a statement. At the very least, the technology of today is unholy, regardless of what a Christian may use it for. After all, this world is not our home.

We can use the things of this world for God's glory, but that does not make it any less unholy or fallen. God's going to burn it all up, regardless (Joel 2:3, 2Ptr 3:10-13)). We can cut down trees and print gospel tracts, books, Bibles, or hymns, or build churches. We can "network" to help spread the Good News of the Lord Jesus Christ. But our goal is not to stay here--WE'RE LEAVING (1Cor. 15:52). In the end, the question is not, "is technology good or evil," but "is man good or evil"? There's no way around it folks, a world of godless, evil men creates godless, evil things. As the Bible says, *"Who can bring a clean thing out of an unclean? not one." (Job 14:4)*, and as such, its technology will never be "good" in the eyes of the Holy God. Note the following verses and tell me that some technologies are not intrinsically evil:

> *"Behold, I know your thoughts, and THE DEVICES WHICH YE WRONGFULLY IMAGINE against me."*
> Job 21:27

> *"For THEY INTENDED EVIL against thee: THEY IMAGINED A MISCHIEVOUS DEVICE..."* Psa. 21:11

> *"...fret not thyself...because of the man who bringeth WICKED DEVICES to pass."* Psa. 37:7

> *"GRANT NOT, O LORD, THE DESIRES OF THE WICKED: further not his WICKED DEVICE..."*
> Psa. 140:8

> *"A good man obtaineth favour of the LORD: but A MAN OF WICKED DEVICES will he condemn."*
> Pro. 12:2

When Noah Webster published his *An American Dictionary of the English Language* in 1828, he relied heavily on the *King James Bible* for defining words in the English language. In many, many instances he even listed scripture to show the meaning of a word. Webster is famous for saying, "Education is useless without the Bible." Here's what his 1828 dictionary said about the word "device":

> "That which is formed by design, or INVENTED; scheme; artificial contrivance; stratagem; project; sometimes in a good sense; MORE GENERALLY IN A BAD SENSE, as artifices ARE USUALLY EMPLOYED FOR BAD PURPOSES."

The Bible says that we, as born-again Christians, *"...look for new heavens and a new earth, wherein dwelleth RIGHTEOUSNESS."* (2Ptr 3:13) That's the key. None of the technology made by the Lord is "neutral," because none of it was conceived in sin. All technology of God is good. The same cannot be said of man who can actually become polluted and corrupted with his works:

> *"Thus were they DEFILED WITH THEIR OWN WORKS, and went a whoring with their own INVENTIONS."* Psa. 106:39

Earlier, we brought to light how that scripture says nothing about man building or inventing anything until after Cain is CURSED and DEPARTS *"from the presence of the LORD"* (see Gen. 4). This first mention of MAN'S CREATIVE ACTS appears to set some kind of general precedent for such things hereafter. It speaks to the fact of how much of the life of man became VAIN AND FUTILE once sin separated him from the Holy God (Gen. 3). As King Solomon wrote:

> *"[2] Vanity of vanities, saith the Preacher, vanity of vanities; all is vanity. ... [14] I have seen ALL THE WORKS that are done under the sun; and, behold, all is vanity and vexation of spirit. "* Ecc. 1:2, 14

> *"...The Lord knoweth THE THOUGHTS OF THE WISE, that they are vain."* 1Cor. 3:20

PART XII

SUMMARY & CLOSING COMMENTS

Satanology - History - Prophecy - Technology

"Thou wilt keep him in perfect peace, whose mind is stayed on thee: because he trusteth in thee." Isaiah 26:3

FINAL WORDS & THOUGHTS

ONE OF THE primary objectives of this study in Satanology was to try and recognize the workings of the Adversary in modern history. This book has attempted to present real-world ways in which the Devil is fulfilling his title of the Prince of the Power of the Air. Scripture leaves no room for belief in the absence of the Devil. For Satan to be torpid or inactive is not the hallmark of a *"principality."* To the contrary, perhaps we're the ones asleep, because scripture informs us that he, and those under his command, are constantly on the prowl. *"Be SOBER, be VIGILANT..."* is our admonishment (1Ptr. 5:8). If an enemy's sitting around doing nothing, there's no need for vigilance. Because we're in enemy territory, we're not here to get comfortable, but to take up the sword and be soldiers (Eph. 6:10-17).

In learning more about the Devil in our age, we first needed to recognize that the God of the Bible is THE GOD OF HISTORY. This means that the Lord is actively moving in man's everyday life. This is likewise true of Satan. Any major history you may read (whether it be world history, church history, the history of the Bible, etc.), if that "history" does not take into account the movements of God or the Devil, then it is a SECULAR HISTORY, regardless of what the work may call itself. In other words, to ignore the Devil's presence in everyday life is to adopt the mindset of a lost man. This should never be the Christian's attitude.

What's been discovered is that the Devil's involvement is linked to his title as the Prince of the Power of the Air. This name has important ties to what's going on in the world today. The direct scripture reference for this designation speaks of the name in the context of being "...*the spirit that now worketh in the children of disobedience...*" (Eph. 2:2). Here's a brief rundown of some of the more outstanding and salient things we've covered:

1.) SATAN CARRIES three important titles of "*prince*": (1) The PRINCE OF THE DEVILS; (2) the PRINCE OF THIS WORLD; and (3) the PRINCE OF THE POWER OF THE AIR. The first name relates to Satan's authority over the DEMONIC REALM; the second communicates his hold over THE WORLD OF MAN; the third speaks to his power over THE EARTH'S ATMOSPHERE. Thus, the Devil is a principality over a SPIRIT REALM (devils), an EARTHLY REALM (kingdoms of this world), and a HEAVENLY REALM (skies of the earth). All these things are interrelated and overlap. Collectively, the titles help encapsulate why the Devil is currently referred to as "*the god of this world*" (2Cor. 4:4).

2.) THE BIBLE PHRASE "*of the air*" primarily relates to "*fowl*" (birds, bats, insects) and the region in which they fly. Therefore, it's no great surprise to learn that the Devil also holds the title of "*Beelzebub*," or "*Baalzebub*." The name means "Lord of the Flies" [207] which, perhaps, may further indicate in a more general sense "Lord of Flying Things"

Owls present an intriguing look into unclean spirits

due to the scope of his authority over the air. If we study the behavior of birds, bats, and bugs, especially those that the Bible describes as "*unclean,*" it will teach us things about devils. One of the more profound, if not obvious, things which fowl make apparent regarding demons is that they're HIGHLY ACTIVE IN EARTH'S ATMOSPHERE. They possibly often travel in swift-moving aerial swarms which appear to operate with a hive-like mentality.

3.) THE DEVIL'S "*power of the air*" extends to weather-related events like the wind. This alone can lead to numerous other types of atmospheric phenomena including straight-line winds, microbursts, macrobursts, downbursts, thunderstorms, dust storms, dust devils, hurricanes, tornados, lightning, hail, as well as falling fire. Satan can interfere with the natural occurrences of these different things, in addition to having the power to create them himself. He does this by manipulating the air in highly sophisticated and elaborate ways comparable to his deep knowledge of it. The Lord God and angels can also create, control, and impact the weather, but this book has not focused on that aspect, it is a separate study. And finally, it's pertinent to stress that none of this has been said to give the impression that the powers of Satan are somehow limited to the air. Rather, the emphasis is to highlight his ADVANCED AUTHORITY in this area

---

[207] FOOTNOTE: The "Zebub" name was not just indicative of "fly" types of insects, but A WIDE VARIETY OF AERIAL CREEPING CREATURES. "The name 'Baal-zebub' means 'the lord of flies'......we entertain little doubt that Baal-zebub, 'the fly-god,' is the name by which this idol [demon] was recognized by his worshippers. ...this Baal obtained the surname of Ze-bub on account of his being considered to protect the town or district...from the visitation of GNATS AND OTHER TROUBLESOME INSECTS...There is however another opinion concerning Baal-zebub, which deserves attention: this is, that Baal-zebub was not a fly-expelling god, but was himself AN INSECT GOD, analogous to the scarabaeus or beetle of the Egyptians... We do not, after all, see why these two opinions may not coalesce, and Baalzebub be at the same time an insect-god and an expeller of insects... Whether he was worshipped in the human or insect form, or as a combination of both, the evidence of Phoenician coins only can determine. We know, however, that in other instances, the same idol may exhibit three varieties of form -- human, animal, and both combined." [SOURCE: *The Holy Bible According to the Authorized Version, Containing the Old and New Testaments: with Original Notes and Pictorial Illustrations.* Volume II. Charles Knight & Co., London, 1837. p. 218]

and to demonstrate why he has been labeled a *"prince"* over it.

4.) THE BIBLE PHRASE *"Satan as lightning,"* (Lk. 10:18) describes another feature of the Devil's aerial power. Natural lightning is an air-centric, electrical, phenomenon as both flashes and bolts are formed in the air and by the air. Thunderbolts carry the earth's most intense heat and were anciently referred to as "fireballs," "the fire of heaven," "the fire of God," etc. Such forces may manifest during thunderstorms, hurricanes, snowstorms, large forest fires, volcanic explosions, surface nuclear detonations, and even out of a cloudless sky. Bolts can materialize both visibly and invisibly. Things like radio waves can also be created by lightning. Lightning is a form of "electricity," and therefore extends satanic influence over into THE REALM OF ELECTRONICS. This bumps us into a major conundrum, as it brings into question Satan's relationship with electrical phenomena in regards to man's recent discovery and utilization of it.

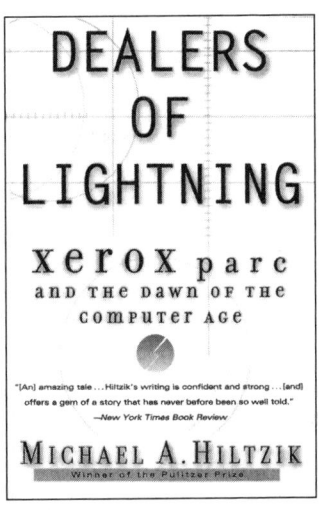

A book addressing an elite group of inventors at Xerox that played a pivotal role in the Computer Age.

5.) THE FORCE we call "electricity" has been a longtime mystery to man, even extending into the twenty-first-century. Much of our advanced technologies today are dependent upon it. One of the strange things about this phenomenon is that it has some kind of UNKNOWN

CONNECTION WITH THE SPIRIT REALM. The fact that the Devil has sway over lightning, unclean spirits, and fallen man should cause the Christian to consider the implications of this. Because, in these things (the three realms of Satan's princeships: air, demons, and the world) THE DEVIL'S INFLUENCE OVER SPIRITS AND ELECTRICITY OVERLAPS. Man's age of electricity directly coincided with an eruption in humanism, materialism, Marxism, liberalism, occultism, demonism, the birth of globalism, advances in knowledge and technology, and theories of "God is Dead" (Nietzsche, 1880s). This history falls in line with scripture which describes an increase in end-times WISDOM AND KNOWLEDGE parallel to an age of EVIL MEN and SEDUCING SPIRITS.

6.) ONE OF THE MOST important issues that's been touched upon in this book is the abject inability of BIOLOGY or ZOOLOGY to recognize the spirits which indwell living men and animals. This is the primary reason why science is unable to distinguish between living matter and dead. This grand lapse in knowledge serves as a wakeup call to the ignorance of science regarding spirit activity in ANY FIELD OF STUDY. What is science incapable of telling us about spirit involvement in PHYSICS? What about ASTRONOMY? What about METEOROLOGY? What about Geology, Cosmology, Psychology, Geography, Sociology, Bacteriology, Entomology, Technology, Crystallography, Electronics? This should help the reader grasp the enormity of the stupidity of science and help illustrate how DEMONIC INVOLVMENT AND ACTIVITY can slip by completely unnoticed in many areas. Now are you beginning to understand why the Bible says "...*the world by wisdom knew not God...*" and why "...*the wisdom of this world is foolishness with God...*"? (1Cor. 1:21, 3:19). I think it can also be fairly stated that, "the world by wisdom, knows not the Devil."

7.) THE SO-CALLED "Age of Enlightenment" and the Industrial Revolutions were proliferate with an explosion in innovation and technology. Mankind began to invent new devices and machines at an unprecedented rate. One stunning aspect to all this was that many of these inventions were conceived by MULTIPLE MINDS during the same era without any of the creators being aware of the other. Generally, scripture speaks negatively of man's imagination and also highlights the fact that higher wisdom and knowledge can be IMPARTED TO MANKIND THROUGH SPIRITS. However, because the Bible does not describe the latter days as an age of god-fearing men, we can know that THE EXPANDING WISDOM OF THE TIME IS NOT FOUNDED IN GOD. Scripture outlines how information can be spread to hundreds of men through the activity of a single lying spirit. Such action provides a foundation for the phenomenon of "SIMULTANEOUS INVENTION." A fact of modern technology which has dogged and baffled the academic world for years.

8.) ONE OF THE INITIAL compelling pieces of evidence which demonstrated a connection with spirits and electrical events, was found by comparing what the Bible says happens to our body at death, with what science says happens to our body at death. One says electrical current ceases, while the other says a ghost departs. This opens a brief window into some type of relationship and gives us a springboard to launch off of in further studying the issue. Throughout history, some individuals that encountered electricity, simultaneously, experienced an awakening to the PARANORMAL. Many native cultures around the world have long been familiar with the mystery between LIGHTNING and OCCULT POWERS. These ancient peoples have admitted that any form of electrical shock, including lighting strikes and fire balls, can enable one to have intercourse with spirits. The evidence shows that the fallout of such is sometimes analogous to the acquiring of mystical abilities including divination, mind-reading, clairvoyance, astral projection, ghost manifestations, and the like. The Bible links these things to demonism. These are BLATANT EXAMPLES OF DEMON ACTIVITY ASSOCIATED WITH LITERAL ENCOUNTERS WITH ELECTRIC PHENOMENA.

9.) THROUGHOUT HISTORY, many accounts of unexplained happenings have had ties to electric-type events. Some of these incidences use the word "lightning" in their names. "Ball lightning" is one example of this. This phenomenon appears as a moving type of AERIAL LIGHT, often spherical. It frequently displays some form of intelligence and cannot be explained by conventional physics. Modern science has long tried to deny this mystery because it upsets their apple cart.

10.) UNDERSTANDING THE BIBLE'S two kinds of supernaturalism helps us to understand how a spirit-electric relationship is possible. The OVERT form of supernatural activity manifests as an outright subjugation of natural law. In this, laws are openly observed to be bent or broken. This is what people generally classify as "supernatural." In its COVERT form, however, no such characteristics are produced. The event outwardly appears "natural," even though it's not. This is a profound

EXAMPLES OF THE TWO KINDS OF SUPERNATURALISM

COVERT: God-manifest-in-the-flesh dies on the cross.

OVERT: God-manifest-in-the-flesh ascends into heaven.

revelation and offers up a scenario of how the Prince of the Power of the Air can be active in our age without us even knowing it. Scripture testifies that spirits can utilize men or the forces of nature without being detected. This ability is not only due to the invisibility of spirits but also to their ability to work through such things without manifesting any outward supernatural signs. Believe it or not, the majority of the Bible's cases of events where something beyond the natural is taking place, yet remained undetected, are more numerous than cases where such things were obvious to the naked eye. There are more Bible examples of COVERT SUPERNATURALISM than there are of OVERT SUPERNATURALISM. Most supernatural events are not presented as a man walking on water, but more like the Star of Bethlehem, where an angel was hidden by what outwardly appeared to be a genuine celestial event (see the book *Star of the King* for more information on this). This leaves us with the question: WHAT PARTS OF SCIENCE TODAY ARE UNKNOWINGLY TEACHING US LIES REGARDING THE OPERATION OF THE SUPERNATURAL? Regardless of the extent, it is most certainly going on. In quantifying this question, the thing that lies at its heart is the breadth and depth of SATAN'S POWER. Is it a little or a lot? Does scripture describe this age as one of minuscule impact from the demonic realm or the opposite?

11.) THE TWENTIETH and twenty-first centuries witnessed an exponential increase in the use of GOLD, DIAMONDS, AND PRECIOUS STONES. This was not due to a growth in fine jewelry or ornaments but in ADVANCED TECHNOLOGIES LIKE ELECTRONICS AND COMPUTERS. Parallel to this, the scriptures had long associated the highest technologies with such things. Quartz stones (like the agate, jasper, onyx, chalcedony, amethyst, beryl, and emerald) represent some of the most common minerals used in industry today. These can be found not only in modern "smart technologies" but in heavenly technologies. While man's devices are enlightened and powered by ELECTRICITY, the Lord's devices are enlightened and powered by THE GLORY OF GOD. Thus, some of today's most advanced technologies may be evolving into counterfeits of God's works. Currently, science is planning an electronic form of "eternal life" -- fake immortality fabricated by a merger in human biology and the computer sciences.

Gold, diamonds and gems are important components in God's technology and modern technology.

12.) RECOGNIZING SOME FORM of deep link between electricity and the spirit realm provides a foundation for understanding how the nineteenth-century ELECTRIC AGE RAN PARALLEL WITH A DEMONIC INVASION. Occult authorities admit outright that the nineteenth-century witnessed substantial growth in occult matters. Spiritism introduced the mainstream public to spirit intercourse and early "New-Age," theosophical-type philosophies. The electrical technologies of the era birthed modern industrialization and paved the way for an electronic, computerized, networked GLOBAL AGE –– one that will eventually enthrone THE PRINCE OF THE POWER OF THE AIR.

13.) THIS STUDY has said quite a lot about modern science and its SADDUCAICAL DOCTRINES––there are no angels, no spirits, and no resurrection (Acts 23:8). This position is one of the foremost mindsets of our time, especially in academic circles. If a thing can't be measured, heard, felt or SEEN, then it doesn't exist. Such a belief means that when the Antichrist finally does make a physical entrance, PULLING DOWN FIRE IN THE SIGHT OF MEN, the whole world will follow this *"God of forces"* (Dan 11:38). Like the sevants of Job who were duped by Satan, they will mistakenly believe:

"... *The fire of GOD is fallen from heaven...*" Job 1:16

In their denial of the spirit realm, secular education has molded its students into HUMANISTIC MATERIALISTS. This creates an atmosphere where the knowledge of man is elevated into a position too high for itself. Scripture speaks of this last-days attitude as highmindedness (2Tim. 3:1-5). Webster says "proud, arrogant":

"... *be not highminded, but fear*"   Rom. 11:20

"[23] *Thus saith the LORD, Let not the wise man glory in his wisdom...* [24] *But let him that glorieth glory in this, that he UNDERSTANDETH AND KNOWETH ME...*"
Jer. 9:23-24

"*PRIDE goeth before destruction, and an HAUGHTY SPIRIT before a fall.*"
Prov. 16:18

"*And the loftiness of man shall be bowed down, and the haughtiness of men shall be made low: and the LORD alone shall be exalted in that day.*"
Isa. 2:17

14.) THE ELECTRIC AGE brought with it ARTIFICIAL LIGHT, while on the same hand marking an age of SPIRITUAL DARKNESS. Contrary to the secular sermons of the day, the universe we live in is not one based on science alone. The basis of reality is a supernatural one, only made possible by "*...the high and lofty One that inhabiteth eternity...*" (Isa. 57:15) Christ and the scriptures are the "*key of knowledge*" which unlock this truth (Lk. 11:52). By these things we realize that history entails real accounts of:

Wingless flying men (Mk. 16:19, Lk. 24:50-51, Acts 1:9-11, Rev. 11:3-12, etc.); Talking animals (Num. 22:28-30 etc.); Giants (Gen. 6:1-4, Num. 13:17-33, etc.); Invaders from beyond earth (Rev. 19:11-15, Joel 2:1-11, Gen. 6:1-4, etc.); Talking images (Rev. 13:11-15); Flying horses (2Kgs. 2:22, Rev. 19:11-14); Monsters from under the earth (Rev. 9:1-6); Plants, animals, and men immune to fire (Ex. 3:2, 2Kgs. 2:11, Dan. 3:19-30, etc.); Animals controlled by devils (Mt. 8:30-32, etc.); Men who literally vanished off the face of the earth (Gen. 5:21-24, Deut. 34:5-6, etc.); Physical, visible wounds inflicted by evil spirits (Lk. 9:39); a man who can literally read minds (Job 42:4, Psa. 94:10, Mt. 9:4, Lk. 11:17, etc.); a man who controls the weather (Mt. 8:23-26, Mk. 4:37-41, etc.); Men who lived for hundreds of years (Gen. 5, etc.); Men with superhuman strength (Mt. 8:23-26, Mk. 4:37-41, etc.) The Bible reveals all these things and more. In grasping these fantastic events, this opens the door to realizing the magnitude of Satan in our time and enables us to shed any feeble beliefs we may have about this enemy. There's no reason for us to believe that demonic operations are any less astonishing (like through the phenomenon of electricity). They may be less obvious, but they're no less miraculous. If we do not return to a supernatural, Bible-based, view of reality, all are doomed to fall under the spell of the demon prince of the empire of the air:

> "...your faith should not stand in the WISDOM OF MEN, but in THE POWER OF GOD." 1Cor. 2:5

The Prince of the Power of the Air and the Last Days has served as a wake-up call of sorts. An admonishing to today's Christian to not fall into the trap of ignoring Satan's hand in the world. We are not to realize this as a weak or superficial thing, but as one hell-bent on leading mankind to a place of no return (Rev. 20:9-13). It is only the power of God, the written words of God, which reveals to us the sweeping scope of the Devil's power. Are you prepared to believe it?

> *"He that committeth sin is of the devil; for the devil sinneth from the beginning. FOR THIS PURPOSE the Son of God was manifested, that he might DESTROY THE WORKS OF THE DEVIL"* 1John 3:8

APPENDIX
THE CURSE THAT GOETH FORTH OVER THE FACE OF THE WHOLE EARTH

In *Part VII: The God of Forces*, under the section titled *Something Unknown is in the Air* (page 101), we talked about the spherical, aerial light phenomenon, more commonly known as "ball lightning." In this appendix I've added a few more notes on the issue that I did not want to put in the body of the book's text. The information contained here is supplementary and elaborates a bit more on the subject. Hopefully, this extra content will edify the reader, if not give them a little more to think about.

> [1] *Then I turned, and lifted up mine eyes, and looked, and behold a flying roll.*
> [2] *And he said unto me, What seest thou? And I answered, I see a flying roll; the length thereof is twenty cubits, and the breadth thereof ten cubits.*
> [3] *Then said he unto me, This is the curse that goeth forth over the face of the whole earth: for every one that stealeth shall be cut off as on this side according to it; and every one that sweareth shall be cut off as on that side according to it.*
> [4] *I will bring it forth, saith the LORD of hosts, and it shall enter into the house of the thief, and into the house of him that sweareth falsely by my name: and it shall remain in the midst of his house, and shall consume it with the timber thereof and the stones thereof.*
>
> Zech. 5:1-4

While it's practically a certainty that the prophet Zechariah is not writing in these verses about "ball lightning." Nevertheless, when this riddle is compared with scripture, tested, proved, and the spirits tried (1Thess. 5:21 & 1Jn. 4:1), this is one of the primary places where we find light. This is because, even thought all the details of the mystery do not align with Zechariah one hundred percent, I believe that these scriptures do provide PARTIAL LIGHT. Here are the details of these verses which best parallel this enigma:

> 1.) Like Zechariah's "roll," ball lightning manifests as a MYSTERIOUS FLYING THING that can sometimes appear "roll" or scroll-shaped – a long, cylindrical rod, sometimes referred to as "cigar" (one witness described his encounter as horizontal shafts of moving light reminiscent of *Star Wars* "light sabers"). On page 183 of this book, we addressed one victim's experience with a rod-shaped, exploding, flying thing.
>
> 2.) Like Zechariah's "roll," ball lightning has entered into houses and consumed the wood and the stone. There are scores of historical accounts of this happening. Is there any mystery, anywhere in the history of the world, that matches the words of Zechariah better on this point than the atmospheric luminous globe? Show it to me.

Regardless if Zechariah is not talking specifically about our puzzling phenomenon, what these scriptures do for us, nevertheless, is that THEY LINK THIS MYSTERY TO SOME KIND OF CURSE FOUND IN THE AIR. Or, as the angel in Zechariah puts it, *"THE CURSE THAT GOETH FORTH OVER THE FACE OF THE WHOLE EARTH"* (Zech. 5:3).

The first curse in the history of the universe was Satan. He became a LITERAL CURSE (Damnation Incarnate – see the book *The Amazing Prophecy of Job* for more information on this) after he sinned and fell. He is now the Prince of the Power of the Air, the God of this World (Eph. 2:2, 2Cor 4:4). Scripture not only demonstrates that the Devil has power over weather phenomena, but he now has some kind of direct connection with, and power over, the force of lightning (Lk. 10:18).

Since time immemorial, the ball-lightning mystery has indeed been a bane to mankind (a curse). All those who DENY GOD and THE SUPERNATURAL, have not been able to explain its existence. For the modern scientist, this is maddening. While the vast majority of physicists ignore it, there are those that have recognized it, honestly evaluated it, and drawn some astounding conclusions:

> "'Ball' or 'globe' lightning...These baffling balls simply do not act like lightning. Their very form is contrary to the laws governing atmospheric electricity and...are inexplicable within the limits of present knowledge. ... The real mystery of ball lightning is not so much in its formation as in its abilities. If it is electrical in nature, why does it occasionally ignore conductors? Balls have skipped over steeples, bells, and transmission wires, yet continued on their merry, mysterious way. ...why does ball lightning sometimes exhibit animal-like curiosity in exploring houses and other structures?" [1]

Author and scientist, William R. Corliss, in his excellent and recommended, 400-plus-page *Handbook of Unusual Natural Phenomena*, reports:

> "Thousands of people have seen ball lightning, and hundreds of scientists have written about it. Nevertheless it remains as inscrutable as ever [impossible to understand or interpret]. Science admits the objective reality of these strange, mobile globes of light, but has been unsuccessful at explaining their origin or their EXPLOSIVE DEMISE. One reason ball lightning resists explanation is that its nature is so variable. It may be as small as a pea or as large as a house. ... Ball lightning is a dynamic thing. It may glide silently and disinterestedly pass an observer

or it may inquisitively explore a room as if directed by intelligence. ... Observers, however, have no doubt that something palpable has visited them because the room is usually filled with the smell of electricity (ozone) and there may be CONSIDERABLE MATERIAL DAMAGE. ... Ball lightning FREQUENTLY EXPLODES VIOLENTLY upon appearing, and in doing so may sometimes CAUSE EXTENSIVE DAMAGE. THE ROD-SHAPED VARIETY, however, ALWAYS SEEMS TO DETONATE WITH CONSIDERABLE VIOLENCE. ... One of the spookiest aspects of ball lightning is its ability to MATERIALIZE INSIDE ROOMS, even in all-metal AIRCRAFT, often with no evidence of penetration anywhere." [2]

Corliss goes on to describe these detonating, "rod-shaped" forms as "malevolent." Or, as the prophet Zechariah puts it, a "curse" like a "flying roll" that can enter into a house and *"consume it with the timber thereof and the stones thereof."* However, not all of these glowing light orbs enter houses or explode. Corliss concludes:

"No reasonable explanation exists for ball lightning. Glowing spheres of plasma created by natural electromagnetic forces have been proposed and found wanting. Others have suggested antimatter meteorites, violent chemical reactions in the atmosphere, and even intense cosmic radiation. The sheer difficulty in accounting for ball lightning has led some scientists to claim that all such observations are illusory—aberrations of the eye and brain. But photographs of ball lightning do exist and we must come to terms with the reality of this phenomena." [4]

"The ancients were well aware of the reality of 'thunderbolts' and 'fireballs,' and considered them to have their origin in the manufactories of the gods. Though the observers of the distant past had no real idea of the true nature of such wonders, they were certainly not so obtuse as to deny their existence. Since the mid-1800s, however, there have been intermittent assaults on the credibility of 'ball lightning' observations, despite INDISPUTABLE EVIDENCE having been published in SCIENTIFIC WORKS such as the *Philosophical Transactions of the Royal Society*." [5]

In his book, *The Taming of the Thunderbolts*, physicist, Maxwell Cade, writes:

> "Because of the strangeness of thunderbolts [ball lightning], their 'other-worldly' behaviour and appearance, they have proved very difficult for orthodox thinkers [scientists] to accept. Many writers who were rational enough in other ways have denied the possibility of thunderbolts...we have followed some of the arguments about ball lightning, and shown the refusal to accept the phenomenon on the part of some eminent authorities... Some of the nineteenth-century writers on thunderbolts made it painfully clear that they were quite unwilling, or unable, to accept anything that was not clearly in accordance with established doctrine [scientific theory]." [6]

A case of indoor ball lightning from southern France as reported by professor M. Schnaufer. The ball rolled over the floor, rose close to the startled girl, without touching her, and left the house by way of the chimney, exploding over the roof with a violent detonation. See *Modern Mechanix and Inventions*. November, p. 99-101

Cade proceeds to accuse mainstream science of "bigotry" regarding this subject:

> "By 'bigotry' is to be understood the contemptuous dismissal by unbelieving orthodoxy [mainstream science] of anything which is not clearly explainable by contemporary theories. It is this attitude which has delayed the acceptance and serious study of ball lightning by scientists for at least a century [mid 1800s]." [7]

The reason why most of modern science refuses to acknowledge this phenomena, is because it throws a monkey wrench into their theories of reality. They're not into "science" for the true purpose of it, many of them. To them, science has become a RELIGION (see pages 179-181, etc). A faith by which they can explain-away the supernatural (namely, God and the Devil). Therefore, anything that threatens this nature-only worldview is scoffed at and discarded. Like the gentleman said, they're "bigots." And, unfortunately, today these men have the upper hand in academia. But be that as it may, the head of the ball lightning division of the UK-based Tornado and Storm Research Organization has rightly assessed:

> "Ball Lightning...presents one of the greatest problems to plague those whose lives are governed by science and logic..." [8]

That quotation was not taken from some backwoods rube of the dark ages, but a secular scientist in the twenty-first century—— an evolutionist, if you can believe it. One that seems to realize that "science" doesn't hold all the answers. Science is not the be-all-end-all of truth, and never will be. But the Lord Jesus Christ, in *"whom are hid all the treasures of wisdom and knowledge,"* is another matter (Col. 2:3).

It is the belief of this author that the "ball lightning" phenomenon may very well be a part of *"the curse that goeth forth over the face of the whole earth"* —— a working of the Prince of the Power of the Air. If Satan can't be classified as a "curse" in operation on the face of the whole earth, then, what is he? (See Job 1:7, 2:2, 1Ptr. 5:8, etc.)

APPENDIX FOOTNOTES:

[1] Gaddis H., Vincent, Mysterious Fires And Lights, New Saucerian Press, London. 2017, p. 49-50

[2] Corliss, William R. Handbook of Unusual Natural Phenomena. (Gramercy Books & Random House: Avenel, NJ, 1977), p. 17, 18, 22 & 25

[[3] Ibid., p. 22

[[4] Ibid., p. 18

[[5] Van Doorn, Peter. "What in Heaven or Hell is 'Ball Lightning' ?" (Ball Lightning and Globular Light-emitting Objects (GLOs), The Nexus Research Project, 2011), www.ball-lightning.info

[[6] Cade, C. Maxwell, and Davis, Delphanie. The Taming of the Thunderbolts. (Abelard-Schuman: New York, NY, 1969) p. 13-14

[[7] Ibid., p. 30

[[8] Van Doorn, Peter. "What in Heaven or Hell is 'Ball Lightning' ?" (Ball Lightning and Globular Light-emitting Objects (GLOs), The Nexus Research Project, 2011), www.ball-lightning.info

INDEX

A

Aamon 41
Aaron 50, 56, 87
Aaron's Rod 50
Abel 15, 108
Abraham 15, 141, 145
Adam 108, 112, 154, 235, 248, 265, 272, 278, 283
Adversary 13, 60, 291
Aerial Phenomena 19, 60, 66, 67, 81, 199, 206
Aeronautics 83
Age of Enlightenment 102, 103, 234, 295
Age of Reason 102
Agnostic 100, 210
Ahab 126, 127
Aholiab 130
Air 14, 17-19, 23-26, 28, 29, 32, 33, 35, 36, 45, 51, 60, 64, 67, 69, 73, 76, 80, 81, 83, 84, 88, 89, 91, 92, 94-96, 125, 126, 145, 147, 148-152, 154-156, 158-160, 168, 169, 177, 181, 183-185, 187, 191, 192, 194, 197, 202, 204, 205, 208, 210, 226, 284, 292, 294, 301
Aircraft 91, 94, 145, 198
Airplane 96, 122, 128, 132
Aladdin's Lamp 147, 226, 227
Alexa (Amazon) 273-276
Alexander, Greta (psychic) 174
Aliens 40, 41, 78, 207, 208, 209

Alien Tornado (film) 7, 77
"A little bird told me." 26
Allegory see *Typologies*
Amazon(.com) 133, 134, 173, 174, 237, 273, 275-277
Amber 125, 253, 254, 327
American Lucifers (book) 132, 133, 328
Anderson, George (psychic) 172, 173
"And God said..." 270
Angel 34, 48, 49, 53, 56, 87, 240, 251, 257, 297, 304
Angelic 48, 53
Angel of Light 56, 257
Animal Magnetism 219
Animals 17, 23, 31, 32, 34, 41, 80, 110, 112, 120, 177, 198, 206, 300
Antediluvian Age 109, 113
Anthrax 81
Antichrist 204, 209, 210, 213, 218, 254, 262, 263, 277, 299
Antichristism 38
Apollo 11 (lunar lander) 114
Apple (Computers) 263-266, 277
Arab legends see *Aladdin's Lamp*
Ark of the Covenant 87, 88, 91, 111, 112, 284
Artificer 107, 108, 127
Artificial Eternal Life 280-284
Artificial Intelligence (AI) 102, 273, 274, 276
Ascending into Heaven 51

312 | Index

Astral Projection 225, 296
Astrology 83
Astronomy 295
Athena (Greek goddess) 37, 39
Athens 37
Atlanta (Georgia) 192
Atlantis 113
Atmosphere 18, 19, 24, 45, 46, 70, 73, 82, 83, 145, 153, 164, 202, 299, 306
Augmented Reality (AR), 278
Automatic Writing 223, 224
Aviation 19, 91-96, 122, 123, 144

B

Baalzebub (Beelzebub) 7, 33, 292, 293
　see also *Lord of the Flies*
Babbel (app) 120
Babel, Tower of 95, 119-121, 123, 236, 276, 285
Baillie, Mike (author) 82, 326
Ball Lightning 167, 181-194, 199 203, 205, 207, 303-308
　see also:
　Ball of fire
　Fireball(s)
　Fire of God
　Fire of Heaven
　Foo-Fighters
　Globular Lightning
　GLOs
　Gremlins
　Kraut Balls
　Kraut Meteors
　Kugelblitz
　Lightning Balls
　Orbs

Ball Lightning Events:
　Ascending a Church Belfry 187
　Appearing inside Aircraft 188
　Barn-sized Red Ball 194
　Bouncing into Tubs 186, 198
　Examining Houses 194
　Chasing Police Helicopter 191
　Destroying Forest 184
　Entering Children's Room 182
　Entering Church 186
　Entering Chimney 198
　Entering Houses 182, 186, 192
　Entering Open Window 198
　Entering Parked Vehicles 194
　Exploding in Forest 185
　Following Person up Stairs 182
　Frightening Rancher 191
　Healing Comatose Child 193
　Killing Man 198
　Melting Metal 186
　Pacing Aircraft 187, 189, 190
　Passing through Keyhole 183
　Going through Bulkhead 188, 198
　Passing through Glass 186
　Opening Door 185
　Rising out of the Sea 185
　Rolling on the ground 198
　Smashing Window 193
　With Strange Creature 195
　Violating Women 184
Ball of Fire 167, 184
　see also *Ball Lightning*
Banbury (England) 183
Clark, Barry (investigator) 195
Bats 31
Battle of the Currents 237
Baum, Frank L. (author) 101, 148

Beaty, William J. 156, 157, 159
Beaver County (Oklahoma) 188
Bees, see *Insect(s)*
Beethoven, Ludwig van 141
Beetles, see Insect(s)
Benson, Sonia (psychic) 173, 174
Bezaleel 130
Bezos, Jeff 275
Bible 13, 15-17, 19, 23-26, 29,
   30, 33, 34, 36, 37, 41, 45, 47,
   48, 50, 51-53, 57, 59, 60, 66, 71,
   73, 76, 78, 79, 80, 81, 91, 94-96,
   99-102, 104-108, 117, 120, 126,
   130, 134, 139, 142, 143, 146
   148, 150, 154, 155, 156, 161-164,
   167, 168, 170, 176, 178, 203,
   204, 207-210, 213, 215, 216,
   218, 225, 233, 235, 236, 240
   242, 245, 247, 249, 250-253,
   256-258, 262, 266, 270, 275,
   283, 285-287, 291-293, 295
   297, 301, 327
Bible-Believing Christian 19,
   167, 178
Bigfoot, see *Humanoids*
Biology 163, 226, 295
Bird(s) 19, 23, 28-31, 81, 122
   Blackbirds 30
   Grackles 30
   Owls 37-41, 292
   Peregrine falcon 32
   Quelea 31
   Starlings 30
   Also see *Fowl*
Black Death (Plague) 82
Blains 81
Blavatsky, Helena 181, 221
Blind 47, 51, 55, 59, 106, 154,
   176, 177, 181, 258
Blowing (air) 17, 36, 47, 67, 94
Boils 81, 83
Bolts 17, 159, 293
   see also *Lightning*
Brain-Computer Interface (BCI)
   278
Brimstone 40
Brinkley, Dannion (psychic)
   168-172
Bugs 33, 292
   also see *Insect(s)*
Bundy, Ted (killer) 141
Burlington (Vermont) 183
Burning Bush 50
Butterfly People, see *Humanoids*

C

Cain 108, 141, 235, 287
Cantore, Jim (meteorologist)
   192, 193
Car 87, 133, 272
Cell Phones 94, 132, 158, 249
Cemeteries 55
Chaldeans 46, 53, 96
Chariot 87, 89
Chariot of the Cherubim
   253, 284
Charmer 58
Chatfield, Chris (artist) 201
Cheetah 32
Cherubim 19, 87, 88, 89, 91, 253,
   254
Chevy Chase (Maryland) 185
Chicago World's Fair, 1938
   237, 238
Chittick, Donald E. (author)
   113, 326

Christian Science 214
Christian Transhumanist Association 282
Chronic Depression 55
Chronic Illness 55
Churchill, Winston 141
Church of Jesus Christ of Latter Day Saints, The 256
see also Mormonism
CIA 275, 276
Cicadas, see Insect(s)
City (cities) 8, 15, 27, 37, 72, 108, 118, 119, 120, 127, 229, 233, 234, 235, 236, 237, 238, 239, 240, 241, 242, 246, 250, 254, 255, 276, 284, 285
see also *Megalopolis*
City of Eternal Day 255
Civil War 218
Clairvoyance 165, 167, 222, 225, 296
Clairvoyant 181
Clelland, Mike (author) 38, 39, 40, 326
Close Encounters of the Third Kind (film) 209
Comet(s) 82-83, 206
Committee for the Scientific Investigation of Claims of the Paranormal 200
Computer(s) 59, 69, 113, 132, 158, 246, 247, 249, 262, 265, 278, 282
Corliss, William (author) 67, 68, 70, 183, 305, 306, 309, 326
Counterfeit(s) 89, 103, 209, 231, 234, 250, 254, 256-258, 270, 280, 283, 299

Covert Supernaturalism
see Supernaturalism
Creator 13, 16, 34, 54, 102, 107, 120, 280
Cult of Sadducees 106
see also *Sadducees*
Curse 25, 162
"...*curse that goeth forth over the face of the whole earth...*" 303-308
Cyclones 63
see also *Weather*

D

Dahmer, Jeffrey (killer) 141
Damascus Steel 113, 114
Daniel 94, 95, 209, 283
Daniels, J.W. (author) 217
Dark Age(s) 95, 101
Darkness 7, 11, 18, 37, 300
Darwin, Charles 141
Darwinism 214
Days of Noe (Noah) 100
Deaf 51, 55, 176
Decentraland 279
Demon 19, 26, 30, 39, 41, 57, 76, 94, 103, 139-142, 148, 194, 224, 225, 227, 256, 257, 285, 293, 301
Demoniacs 29, 130, 218
see also *Legion*
Demonic Counterfeits Doctrine 258
Demonic 18, 40, 48, 126, 168, 226, 292, 299
Demonic Miracles 176
Demonism 165, 221, 225, 226, 295, 296

Index | 315

Demonology 204
Demon-possessed 30, 41, 55, 56, 57, 77, 103, 139, 141, 142, 143, 154, 209
Destroyer 81
Device(s) 91, 104, 132, 135, 163, 216, 249, 252, 253, 284, 286
Devil 13-19, 24, 27, 28, 32, 36, 39, 41, 45, 46, 53, 55, 57, 60, 67, 70, 73-82, 84, 87, 89, 91, 94, 95, 96, 101, 103, 104, 117, 144, 145, 147-152, 154, 155, 156, 163, 164, 168, 178, 202-204, 206, 207, 209, 210, 225, 227, 234, 239, 250, 254, 256-258, 263, 265, 266, 272, 277, 279, 280, 284, 285, 291-294, 301, 305, 308
Devils 18, 26, 28, 45, 149, 221, 292
Devil Spirits 27, 76
Devon (England) 187, 193, 194
Diamond Valley 248
Disease 80-84, 103
Dissociative Identity Disorder 141
Divination 56, 58, 139, 165, 215, 225, 296
Downbursts 293
see also *Weather*
Downs, Kenny 191
Dragons 40
Driverless Cars 133
Dr. Seuss 156
Dumb (mute) 47, 176
see also *Muteness*
Dust devils 293
see also *Weather*

Dust storms 293
see also *Weather*

E

Earth 19, 24, 78, 80, 99, 107, 231, 251, 292, 293, 303, 304
Echo Dot (Amazon) 133, 273, 276
Edison, Thomas (inventor) 128, 129, 233, 237
Egypt 81, 114, 122, 273
Einstein, Albert 100
Electric Age 205, 213, 215, 220, 237, 240, 300
Electric Conductors 147, 160, 201, 248, 227, 305
Electric Insulators 160
Electrical Activity 83, 160, 162
Electricity 19, 101, 134, 146-151, 155, 156-163, 165, 171, 178, 181, 214, 220, 226, 227, 232, 233, 240, 242, 246, 249, 254, 255, 284, 294, 296, 299, 305, 306
Electroencephalogram 162
Electronics 133, 147, 242, 245, 248, 249, 255, 295
Elisha 25, 26, 51, 124, 128
Ellickson, Erin 174, 175, 176
Elymas the Sorcerer 57
Empire State Building 153
Enchanter 58
Entities coming through a hole in the ceiling, see *Humanoids*
End-Times 14, 123, 155, 295
Enoch 15, 154, 235
Envy 129
Eternal life 280, 281, 282, 283, 299

EU (European Union) 121
Euroclydon 73-77
Ever-Learning 94, 95, 102, 163
Example, see *Typologies*
Eyes 47-49, 59, 101, 112, 191, 254, 258, 265, 286, 303
Ezekiel 87, 89, 90, 253, 254

F

Facebook 134, 277
Familiar Spirits 56-58, 168, 176
    see also *Unclean Spirits*
    see also *Devils*
Feminism 221, 231
Figure, see *Typologies*
Fire 46, 51, 151, 169, 186, 206, 253, 299
Fireball(s) 47, 60, 82, 83, 151, 153, 182, 184, 185-187, 195, 199, 294, 306
    see also *Ball Lightning*
Fire of God 294, 299
    see also *Ball Lightning*
Fire of Heaven 294
    see also *Ball Lightning*
Flammarion, Camille (author) 154, 176, 177, 178, 185, 186, 198, 326
Flatwoods Monster
    see *Humanoids*
Florida Institute of Technology 160
Flu 81, 83
Fly, see *Insect(s)*
Fly-god 293
    see also *Baalzebub,*
    see also *Lord of the Flies*

Flying 17, 25, 30, 31, 33, 34, 39, 71, 81, 88-92, 94, 122, 145, 182, 192, 194, 197, 198, 253, 254, 300, 303, 304, 306
Flying Roll 303, 306
Flying Saucer(s) 90, 197
    see also *UFO(s)*
Foo-Fighters 188, 199
    see also *Ball Lightning*
Footprints 146
Forest Fires 294
Fortnite (video game) 277
Fowl 23, 24, 27, 31-34, 37, 83, 206, 292, see also *Bird(s)*
Fox sisters (Leah, Margaret, and Kate) 170, 222
Franklin, Benjamin (inventor) 101, 128, 145
Frogs 81
Fruit 263, 264, 265, 270, 272, 283

G

Gadarenes 7, 29, 75, 76, 139
    see also *Gergesa*
Gaddis, Vincent (author) 152, 153, 159, 183, 186, 202, 309, 326
Galilee, Sea of 51, 76
Gaverluk, Emil (author) 115, 116, 327
Gemstones (gems) 246-250, 252, 254, 283, 299
    Agate 247, 249, 252, 299
    Amethyst 247, 249, 252, 299
    Beryl 247, 249, 252, 253, 254, 299
    Carbuncle 252, 254

Chalcedony 247, 249, 299
Crystals 246, 247
Diamond 248, 249, 252, 254
Emerald 247, 249, 252, 254, 299
Jasper 247, 249, 252, 254, 299
Onyx 247, 249, 252, 254, 299
Quartz 124, 246, 247, 249, 250, 254, 299
Sapphire 89, 252, 254
Sardius 252, 254
Topaz 252, 254
Genie 140, 147, 226
  see also *Jinn*
Genius(es) 130, 134, 140, 141, 144, 161
Geology 295
Westinghouse, George 237
Gergesa 76, 77
  see also *Gadarenes*
Ghost 36, 145, 225, 295, 296
Giza Pyramids 113, 114
Global Age 16
Globalism 216, 295
Globular lightning 199
  see also *Ball Lightning*
Glory of God 102, 234, 250-254, 285, 298, 299
GLOs 201, 309
  see also *Ball Lightning*
Glouchestershire (England) 182
Gnats, see *Insect*(s)
Goblins 178
God 13, 15, 16, 23, 26-29, 32, 34, 35, 37, 41, 46, 47-49, 53, 54, 57-59, 65, 66, 69, 72, 74, 75, 77, 79, 81, 87-89, 91, 95, 96, 100-102, 103, 105, 106, 107, 110-113, 116, 120, 127, 130, 134, 140, 142, 146, 147, 149, 150, 155, 171, 172, 175, 176, 180, 202-206, 209, 216, 218, 224, 225, 227, 231-236, 240-242, 250-252, 254-258, 264, 265, 267, 270-272, 274, 275, 280-287, 291, 293-295, 297-299, 301, 303, 304, 308, 328
"God is dead" 103
  see also *Nietzsche*
God of Forces 209, 283, 299, 303
  see also *Prince of the Power of the Air*
God of History 291
God's Throne 23
  see also *Chariot of the Cherubim*
Gold 34, 147, 209, 227, 249, 250, 252, 254, 283, 284, 299
Gomorrha 236
Google 134, 277
Gopher Wood 110
Gordon, Stan (author) 194-197, 221, 327
GPS 263
Grackles, see *Bird*(s)
Graham, Kenny 191
Grasshoppers, see *Insect*(s)
Graveyards 55
Gravity 180
Gray, James Martin (author) 218
Great Flood 111, 112
Great Mortality 82
  see also *Black Plague*
Great Red Spot, The 79
Great Tribulation 210
  see also *Tribulation*
Greek Fire 113, 114

Gremlins of WWII 187, 188
  see also *Ball Lightning*
Marconi, Guglielmo (inventor)
  128
Gutierrez, Kathy (author) 217

H

Haag, Dr. Bill (teacher) 142
Hail see *Weather*
Hall, Manly Palmer (author)
  154, 159, 164, 327
Halloween 37, 38
Ham 116, 130
Hamburg (Germany) 186
Hancock, Graham (author) 115,
  128, 191, 327
Haunted Houses 40, 41
Healing 54, 165, 225
Heart 99, 101, 285
Heaven(s) 13, 19, 23, 32, 46, 51,
  54, 88, 117, 119, 126, 149, 150,
  151, 171, 176, 208, 220, 221,
  242, 270, 283, 294, 297, 299
Heavener, David (author)
  143, 327
Hedonism 102
Heinkel He-178 (jet plane) 94
Helicopters 92, 96
Hell 170, 171, 220
Hollerith, Herman (inventor)
  261, 262, 263
H.H. Holmes (murderer) 237,
  238
  see also *Mudgett, Herman*
Hitler, Adolf 141
Hive Mind 29, 31
Hollywood 36, 78
Holy Spirit 25, 26, 134, 252, 255

Homosexual 264
Hopkinsville (Kentucky) 39
Hornets, see *Insect(s)*
Horses 51, 131, 191, 300
Hot-air Balloon 91, 92
HTML see
  Hypertext Markup Language
Humanism 102, 105
Humanoids 38, 41, 71
  Bigfoot 41
  Butterfly People 71-72
  Entities coming through a
    Hole in Ceiling 195
  Flatwoods Monster 39
  Hair-covered, green-eyed 194
  Mothman 38, 40, 41
  Non-Physical Entities 196
  Strange Creatures 40
  Woman with Wings 193
Hurricane 60, 63, 67, 70, 79, 84,
  293, 294
  see also *Weather*
Hydesville (New York) 214
Hypertext Markup Language
  267

I

IBM 261
Ice 63
  see also *Weather*
Image of the Beast 277
Imagination(s) 99, 100, 101, 107,
  147, 207, 214, 295
Immortality 103
Immortal Sinners 283
Incarnate Word 270
  see also *Lord Jesus Christ*
Industrial Revolution(s) 102,

103, 123, 205, 237, 295
Infirmities 81, 176
Influenza 83
Insect(s) 33, 34, 293
  Bees 31
  Beetles 293
  Cicadas 31
  Flies (fly) 23, 33, 81, 83, 88, 292, 293
  Gnats 31, 293
  Grasshoppers 31, 33
  Hornets 31
  Locusts 31, 32, 33, 34, 81
  Lice 81
  Mayflies 31
Insect-god 293
  see also *Baalzebub*
  see also *Lord of the Flies*
Inter-dimensional 196
International Business Machines
  see *IBM*
Internet 95, 133, 134, 146, 201, 215, 226, 266, 267, 270, 271-273, 277, 278, 282
Internet of Things (IoT) 272, 273, 276
Invisible Things:
  Aerial Phenomena 153
  Forces 163
  Lightning Formation 151
  Lightning Bolts 153
  Tornados 64, 65
  Preternatural Entities 205
  Some things God made 270
  Spirits 29, 35, 36, 41, 48, 155, 220
Influences 83

J

Jack the Ripper 237-238
Japheth 116, 130
Jehovah's Witnesses 214, 257
Jets 92, 96, 113, 122
Jewish High Priest's Breastplate 250
  see also *Urim & Thummim*
Jim Thorpe (Pennsylvania) 186
Jinn 140, 147, 226
  see also *Genie*
Job 24, 37, 45-48, 53, 59, 60, 64, 66, 67, 72, 73, 83, 94, 96, 104, 105, 144, 145, 151, 152, 154, 206, 210, 227, 280, 281, 286, 299, 300, 304, 308
Kass, John (reporter) 66
Jonah 53
Joplin (Missouri) 71, 72
Smith, Joseph 214, 256
Judas (Iscariot) 55-57, 207
Jupiter (planet) 78-80

K

Kaczynski, Ted (killer) 141
Kentucky 39, 191, 192
Keyhole 183
Killers 19, 141, 239
King James Bible 29, 99, 209, 252, 286
King of Syria 25, 26
Knapp, George (host) 169
Knowledge 15, 19, 37, 57, 60, 84, 94-96, 99, 100, 102-105, 107, 108, 112, 113, 115-120, 122, 123, 126, 130, 141, 143-145, 154,

155, 161, 163, 178-180, 220, 221,
231, 232, 250, 258, 264, 273,
281, 282, 285, 293, 295, 299,
300, 305, 308
Kohath 87
Kohathites 87, 88
Kraut Balls 188
 see also *Ball Lightning*
Kraut Meteors 188
 see also *Ball Lightning*
Kudrovo (Russia) 241
Kugelblitz 199
 see also *Ball Lightning*
Ku Klux Klan 214

L

LaFrance, Adrienne (author) 66
Lamb 41
Lamb of God 29, 79
Laser-like Effects 252
LaVey, Anton Zandor 152, 256
Legion 29, 76, 77
LEGO (block toys) 277
Leprosy 79
Lewis Center (Ohio) 182
Liberal (politics) 100
 also see Progressive
Liberalism 221, 295
Lice, see *Insect*(s)
Light Bulbs 132
Lightning 17, 19, 60, 91, 134, 145,
 147, 149-155, 157-161, 164-168,
 170-178, 180, 182, 186, 191, 193,
 194, 199-201, 203, 205, 207
 210, 225, 226, 232, 283, 293,
 294, 296, 303-309
Lightning Events:

Conveying Occult Powers 165-169, 172-175
Creating Sulfurous Odors 177
Healing People 176
Human Petrification 177
Invisible Bolts 153
Killing People, Animals 177
Orange Lightning 194
Removing Clothes 177
Splitting People in Half 177
Throwing People 177
Turning People to Ash 177
Lightning Balls 199
 see also *Ball Lightning*
Lightning Rod 128
Limp, David 273, 275
Lincoln, Abraham 141
Lincoln, Mary Todd 222
Locust(s), see *Insect*(s)
Lord Jesus Christ, The 13, 14,
 16, 17, 28, 29, 35, 41, 51-56,
 76, 77, 79, 81, 100, 106, 110,
 148, 149, 150, 152, 164, 168,
 171, 173, 204, 213, 251, 252,
 254, 256, 258, 274,
 279, 281, 284, 285, 300, 308
Lord of the Flies 292
 see also *Baalzebub*
Lord's Chariot 87, 250
 see also *Chariot of the Cherubim*
Louisville (Kentucky) 191
"...*love of money*..." 134, 277
Lucifer 59, 87, 88, 91, 257

M

Macintosh 263
Macrobursts 293
 see also *Weather*

Madness 130, 144
Magic 37, 113, 139, 167
Magicians 50, 56, 57, 58, 139
Mammals 34
Manoah 48, 49
Marian Apparitions 256
Mark of the Beast 262
Marxism 214, 295
Master Key, The (book) 148
Materialism 102
McIntosh Apple 263
Measles 81
Megalopolis 239, 241
  see also *City*
Melting Metal 186
  see also *Ball Lightning Events*
Mercy Seat 88, 91
  see also *Ark of the Covenant*
Metaverse 277, 278, 279
Meteorologist(s) 64, 193
Microbursts 293
  see also *Weather*
Microchip 128
Microsoft 277
Millennium 35
Mind 99, 223, 250
Mind of Christ 254
Mind-Reading 169, 296
Ministers of righteousness 56, 257, 258
Missouri 71, 72
Moody Bible Institute 218
Moon 92, 94, 113, 114, 255
Mothman see *Humanoids*
Mormonism 214, 257
Morse, Samuel (inventor) 128, 215, 216
Moses 15, 50, 56

Mothman see *Humanoids*
Mozart, Wolfgang Amadeus 141
Mudgett, Herman (killer) 237, 238
  see also *Holmes, H.H.*
Multiculturalism 220, 231
Multiple Personality Disorder 141
Mumps 81
Murmuration 30, 31
Murmuring 30
Muteness 55
  see also *Dumb*
Mystical 147, 172, 296

N

Nakedness 55
NASA 79, 92, 113
National Education Association 103
National Oceanic & Atmospheric Administration 63, 69, 159
  see also *NOAA*
National Security Agency 276
National Severe Storms Laboratory 150, 151, 159
National Weather Service 63
Native American(s) 165, 167, 168
Natural 16, 47, 51, 53
Naturalism 47, 203
Near-death experience (NDE) 166, 169, 172, 175
Nebuchadnezzar 79
Necromancer 58, 172
Necromancy 165, 214, 215, 225
New Age 165, 168, 170, 217, 221, 327, 328

Newark (New York) 214
New Jerusalem (Heavenly City) 241, 250, 254, 255, 284
Newspaper clipping 189-191
Newton, Isaac 141
New York Daily News, The 246
New York Times, The 101
Nietzsche, Frederic (philospher) 103, 232, 295
Tesla, Nikola (inventor) 128, 141, 161, 237, 326
NOAA 63, 150, 151, 159
Noah 15, 47, 100, 107-120, 130 154, 236, 286, 328
Noah's Ark 107-120
Nohl, Johannes (author) 82, 327
Nuclear Detonations 294
Numbering People 262

O

Observer of Times 58
Occult 36, 56, 101, 140, 172, 213, 214, 216, 225, 231, 296
Occultism 36, 140, 152, 219, 221, 328
"*of the air*" 17, 19, 23-28, 32, 33, 35, 45, 60, 73, 76, 80, 83, 84, 89, 91, 94, 145, 147, 151, 152, 155, 156, 168, 204, 210, 284, 292, 293, 301
OOPArts (Out-of-Place artifcts) 118
Operators (telegraph, telephone) 224
Orbs 194, 199, 206, 207, 225, 306
see also *Ball Lightning*
Ouija Board, see *Planchette*

Out-of-Body experiences 165
Overt Supernaturalism see *Supernaturalism*
Owls, see *Bird*(s)

P

Parable see *Typologies*
Paranormal 38, 48, 51, 195, 296
Paranormal Powers, see:
  Astral Projection
  Automatic Writing
  Astrology
  Charmer
  Clairvoyance
  Clairvoyant
  Divination
  Magic
  Mind-Reading
  Near-death experience (NDE)
  Necromancy
  Observer of Times
  Out-of-Body experiences
  Psychics
  Seance
  Shamanism
  Travel into other Dimensions
  Turn the Tables
  Witchcraft
Pattern, see *Typologies*
Paul (Apostle) 18, 37, 57, 73-76, 81, 199, 200, 208, 257, 328
Pennsylvania 186, 194-196
Peregrine falcon, see *Bird*(s)
Pestilence 80, 82, 84
"*...pestilence that walketh in darkness...*" 82
Phenomena 35, 83, 146, 147, 162, 168, 182, 225, 297

Phonograph 128
Physics 51, 160, 164, 182, 199, 200, 225, 295, 297
Pit 35
Plague(s) 31, 32, 81-83, 214, 308
Planchettes 224
Planes 92, 198
Point Pleasant (West Virginia) 40
Poltergeist 165, 209, 219
Power Lines 196
Powers (spiritual) 18, 168, 173
see also *Principalities*
Precious Stone 252
Prince 16-19, 24, 28, 35, 80, 91, 134, 292, 299
Prince of the Devils 16-18, 28, 292
Prince of the Power of the Air 13, 16, 17, 19, 23, 28, 35, 46, 74, 77, 79, 81, 95, 134, 144, 148, 149, 150, 156, 164, 206, 210, 226, 228, 258, 292, 297, 299, 301, 304, 308
Prince of this World 18, 292
Principalities 18
see also *Powers*
Progressive (politics) 221, 222, 231, also see *Liberal*
Prophets of Baal 144
Proud, Lewis (author) 165, 174, 178, 328
Psychic(s) 165, 168, 169, 172, 174
Putin, Vladimir 141

Q

Quartz, see *Gemstones*
Quelea see *Bird*(s)

R

Radio 94, 96, 128, 163, 169, 181, 194, 196, 226, 294
Ramsey, William (author) 14, 223, 328
Red Herring 207
Red Sea 50
Religious Pluralism 220, 222
Revelation 14, 34
RFID chip 263
Rocket 92, 94, 113
see also *Saturn V*
Roman Catholic Church 89, 256
Roman Catholicism 257
Rome 73-75
Rowling, J.K. (author) 100
Rulers of the Darkness of this World, The 18, 45, 47, 231
see also *Powers, Principalities*
Russia 202, 241

S

Sabeans 46, 53, 96
Sadducaical 106, 299
Sadducees 106, 227
Samson 15, 48, 49
Sapphire, see *Gemstones*
Saqqara Bird 122
Sandbox, The 279
Sardius see *Gemstones*
Satan 13-29, 33, 35, 37, 43-48, 53, 55, 56, 59-61, 70-75, 78, 80, 81, 85, 88, 91, 95, 96, 97, 117, 130, 137, 144, 145, 147, 149, 150, 151, 155, 156, 162-164, 206-209, 211, 226, 227, 229, 240, 242, 243, 256-259, 262,

266, 272, 277, 283, 289, 291-294, 299, 301, 304, 308
Satan as Lightning 149, 151, 208,
226, 283, 293
Satanology 204, 291
Satellites 96
Saturn V 92, 93, 113
see also *Rocket*
Saul (king) 56, 103, 251
Scarabaeus (scarab) 293
see also *Insect*(s), *Beetle*
Schizophrenia 141
Science 15, 16, 34, 36, 47, 59, 66, 69, 78, 80, 99, 103, 104, 108, 109, 112-118, 125, 130, 133, 140, 144, 146, 155, 157, 159, 161-163, 178-182, 201-208, 220, 225 227, 249, 264, 273, 275, 278, 280, 281, 295, 296, 298, 299, 300, 307, 308
Science Fiction 78, 99, 207, 208, 273, 278
Scientism 178-179
Scroll see *Flying roll*
Seance 215
Sedan 89
Seed 26-28, 32, 205, 235, 270
Self-mutilation 55
Self-torture 55
Serial killers 19, 141, 237, 239
Seventh-Day Adventism 214
Shadow see *Typologies*
Shaman 166, 167, 257
Shamanism 165
Smith, Shane 174-175
Shem 116, 130
Shinar 118

Siberia 202
see also *Tunguska Event*
Sickness 80
Silicon Valley 248, 249, 280, 282
Similitude, see *Typologies*
Simon, Linda (author) 132, 157, 216, 232, 233, 328
Simultaneous Invention 123, 130, 141, 295
Sin 13, 79, 80, 88, 109, 255, 280-282, 287, 301
Six, six, six (666) 63, 263, 266, 272
Skeat, Walter (author) 139, 140, 267, 328
Skyscraper 234, 241
Smart (technology) 15, 164, 245, 247, 250, 255, 266, 275, 276, 283, 299
Smart City(ies) 242, 255
Smart Materials 246, 247
Snow 63, see also *Weather*
Sodom 236
Sodomite 264
Sons of God 113
Soothsayer 139
Sorcerers 50, 56, 139
Sower 26, 27, 28
Speilberg, Steven (director) 209
Spence, Lewis (author) 36, 140, 219, 328
Sphere Lightning 199
see also *Ball Lightning*
Spirit(s) 16, 21, 24-28, 34, 35, 58, 75, 76, 91, 126, 131-135, 140, 149, 162, 167, 173, 174, 211, 225, 226, 252, 255, 294, 295

Index

Spiritism 214, 215, 218, 219, 299, 327
  see also *Spiritualism*
Spirit of Infirmity 81
  see also *Thorn in the Flesh*
"...*spirit that now worketh in the children of disobedience...*" 27, 144, 292
Spiritualism 14, 168, 214-221, 223, 225, 282, 326-328
Spiritualism Versus Christianity (book) 168, 217, 218, 326
Spiritualists 217-222
Spiritual Wickedness in High Places 18
  see also *Powers, Principalities*
Stalin, Joseph 141
Starlings, see *Bird(s)*
Star of Bethlehem 297
Star Trek (tv series) 273
Star Wars (film) 233, 304
Steinbeck, John (author) 100
Stones 209, 247-250, 252, 254, 283, 299, 303, 306
  see also *Gemstones*
Storm(s) 17, 19, 60, 63-68, 70, 73-80, 84, 116, 145, 149, 153, 160, 161, 173, 194, 199, 207, 293
  see also *Weather*
Storm Prediction Center 69
Straight-Line Winds 73, 293
  see also *Weather*
Suicidal Thoughts 55
Sun 31, 32, 35, 78, 150, 233, 255, 287
Sunday School Times, The 219
Supercell 64
  see also *Weather*

Superhuman Strength 55, 301
Supernatural 15, 16, 47, 53, 59, 103, 106, 154, 203, 207, 209, 299, 305
Supernaturalism 47-49, 52, 54. 59, 77, 107, 180, 203, 206, 297
  Covert 48, 49, 52-54, 57-60, 77, 107, 139, 158, 206, 297, 298
  Overt 50-52, 55, 60, 102, 139, 297, 298
Swarm(s) 29-32, 34, 195, 293
  see also *Fowl, Insect(s)*
Swine 77

T

Technocracy News & Trends (website) 132, 280, 282
Technocrats 132, 246, 280
Technology 19, 35, 66, 93, 99, 103, 107, 108, 111-118, 120, 122, 124, 132, 134, 144, 145, 149, 158, 179, 197, 220, 228, 233, 234, 236, 237, 240, 245, 246, 248, 249, 250, 254-256, 258, 262, 263, 270-273, 275, 278, 280-287, 295, 299
Telegraph 94, 128, 132, 215, 216, 220, 224, 278
Telephone 94, 101, 124, 125, 128, 132, 163, 174, 224, 278
Telescope 125
Television 96, 132, 133, 208, 249, 272
Theosophical Society 221
Theosophy 101, 214, 221
Thermometer 125
Tunguska Event, The 202

"...things not seen..." 15, 55, 112
  see also *Invisible*
Thorn in the Flesh 81
  see also *Spirit of Infirmity*
Throne 23, 87
Thuesen, Peter J. (author) 65, 69, 328
Thunderbird 167
Thunderbolts 199, 306, 307
Thunderstorm(s) 63, 69, 151, 158, 160, 183, 192, 193, 293, 294
  see also *Weather*
Tombs 55
Topaz, see *Gemstones*
Tornado and Storm Research Organization 150, 187, 308
Tornado(s) 19, 60, 63 67, 69-72, 77, 84, 180, 187, 293
Torpedo-Shaped (light orb) 183
Totem Pole 167
Transhuman 280, 282
Transhumanism 280
Transhumanists 283
Travel into other Dimensions 169
Treasure Chest 111
Tribulation 80, 207
Tuberculosis 81
Turing, Alan 264
Turn the Tables 223
Twister 64, 67
  see also *Tornado*(s)
Typewriting Machines 125
Typhoons 63
  see also *Weather*
Typologies 29

Allegory 29
Example 29, 268, 269
Figure 29
Parable 26, 27, 28
Pattern 29
Shadow 29
Similitude 29

U

UFO(s) 38, 39, 94, 192, 196, 197, 201
  see also *Ball Lightning*
Unclean Spirits 25, 35, 126, 140, 211
  see also *Demons*
Unexplained 19, 38, 39, 160, 188, 194, 199, 203, 225, 296
UPC 262-263
Urbanization 239, 240
Urim and Thummim 252
  see also *Jewish High Priest's Breastplate*
U.S. Census Bureau 262

V

Van Doorn, Peter 200, 201, 205
Vatican City 242
Virtual Reality 267, 270, 278
Viruses 81
Voice out of the Cloud 273, 274
Von Braun, Werner (inventor) 93

W

War of the Worlds, The (films or book) 207, 208
Washington, D.C. 183
Weather 24, 63, 66, 68, 70,

153, 156, 187, 192, 194, 199, 209, 293, 300, 305
see also:
Cyclones
Dust devils
Dust storms
Hail
Hurricanes
Ice
Macrobursts
Microbursts
Snow
Storms
Straight-Line Winds
Thunderstorms
Tornados
Supercell
Wind
Windstorms
Whirlwind
Weather Channel, The 68, 192, 193
Web 201, 246, 266, 267, 271, 272, 273, 279, 280, 284
Web 3.0 279
Webster, Daniel (author) 83, 107, 140, 245, 246, 286, 299, 328
West Virginia 38, 40
Whale 53
What Dwells Beyond (book) 78, 208
Wheels 91, 253, 281
Whirlwind 64, 253
see also Tornado(s)
see also *Weather*
Widecombe Church 187
Wind 19, 26, 35, 36, 45, 51, 63, 64, 68, 73, 76, 79, 83, 89, 91, 155, 180, 184, 186, 198, 210, 293
see also *Weather*
Windstorms 63, 64
see also *Weather*
Wings 25, 26, 33, 34, 37, 51, 71, 72, 89, 162, 193, 263
Wires 157, 201, 216, 252, 255, 305
Wisdom 16, 19, 37, 39, 47, 57-59, 91, 96, 99, 101, 104-107, 112, 119, 127, 129, 140, 144, 180, 225, 258, 281, 295, 299, 301, 308
Witchcraft 37, 41, 165, 219
Witch(es) 38, 41, 56-58, 139
Witch of Endor 56
Wizards 56-58, 139
Wizard of Menlo Park, The 233
see also *Edison, Thomas*
Wonderful Wizard of Oz, The (book) 101, 148
World Economic Forum (WEF) 277, 278
World War I 93, 218
World War II 187
Wright Brothers 95, 128
Wright Flyer 92
Wyoming, The (ship) 108-109

Z

Zechariah 304, 306
Zeus 160
Zoology 295

BIBLIOGRAPHY

Baillie, Mike. New Light on the Black Death. Stroud, Glouchestershire: Tempus Publishing Limited, 2006.

Basalla, George. The Evolution of Technology. New York, NY: Cambridge University Press, 1988.

Bord, Janet and Colin. Unexplained Mysteries of the 20th Century. Chicago, IL: Contemporary Books, 1989.

Cade, C. Maxwell, and Davis, Delphanie. The Taming of the Thunderbolts. New York: Abelard-Schuman, 1969.

Carlson, W. Bernard. Tesla: Inventor of the Electrical Age. Princeton, NJ: Princeton University Press, 2015.

Chittick, Donald E. The Puzzle of Ancient Man. Newberg, OR: Creation Compass, 1997

Clelland, Mike. The Messengers. Los Angeles, CA: Richard Dolan Press, 2020.

Corliss, William R. Handbook of Unusual Natural Phenomena. Avenel, NJ: Gramercy Books & Random House, 1977.

Craffert, Pieter F. The Life of a Galilean Shaman. Eugene, OR: Cascade Books, 2008.

Daniels, J. W. Spiritualism Versus Christianity. London, England: Forgotten Books, 2015 [reprint of a 1856 ed].

Doe, Robert K. Extreme Weather. Chichester, West Sussex, UK: John Wiley & Sons, 2016.

Flammarion, Camille. Thunder and Lightning. London, England: Chatto & Windus, 1905.

Friedman, John S. Out of the Blue. New York, NY: Delta, Random House, Inc., 2009.

Gaddis, Vincent H. Mysterious Fires and Lights. New Saucerian Press, 2017.

Gaverluk, Emil. Did Genesis Man Conquer Space? Nashville, TN: Thomas Nelson Inc. Publishers, 1974.

Gordon, Stan. Silent Invasion. Greensburg, PA: Stan Gordon, 2010.

Gray, James Martin. Spiritism and the Fallen Angels in the Old and New Testaments. London, England: Forgotten Books, 2018 [reprint of a 1920 ed].

Hall, Manly Palmer. The Mystery of Electricity. Los Angeles, CA: The Philosophers Press, 1939.

Hancock, Graham. Fingerprints of the Gods. New York, NY: Three Rivers Press, 1995.

Heavener, David. End-Times Investigations with David Heavener. Crane, MS: Defender Publishing, 2022.

The Holy Bible According to the Authorized Version, Containing the Old and New Testaments: Volume II. London: Charles Knight & Co., 1837.

Jackson, Tom. Engineering: An Illustrated History from Ancient Craft to Modern Technology. New York, NY: Shelter Harbor Press, 2016.

Kelly, Kevin. What Technology Wants. New York, NY: Penguin Group, 2011.

Kernahan, Coulson. Spiritualism: A Personal Experience and a Warning. Chicago, New York, London: Fleming H. Revell Company, 1920.

Krohn, Elizabeth G., Kripal, Jeffrey J. Changed in a Flash. Berkeley, CA: North Atlantic Books, 2018.

Lewis, James R., Melton, J. Gordon. Perspectives on the New Age. Albany, NY: State University of New York Press, 1992.

Muimba-Kankolongo, Ambayeba. Food Crop Production by Smallholder Farmers in Southern Africa. San Diego, CA: Academic Press, 2018.

Mysteries of Mind, Space & Time. Tarrytown, NY: Websters Unified H.S. Stuttman, Inc, 1992.

Nohl, Johannes. *The Black Death: A Chronicle of the Plague.* Unwin Books: London. Hassell Street Press, a reprint of the original 1924 edition.

Park, Benjamin. The Age of Electricity From Amber-Soul to Telephone.

Boston, MA: Berwick & Smith, 1886.

Partridge, Christopher. The Occult World. New York, NY: Routledge, 2016.

Proud, Louis. Strange Electromagnetic Dimensions. Pompton Plains, NJ: New Page Books, 2015.

Ramsey, William. Spiritualism, a Satanic Delusion and a Sign of the Times. Peace Dale, RI: H. L. Hastings, 1856.

Sagan, Paul. Ball Lightning: Paradox of Physics. Lincoln, NE: iUniverse Inc., 2004.

Scott, Irena McCammon. Inside the Lightning Ball. West Yorkshire, England: Flying Disk Press, 2018.

Simon, Linda. Dark Light. San Diego, CA: Harcourt Inc., 2004.

Skeat, Walter W. An Etymological Dictionary of the English Language. Garden City, NY: Dover Publications, 2005 [reprint of a 1910 ed].

Spence, Lewis. An Encyclopedia of Occultism. Secaucus, NJ: Citadel Press & Carol Publishing Group, 1996 [reprint of a 1920 ed].

Story, Ronald. The Encyclopedia of Extraterrestrial Encounters. New York, NY: New American Library, 2001.

Sutcliffe, Steven J. Children of the New Age. New York, NY: Routledge, 2002.

Sword, Helen. Ghostwriting Modernism. Ithaca, NY: Cornell University Press, 2002.

Thuesen, Peter J. Tornado God. New York, NY: Oxford University Press, 2020.

The Timechart History of Aviation. Ann Arbor, MI: Lowe & B. Hould Publishers, 2001.

Webster, Noah. An American Dictionary of the English Language [1828 Ed.]. Springfield, MA: George and Charles Merrian, 1854.

Zallen, Jeremy. American Lucifers. Chapel Hill, NC: University of North Carolina Press, 2019.

ABOUT THE AUTHOR

CHRISTIAN author Jeffrey W. Mardis has been reading, writing, and researching on Bible discernment issues since the late 1990s. He has read and studied the scriptures from *Genesis* to *Revelation* 28 times thus far; written personal summaries on all 1,189 chapters; taken thousands of pages of notes; and written other books (these things are mentioned merely to show the author's qualifications, as he has no theological degree, only a love of the Bible). He founded *Sword-In-Hand Publishing* in 2009 to provide an outlet to teach and edify others. His passion is in writing about the supernatural aspects of scripture and why modern Christians need to return to this foundation (1Cor. 2:5). His mission is to make the Bible real again, while instilling a deeper love for the Lord Jesus Christ, and strengthening one's faith in the Final-Authority of the *King James Bible*. Jeffrey's works have appeared on Christian websites, radio, and television, including Southwest Radio Church, Prophecy Watchers, SkyWatch TV, and Now The End Begins (NTEB).

Jeffrey has served in the graphic design field since graduating college in 1993. He is a former internationally recognized logo and trademark designer, whose work has been showcased numerous times in top peer publications. In 2009, Jeffrey began serving in the independent, book and book design industry, and has had the privilege to work with several widely published Christian authors.

Jeffrey resides in Campbellsville, Kentucky, and has been a born-again Christian since 1979. He is an Independent, *King James Bible*-Believing Baptist.

"Even so, come, Lord Jesus." Rev. 22:20

SWORD™ IN HAND
PUBLISHING

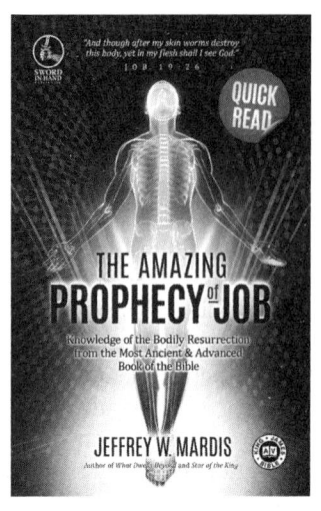

The Amazing Prophecy of Job:
Knowledge of the Bodily Resurection from the Most Ancient & Advanced Book of the Bible

"Over the years, after reading several commentaries on Job, including E. W. Bullinger's *The Book of Job* (1904), not one has been as informative, helpful, and scriptural as *The Amazing Prophecy of Job* - an exceptional work in dealing with the doctrine of the present body's death and future bodily resurrection."
-- Dr. Dave Reese, BA, MRE, DRE, PhD, ThD, Open Bible College International

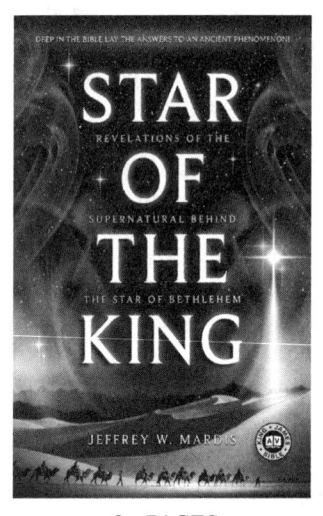

165 PAGES

Star of the King:
Revelations of the Supernatural Behind the Star of Bethlehem

"The thing I like about Jeffrey Mardis is he really goes into detail, fine detail. You want to know about the Christmas star? This is your book, because, I mean, he goes passed the surface level, he goes two or three layers deep. *Star of the King* is really a marvelous book!" -- Gary Stearman, author, *Prophecy Watchers* magazine

"You have given the body of Christ an invaluable tool for clarifying a Christmas issue." -- Pastor Michael Schreib, Bible Baptist Church International

180 PAGES

www.swordinhandpub.com

SWORD IN HAND PUBLISHING

What Dwells Beyond:
The Bible Believer's Handbook to Understanding Life in the Universe

"Your book, *What Dwells Beyond*, is an absolute must-read for all Believers....so much information, crammed between the covers of one book, and wrote in a way that you make one not want to put it down. Excellent book, from cover to cover. God has truly blessed you. And your chapter on darkness? Awesome! Never have I read so much meat on this topic. Thank you, once again, and may God continually bless you and your ministry." -- C.E. Kiluk Sr.

520 PAGES

"Jeffrey Mardis is really a great authority from a Bible-Believing standpoint concerning aliens and life in outer space."
-- Dr. Gene Kim, MA, ThD, pastor, San Jose Bible Baptist Church

"*What Dwells Beyond* was super helpful! And interesting. Maybe a tiny bit creepy. It really helped me to be able to see life in space and creatures like that from a Biblical perspective. Saturated with scriptural support, every point made was strongly supported. This man knows his Bible very well!"
-- Joey T., Goodreads Review

"Brother Jeff, I put the finishing touches on your book, *What Dwells Beyond*. I will save you a long review, but I want to tell you that this is *THE* best book on this subject, bar none. I will give this book my hearty recommendation and when anyone tells me they are interested in this subject matter or just want to read a good book, I will be recommending it. ...it is an *INSTANT CLASSIC*, in my opinion. God bless your hard work, brother."
-- Pastor Greg Miller, Bible-Believers Fellowship

"*What Dwells Beyond* may be the best work ever produced on the question of extraterrestrial life from a conservative Christian worldview."
-- Dr. Thomas Horn, author, publisher, CEO SkyWatch TV

www.swordinhandpub.com

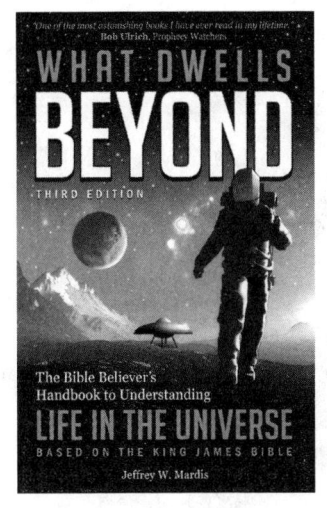

DEFENDER
PUBLISHING

The Prince of the Power of the Air and the Last Days:
Satanology – History – Prophecy – Technology

One of the objectives of this book is to give the reader an opportunity to shed any feeble beliefs they may have about Satan. You might even say that this study does an "about face," and travels one hundred and eighty degrees in the opposite direction. Scripture doesn't present any sort of weak presence on the part of the Devil, so we have no excuse to hold beliefs reflective of such things. Satan is alive and well in the twenty-first-century–and working!

www.swordinhandpub.com

DEFENDER
PUBLISHING